Modern Masters Volume Eleven:

D1295756

MODERN MASTERS VOLUME ELEVEN:
CHARLES VESS

edited by Eric Nolen-Weathington and Christopher Irving
designed by Eric Nolen-Weathington
front cover art by Charles Vess
all interviews in this book were conducted by Christopher Irving
proofreading by Fred Perry

TwoMorrows Publishing
10407 Bedfordtown Dr.
Raleigh, North Carolina 27614
www.twomorrows.com • e-mail: twomorrow@aol.com

First Printing • February 2007 • Printed in Canada

Softcover ISBN: 978-1-893905-69-6

Dedication

To Cindy Jackson of Virginia Commonwealth University Special Collections, the biggest Sandman fan I know. — Christopher

To Sue Claybrook and Barbara Rouse—the coolest English teachers ever. And, as ever, to Donna, Iain, and Caper. — Eric

Acknowledgements

Charles Vess, for his time and for letting us rummage through his closet for artwork.

Michael Kaluta, for his invaluable input.

Special Thanks
Edwin & Terry Murray
Rick McGee and the crew of Foundation's Edge,
Russ Garwood and the crew of Capital Comics,
and John and Pam Morrow

Modern Masters Volume Eleven:

CHARLES VESS

Table of Contents

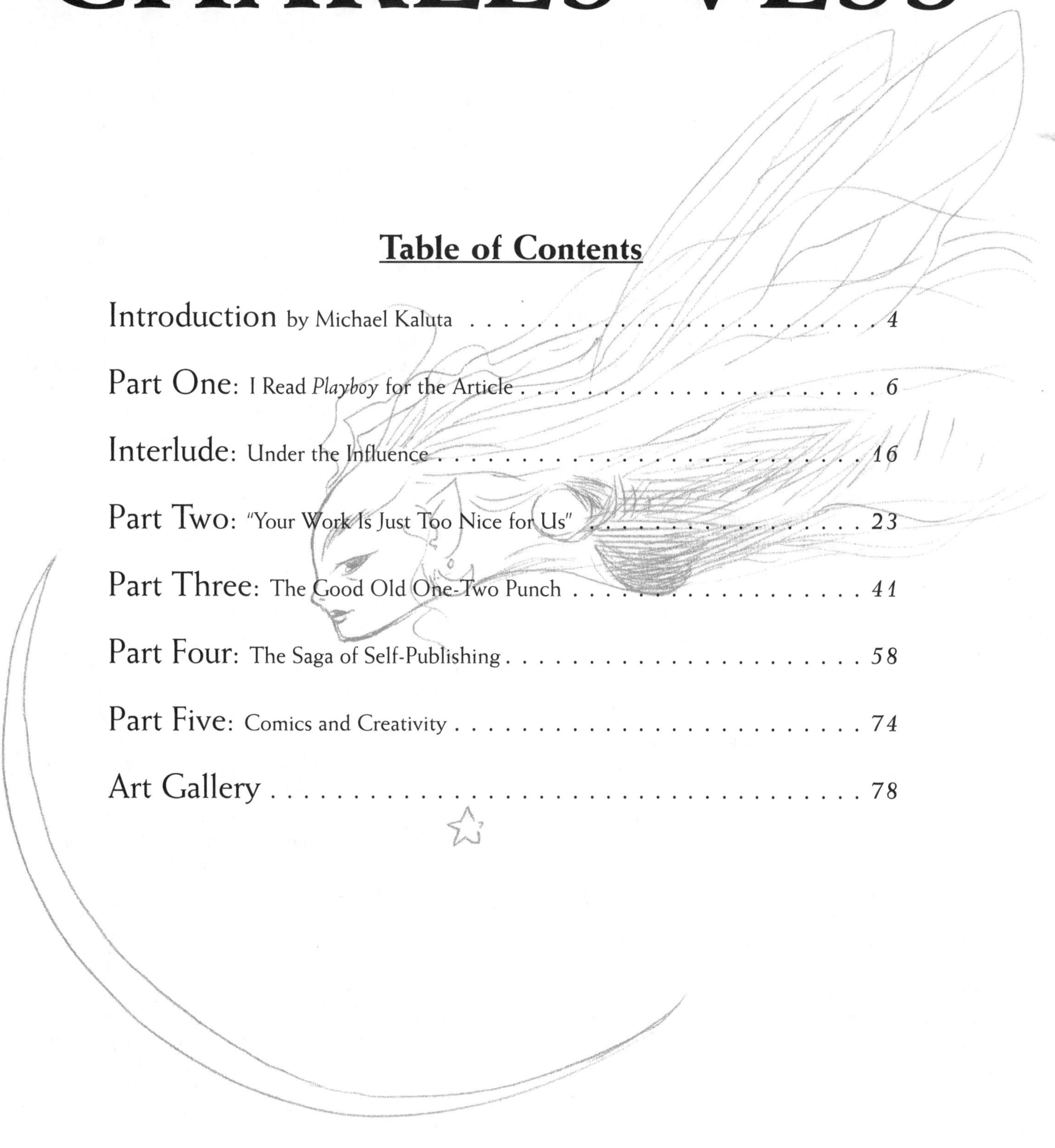

Introduction

During one of my personal ghost-hunting visits to Richmond, Virginia, in 1975 (home of my alma mater: Richmond Professional Institute, now Virginia Commonwealth University) my host, and old college chum, Phil Trumbo, made mention of a young student that had joined up with The Richmond Artist's Co-op; someone he knew I'd like to meet and whose work he knew I'd admire. Phil handed me a local newspaper, produced by the artists and writers at the college, pointing me to the comic strip section. Expecting some variant of the underground comics I was familiar with, or the comic strip pages of *The East Village Other* I'd contributed to in New York City, I was not ready for what I saw here: the Charles Vess strip had the pure essence of everything I'd ever admired in 19th century art, while blending the compositional movement of modern experimental film and 1930s cartoons with the poetry of dream. Being a fan of pen rendering, and especially the technique of cross-hatch, I was struck by the unique use of same in the rendering of the familiar objects Charles had used to move his story strip forward: The result was an alluring soft-light modeling that lent incredible depth to the panels and a palpable reality to all that was in them. Without use of grey wash toning, he'd effectively "painted" the strip with his deft pen work.

It was then, and has been for over 30 years, a treat to be a friend to that artist, as well as a fervent admirer and student of his work. Learning how Charles mixed his humor and incredible work focus with his admirable collection of techniques, his adopting of whatever idea struck him as applicable to furthering his personal take on Fantasy and the picturing of same, has been a big part of my own artistic growth. It is such an asset to have someone's work to turn to knowing it'll constantly amaze and challenge me.

New York became one big cornucopia of delights for Charles: from his earlier visiting days to his advent in the city as a resident, it was Charles For The City and The City For Charles… just as he'd show me another way to think about drawing, he showed me, by his example, how marvelous The City was, even beyond my own delvings. To this day I have a pair of Charlie Vess Eyes in my sketch bag, for use when my own get tame and tired.

In his personal Palette of Life, Charles has always mixed his vision, talent, and colors with enlightened self-interest. If the world is luckier than it deserves, Charles will write a "How To…" book that'll include his no-nonsense approach to doing the work, as well as his insights into the why and wherefore of Fantasy Art creation.

He never turns his back on monumental tasks, but removes that task from the appearance of being overwhelming, so the viewer, rather than be over-awed, is invited in… offered the gift of deep color, like light frozen in water: organic, loamy, rich, as awesome as Loie Fuller's scarf dances.

He defines his path and walks it. One look at his work shows he is as delighted with the world he is presenting as if he had just discovered it himself. That personal delight pours over the brim of the image and swallows us in its flood. Welcomed, we get Charles' point of view: the best vantage point from which to peer at his passing parade.

Charles is a master of both the epic moment and the casual event, melding archaic nature with a conscious design, offering the viewer a request to linger in a bower of ropy originality (not without dynamism, especially to the tutored, knowing eye). His drawings redefine common objects, not by gilding them out of recognition, nor by artificially enhancing them, but by presenting their essences with an un-self-consciousness that charms as quietly as it lures. A Charles Vess Tree is still a tree, but ever so much more a tree. The familiar is made more so when Charles brushes it with his brand of moon and starlight. His pictures offer treasure maps to all the hiding places in Faerie—it's such a pleasant way to be immersed into the unknown, captured in world that Charles holds. As viewers we metamorphose through Charles' talent, becoming translucent: shadows in partial twilight immersed in his liquid imagination, coated by his luminous dreams, comfortably imbued with the second sight Charles lends us through all his work. There's an invitation to recline in these private shadows beneath the flowers, lulled with soft guitars, lit by golden lamps, as our eyes open the crystal door: smoke, petals, feathers, leaves eddy on the breeze that curls like smoke, smoke that flows like a torrent, a torrent that snakes like roots, roots that wind like the hair on a shepherdess, hair that gathers like cloud, clouds that blossom and bloom like milk in blood.

Searching into the pictures uncover more and more levels of satisfaction—still surprising, but rarely unsettling for more than a bright flash moment. Trust in your gaze. While there may be an unanticipated face or fairy figure as your eye wanders through the art into the glade beyond, you feel at home, welcomed. Rest assured: you are an expected part of the composition, no matter how secret the subject may appear to be.

Michael Kaluta
New York City
January, 2007

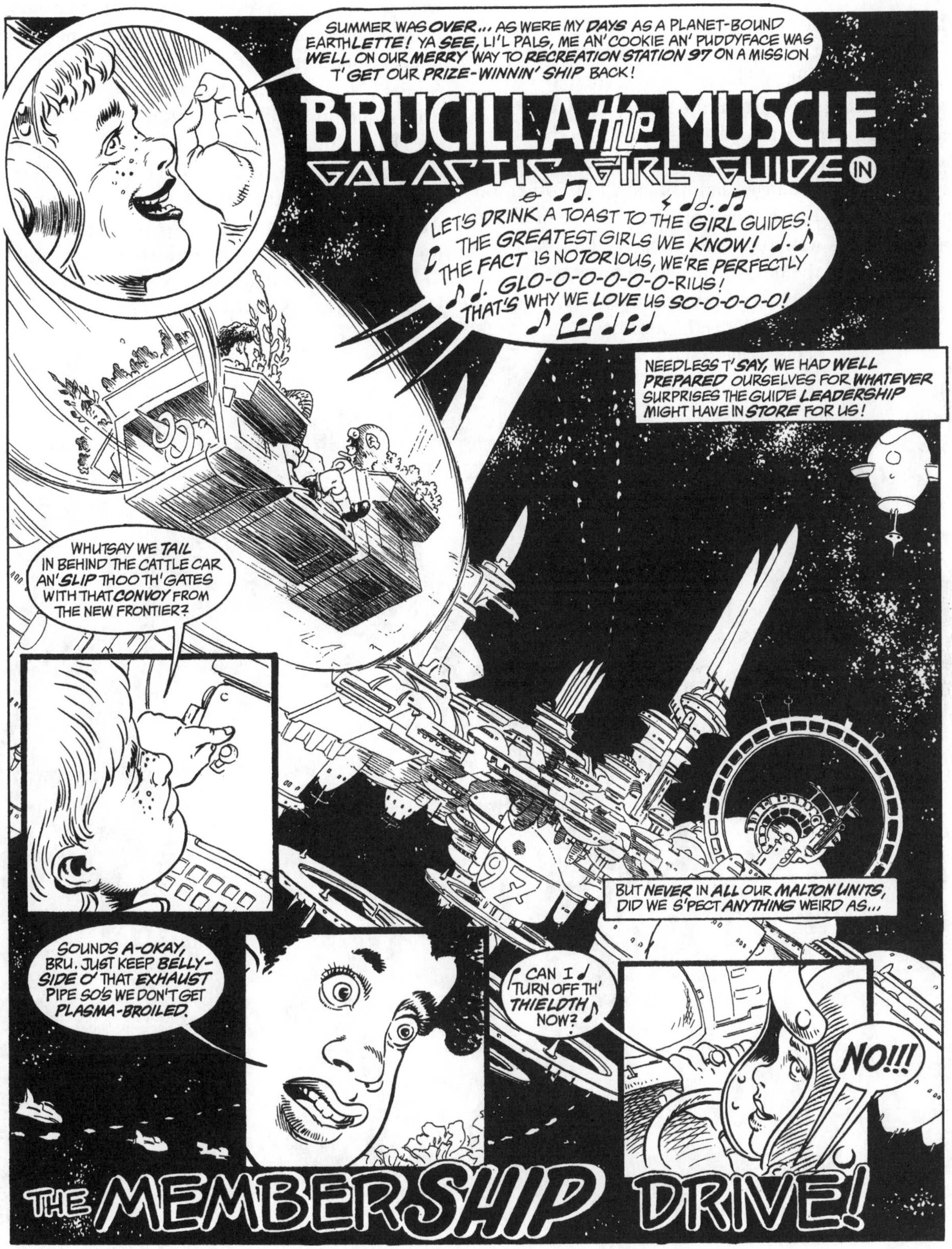

SUMMER WAS OVER... AS WERE MY DAYS AS A PLANET-BOUND EARTHLETTE! YA SEE, LI'L PALS, ME AN' COOKIE AN' PUDDYFACE WAS WELL ON OUR MERRY WAY TO RECREATION STATION 97 ON A MISSION T' GET OUR PRIZE-WINNIN' SHIP BACK!
BRUCILLA the MUSCLE
GALACTIC GIRL GUIDE IN
LET'S DRINK A TOAST TO THE GIRL GUIDES! THE GREATEST GIRLS WE KNOW! THE FACT IS NOTORIOUS, WE'RE PERFECTLY GLO-O-O-O-O-O-RIUS! THAT'S WHY WE LOVE US SO-O-O-O-O!
NEEDLESS T' SAY, WE HAD WELL PREPARED OURSELVES FOR WHATEVER SURPRISES THE GUIDE LEADERSHIP MIGHT HAVE IN STORE FOR US!
WHUTSAY WE TAIL IN BEHIND THE CATTLE CAR AN' SLIP THOO TH' GATES WITH THAT CONVOY FROM THE NEW FRONTIER?
97
BUT NEVER IN ALL OUR MALTON UNITS, DID WE S'PECT ANYTHING WEIRD AS...
SOUNDS A-OKAY, BRU. JUST KEEP BELLY-SIDE O' THAT EXHAUST PIPE SO'S WE DON'T GET PLASMA-BROILED.
CAN I TURN OFF TH' THIELDTH NOW?
NO!!!
THE MEMBERSHIP DRIVE!

Part 1: I Read *Playboy* for the Article

MODERN MASTERS: Should we start with *Stardust*?

CHARLES VESS: I guess so, because everything's sort of focused around that at this point. With the movie coming out, there's lots of peripheral fall-out, all of it good, but still making me work every day at the studio. DC Comics is reissuing the hardcover, as well as a softcover, both with new covers. They also wanted supplemental material, so I said that I had at least six new paintings and all this other work that they could use to stimulate interest in the book. These new paintings weren't actually done yet, but I had been wanting to find the time to draw them for years and years and years. There were, and still are, many scenes in the book that I hadn't been able to illustrate, either because of the very tight deadline or because there were too many pictures for a little bit of text, so this was going to give me a chance to illustrate some of those "lost" images from the book that I've always thought about.

And Neil, for years, has always said that if we ever do a sequel, the image he had in his head to start from was Tristan in a hot-air balloon descending into hell, and he wanted me to draw it. There's one other person in the carriage of the balloon, but he didn't know who it would be. So in drawing that particular scene, as I did for the new edition, I'll be directly influencing the flow of that story. Not that either Neil or I can even think about starting to work on a sequel anytime soon.

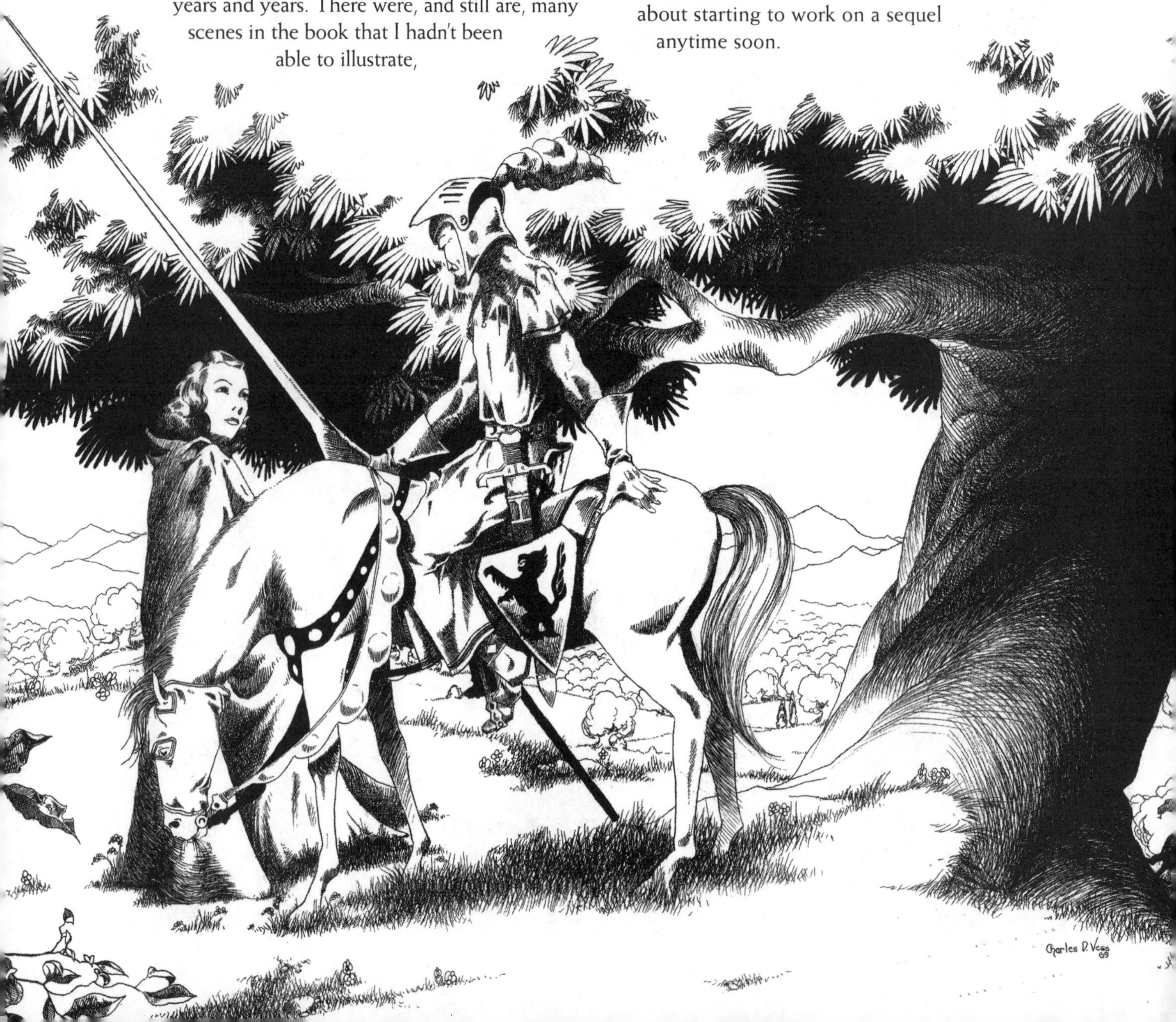
Charles R. Vess 69

MM: Wow.

CHARLES: So I've started drawing/painting these new images. At the same time that this was happening, Paramount Pictures—who will be releasing the movie—has begun development of an extensive promotional website for the movie, and they were approaching me about doing work for it. Also Titan Publishing is doing a "Making Of..." book, and they were approaching me about doing work for their book. And at the same time, for years and years my Green Man Press has been publishing a limited edition signed and numbered portfolio set of *Stardust* prints, and I needed six more images for that. So all of these are one and the same.

MM: Nice, nice.

CHARLES: And they've all sort of piggybacked off one another. The DC images will be in a very rendered pencil style, because there's not really enough time to paint them for the book, but there are one or two of them that will be painted. The website will have the painted versions and I'll also issue those limited edition prints. I'm also producing a new, large-scale faerie market scene that will be used, in pencil form, for the new end papers to the hardcover book, then in full color on Paramount's website and issued as a limited edition print from Green Man Press.

It's been really fun to reread the book, which I hadn't done in a number of years. Neil kept talking about certain characters and I was thinking to myself, "Hmm, I don't remember that." It's been ten years and lots of book projects under the bridge, as it were. So it was really fun to go back and think about it all and get into that world.

Once back in the world of *Stardust* it was all I wanted to do, but at the same time I had a book project for Bloomsbury Press that just came out, 20 black-&-white illustrations for Susanna Clark's *The Ladies of Grace Adieu*. Coincidentally, one of the stories in the book was a *Stardust* story that she'd written for the benefit portfolio I'd produced years ago when my wife was in the car accident. So, really, it's all one big web.

MM: It's come full circle.

CHARLES: I finished those illustrations—as well as some 20 paintings, in collaboration with art pal Michael Kaluta, for *Fables: 1001 Nights of Snowfall*—late last spring and summer. Right now I'm working on a 32-page picture book with Neil called *The Blueberry Girl* for Harper-Collins, and another book called *Coyote Road, Trickster Tales* for Viking that'll have a painted cover and some black-&-white drawings by me. So, I'm juggling lots of deadlines. Also, I'm designing and sculpting several sculptures for the direct market through DC and Dark Horse.

MM: Wow.

CHARLES: And that's not all folks! There are several local projects being worked on at the same time, so it's a very interesting time for me right now. One of those local pieces is a 16' bronze sculpture that I've designed that's going to probably take a year-and-a-half to complete and cast.

MM: Oh my goodness. What's—?

CHARLES: It's been commissioned by the state theater of Virginia and is based on *A Midsummer Night's Dream*. When completed it's going to be placed in the middle of downtown Abingdon, where my studio is located.

MM: Speaking of *A Midsummer Night's Dream*, when I was reading the letters column from the "Midsummer's Night" issue of *Sandman*, Neil referred to you as "an unusual choice for *Sandman*." [*Vess laughs*]

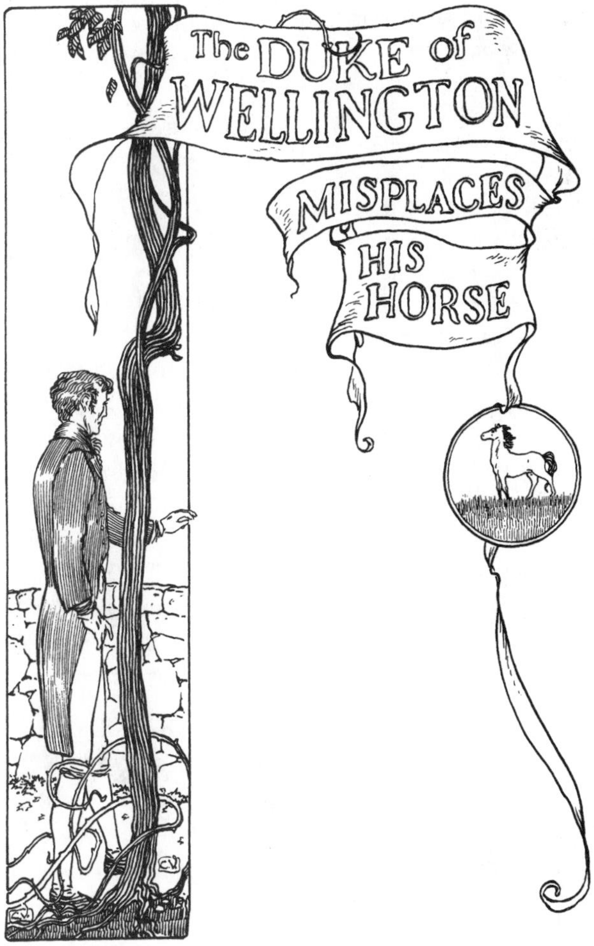
The DUKE of WELLINGTON
MISPLACES
HIS
HORSE

Previous Page: Charles: "The woman's face is swiped from Dale Arden in *Flash Gordon*, and the knight on the horse is from an Angelo Torres story from *Creepy* or *Eerie*. It was a sword-&-sorcery story called 'The Ogre's Castle' with this beautifully drawn knight, and I decided 'That looks good, I'm swiping that.' I believe the dragon is also swiped from Al Williamson. My drawing wasn't so good, but I could always kind of ink. The leaves of the trees were inspired by Russ Manning's *Tarzan* drawings."
Above: Illustration from Suzanna Clark's *The Ladies of Grace Adieu*, for a story which first appeared in the *Fall of Stardust* portfolio.

Below: Charles' homage to a few of his early influences.

Next Page: Charles was able to draw his own "tale of Asgard" as a back-up in *Thor* #400. "Evil Aborning," written by Randall Frenz, showed how Loki learned magic. Charles really liked this story.

From my perspective at the time, I only knew your work starting from *Sandman* up, and so, to me, you're naturally this fantasy illustrator. But you weren't always. You were really well known for your Spider-Man covers, for your "Warriors Three".... And it just amazes me that you were a comic book artist of primarily super-hero or super-hero-related work, and now you've just kind of evolved into not just a comic book artist of fantasy material, but you're also doing lots of illustration and sculpting. How would you classify yourself if you needed to, an illustrator?

CHARLES: As a storyteller. There are many, many avenues that, as an artist, are interesting to follow and eventually you work in a medium you've never used before. When you come back to work in your chosen medium again, you bring with you all that you've learned "outside," and that knowledge radically informs your art, makes it better, fresher. It also keeps you from being bored.

MM: I want to go back to your early days at Virginia Commonwealth University in Richmond, Virginia, primarily, because that's where I went. I understand you grew up in Lynchburg, Virginia, in the early '50s.

CHARLES: Yes. I was born in 1951.

MM: How would you describe Lynchburg in contrast to Abingdon, where you live now?

CHARLES: Lynchburg's a much bigger city. It's also much more conservative. There was very little art or culture at the time. For example, I wasn't even aware that movies were being made anywhere other than Hollywood. There were no bookstores to speak of other than a downtown newsstand. There were libraries to go to, but I had very few friends that shared my interest in fantasy, super-heroes, any of that stuff, so I had no one to suggest, "Oh, well, have you read that?" I had to discover everything myself, so most of the time I was the lone comics fan or Harryhausen/*Tarzan* movie buff or Bradbury/Asimov/Heinlein book nut.

MM: So you were a lonely comics fan in a small city. What was your first experience with comics?

CHARLES: This would have been in the late '50s to early '60s, on a Saturday morning at the barber shop. My brother handed me an *Uncle Scrooge* comic, which had a Carl Barks story—nobody knew that [it was Barks] at the time—and I really enjoyed it. The [Dell] *Tarzan* comics were also in the mangled pile of reading material at the shop. I loved the "Brothers of the Spear" serials that ran in the back.

But it wasn't until I read a copy of *Fantastic Four* #4 there, that I said to myself, "I have to own this!" So I saved up my money, and by the time I had

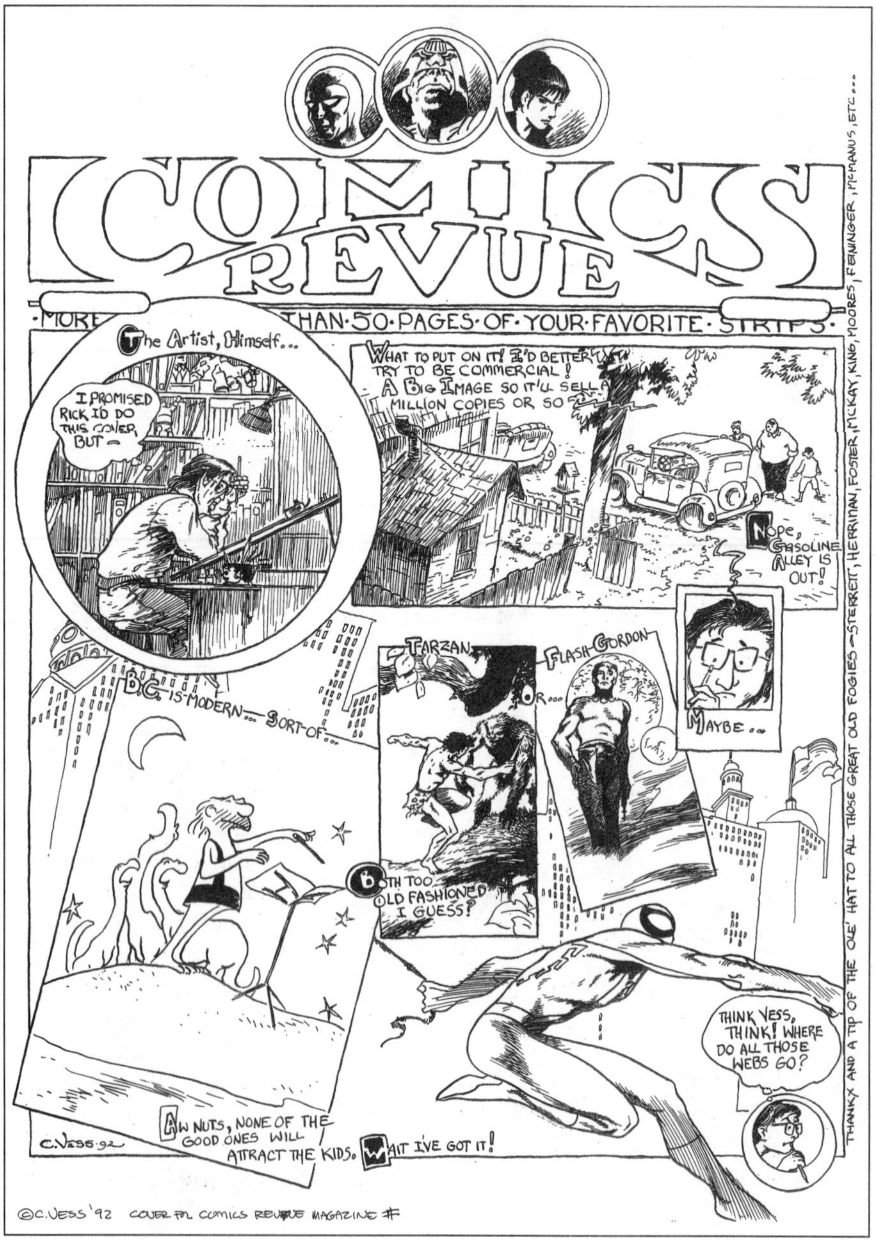

COMICS REVUE
·MORE THAN·50·PAGES·OF·YOUR·FAVORITE·STRIPS·
The Artist, Himself...
I PROMISED RICK I'D DO THIS COVER, BUT –
WHAT TO PUT ON IT! I'D BETTER TRY TO BE COMMERCIAL! A BIG IMAGE SO IT'LL SELL A MILLION COPIES OR SO
NOPE, GASOLINE ALLEY IS OUT!
B.C. IS MODERN... SORT-OF...
TARZAN
OR...
FLASH GORDON
MAYBE...
BOTH TOO OLD FASHIONED I GUESS?
THINK VESS, THINK! WHERE DO ALL THOSE WEBS GO?
AW NUTS, NONE OF THE GOOD ONES WILL ATTRACT THE KIDS. WAIT I'VE GOT IT!
C.VESS·92
THANKS AND A TIP OF THE OLE' HAT TO ALL THOSE GREAT OLD FOGIES—STERRETT, HERRIMAN, FOSTER, MCKAY, KING, MOORES, FEININGER, MCMANUS, ETC...
©C.VESS '92 COVER FOR COMICS REVUE MAGAZINE #

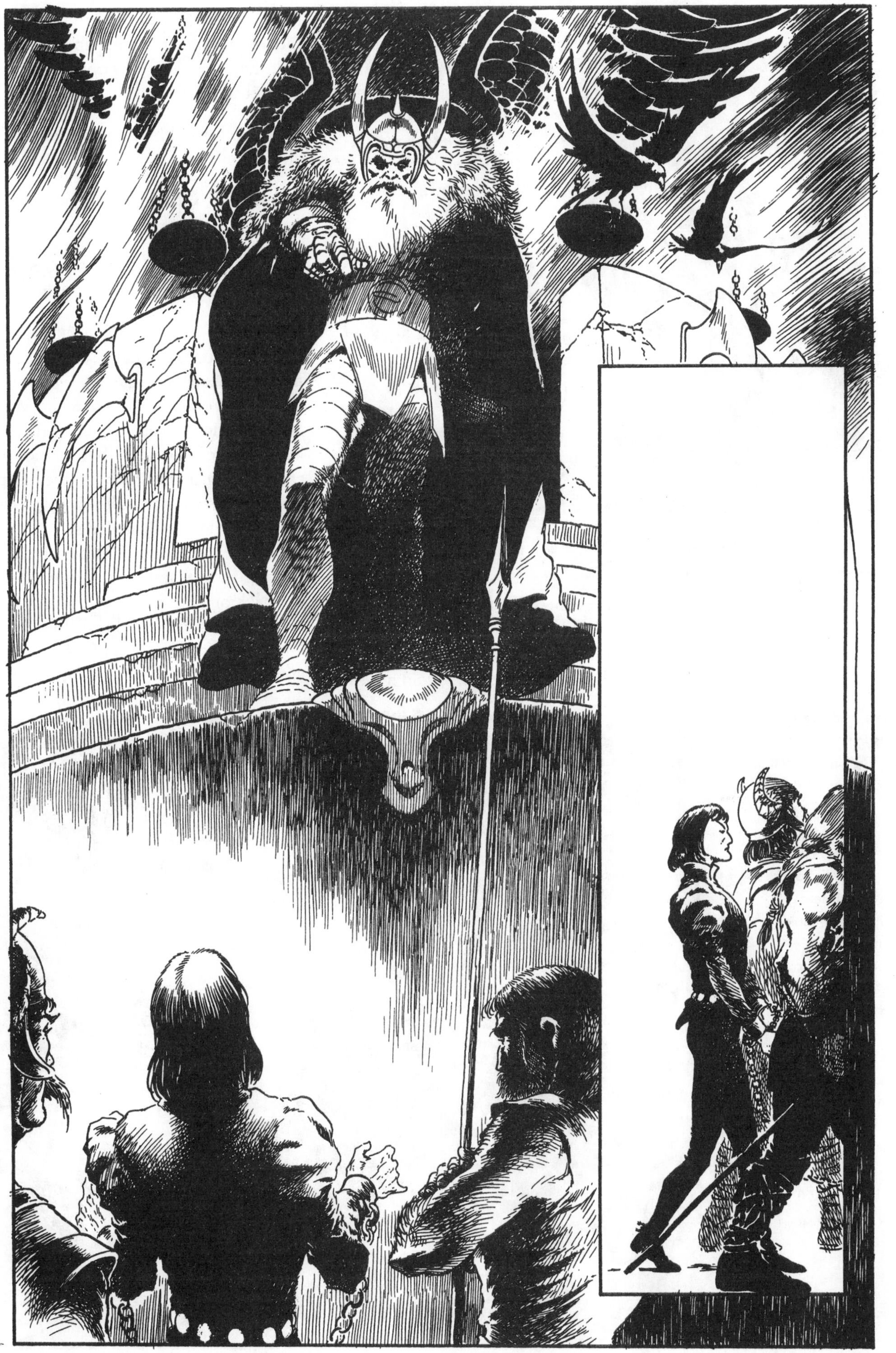

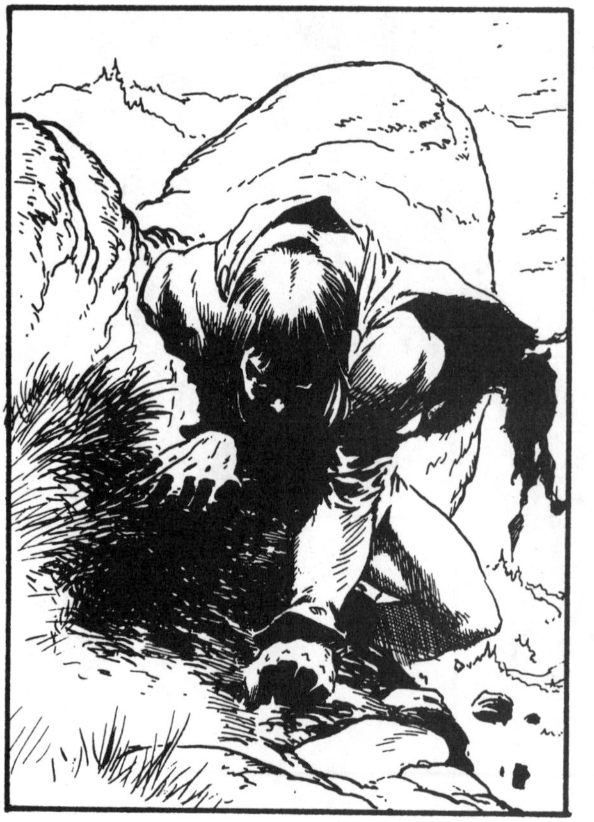

enough—we weren't getting much for allowances back then—and had convinced my parents to drive me down to the newsstand in downtown Lynchburg, Peter's Newsstand, and *Fantastic Four* #6 was on the rack, so I bought that and I'm like, "Wow!" Hooked. Totally hooked.

And right around then, I started making friends with the man down the street who had the coin and stamp shop that sold old comics that he'd find in attics. I got to be a regular customer, and he'd call me up as soon as he had gotten the latest gold mine from some attic, and I got to go through them first. The best thing about them was that they were half cover price, so the older it was, the cheaper it was.

MM: So how old were you, again, when you discovered—?

CHARLES: Oh, this would be ten, eleven, twelve.

MM: What was it about *Fantastic Four*—or even just Kirby's art—that really drew you in?

CHARLES: I guess the humanity of the characters and the dynamic drawings. It was the perfect time for me to see that. I also bought lots of *Strange Adventures* and *Mystery in Space* and those absolutely, sublimely ridiculous "Atomic Knights" with the armor riding around the giant Dalmatians—the Murphy Anderson drawn stories. It was gorgeous, and I just fell in love with all that stuff.

I was enjoying the fantasy aspects of it all, but it wasn't until "Tales of Asgard" in the back of *Thor* that I realized that there was some world mythology other than the Greek. I'd watched a lot of sword-&-sandal epics on TV—which usually featured a

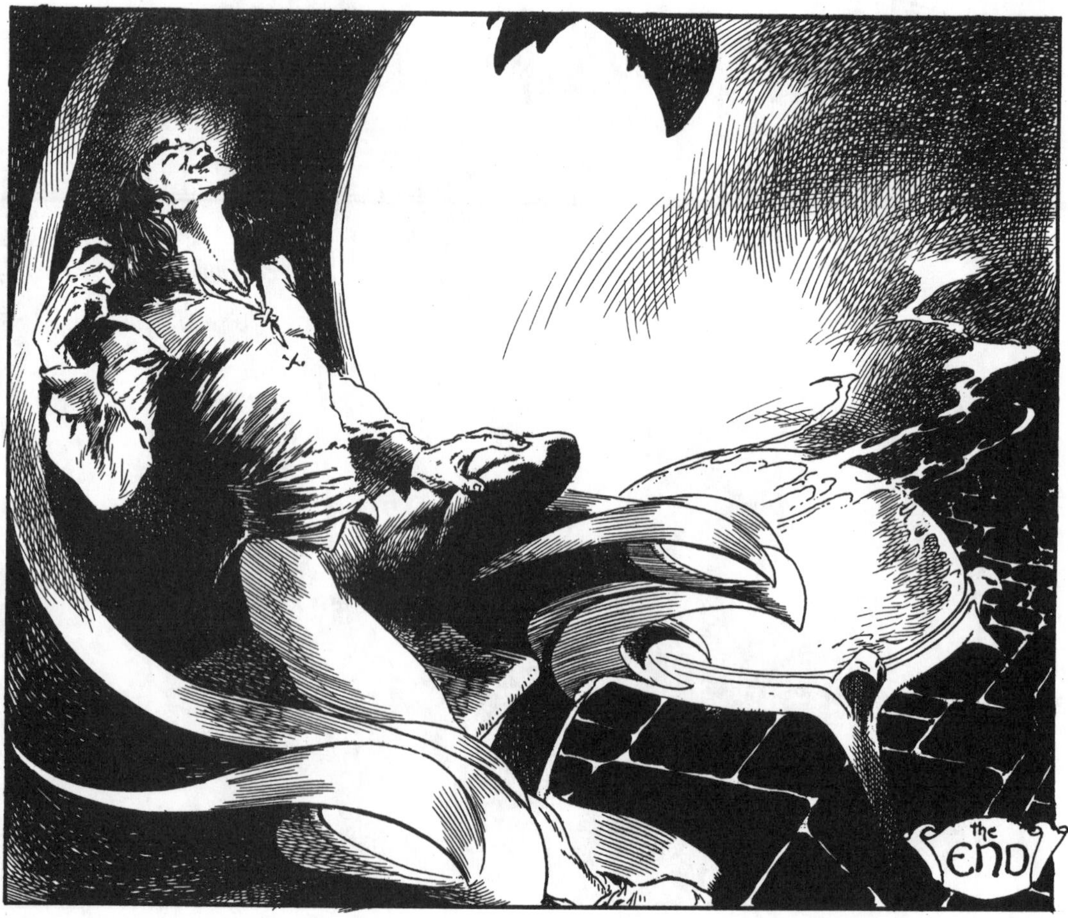
the END

Above and Right: Panels from "Evil Aborning" in *Thor* #400. **Next Page:** Of this ink wash drawing Charles says, "It was a copy of one of Frank Frazetta's *Creepy* or *Eerie* covers—just a magnificent painting that I couldn't get enough of. I reproduced his art in black-&-white as best I could with primitive tools and materials, but there's a lot of love there. I was 15 when I did that? I used to do a lot of copying, and learned a lot that way. I was a huge fan of Frazetta at the time."

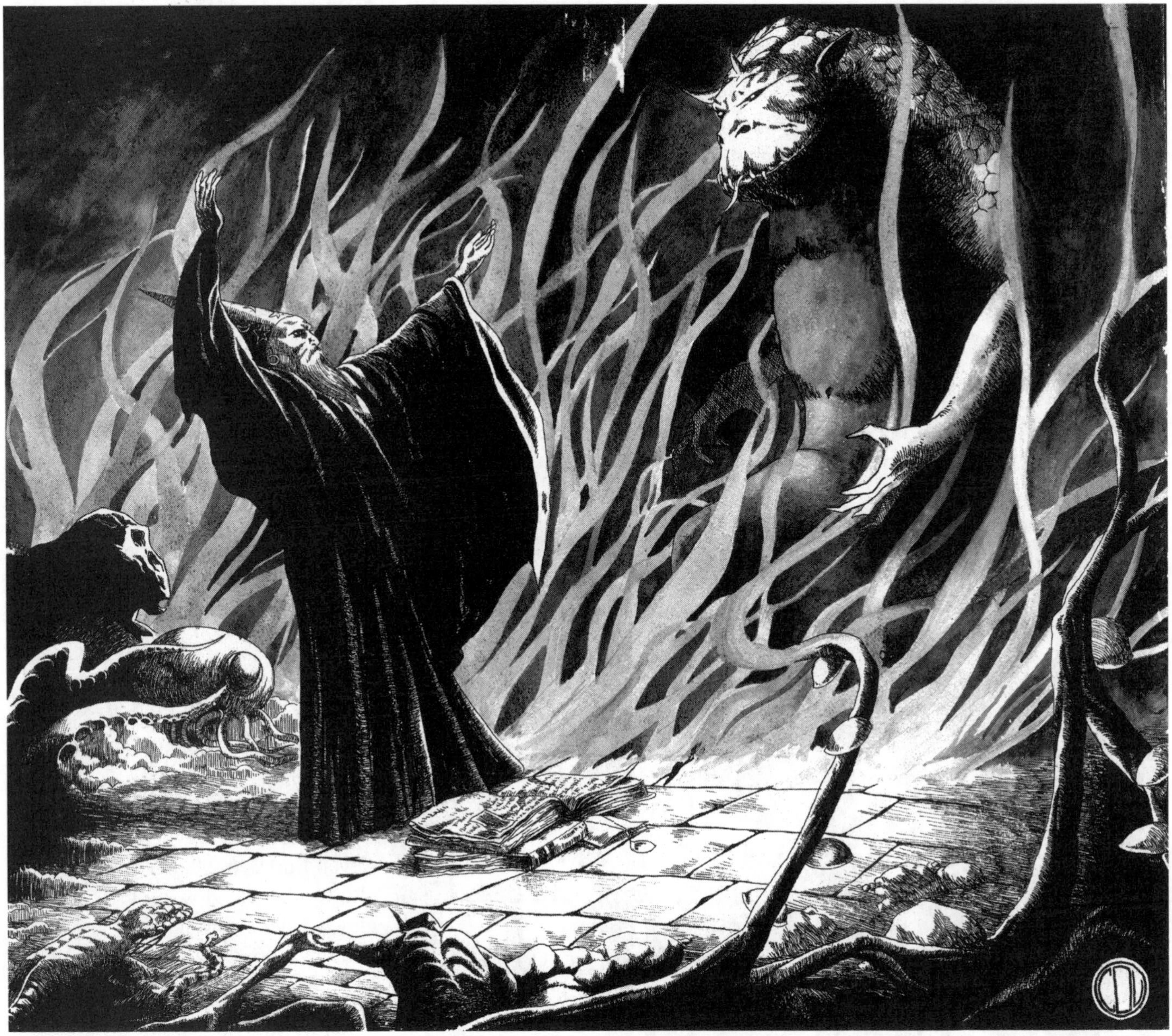

mangled version of the Trojan War or the quest for the golden fleece—and found it really exciting. And you could find *Bullfinch's Greek Mythology* in the library, but again, I didn't have anybody pointing anything out, so I had to stumble across something, see a connection, and go after it. And once I realized that there was some other mythology other than Greek mythology, I went to the library and looked it up and began to read all those dark and stormy Nordic Sagas. I was in early adolescence and that type of story was very appealing to my raging hormones, perfect timing I would say.

MM: So you watched a lot of sword-&-sandal epics; were there any movie serials being shown at the time?

CHARLES: They didn't have too many of those. I watched those Ray Harryhausen films... of course, at that point, I didn't know Ray Harryhausen was *Ray Harryhausen*, but just that there were these cool films that all had the same quality of imagination that I liked! Somewhere in there I was reading *Famous Monsters of Filmland*, as well as *Castle Frankenstein*, their low-rent rival, which printed the work of a lot of illustrators I'd never seen before.

It wasn't like you could go to the Internet and look up this stuff, and there weren't any art books. I was desperate to find the history of the art and stories that I was interested in. One absolute vivid memory was finding out from the *Castle Frankenstein* magazine that Jules Feiffer was writing a book called *The Great Comic Book Heroes*, and that months before the book was to come out there was going to be an article in *Playboy* magazine. I knew what issue the article was going to run in, but I was twelve years old and also knew that there was absolutely no way I would ever be able to buy the magazine. So I went into this rather large department store with its magazine rack located far in the rear, and waited for any noise to happen in the store, and slowly ripped the article out of the magazine. I just had to read it!

Below: Page 4 of *The Dark Rider.*

Next Page: Charles on "Jack Tales": "After Archie Goodwin asked me for a story, it took me eight months to write and draw this 8-page story. In 1968, when I was still in high school, I'd drawn a barbarian strip, 'Tros,' and a friend gave me a great twist-ending, which I used again for this story."

MM: So you were the first kid who actually looked at *Playboy* for the articles. [*laughter*]

CHARLES: Yeah, I did, for the article. And then my parents bought me the actual book as my Christmas present that year.

MM: Did you latch on to Kirby specifically, or could you tell it was him?

CHARLES: Oh, I could tell. Actually, with all the art I'd studied up until that time, it didn't occur to me until I saw Jack Kirby's signature on a splash page of the *Fantastic Four* that an actual, living, breathing person had done the art. Where before I had had no idea, or even questioned where a particular piece of art would have come from, that signature made a connection in my mind—an actual human being had done that art. Then I immediately thought, "Maybe I could do the same!"

As a fanatic of comics, I quickly began to identify the styles of various artists at that time when hardly anybody would sign their work. Marvel had the occasional signatures, but not DC. I didn't know who Gil Kane or Carmine Infantino were, but I knew their styles. And what was really difficult—before the signatures—was when somebody who had a very distinctive style, like Murphy Anderson, would ink somebody else like Carmine Infantino and make it, at least superficially, look like his. Which caused me to think, "That looks like artist A, but the way the figures are posed looks like artist B."

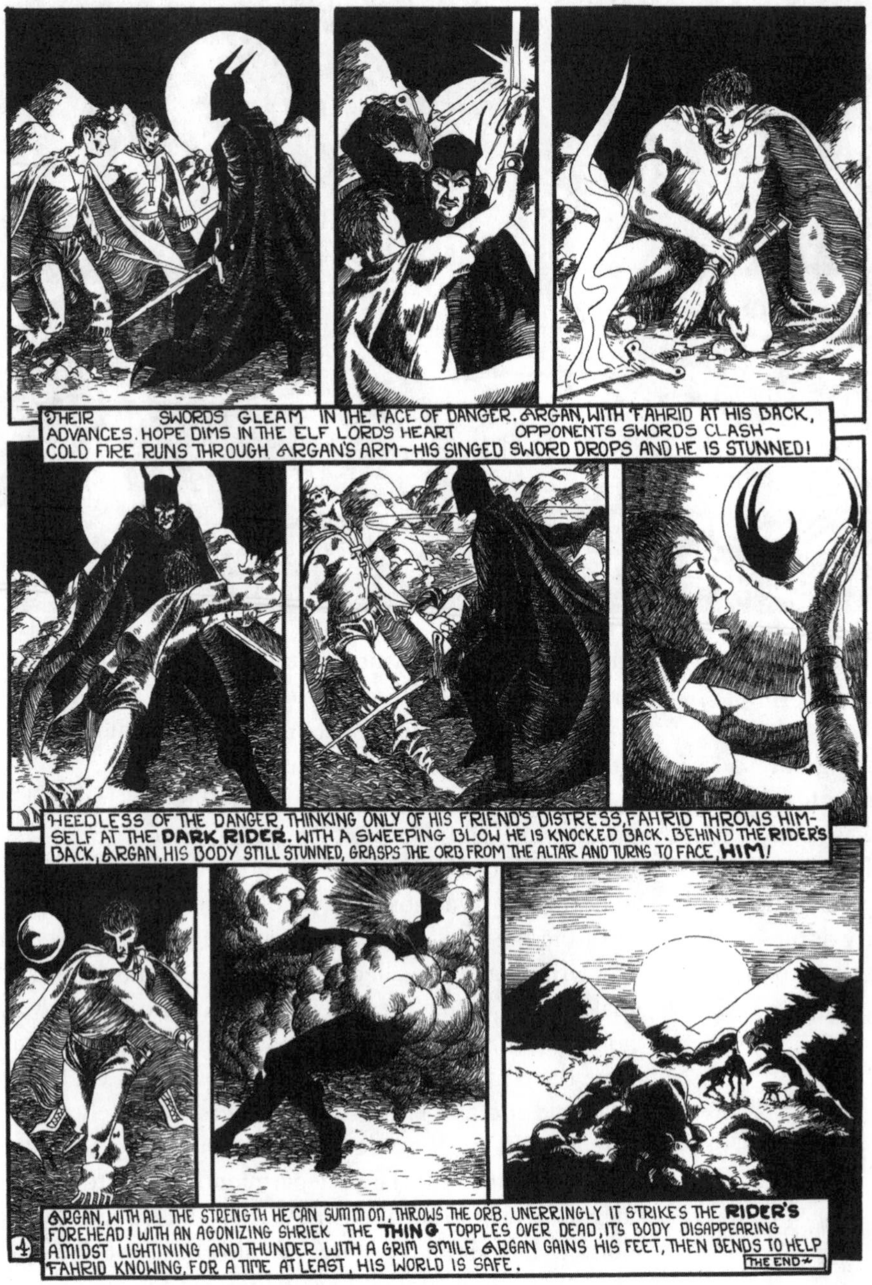
THEIR SWORDS GLEAM IN THE FACE OF DANGER. ARGAN, WITH FAHRID AT HIS BACK, ADVANCES. HOPE DIMS IN THE ELF LORD'S HEART OPPONENTS SWORDS CLASH~ COLD FIRE RUNS THROUGH ARGAN'S ARM~HIS SINGED SWORD DROPS AND HE IS STUNNED!
HEEDLESS OF THE DANGER, THINKING ONLY OF HIS FRIEND'S DISTRESS, FAHRID THROWS HIM-SELF AT THE DARK RIDER. WITH A SWEEPING BLOW HE IS KNOCKED BACK. BEHIND THE RIDER'S BACK, ARGAN, HIS BODY STILL STUNNED, GRASPS THE ORB FROM THE ALTAR AND TURNS TO FACE, HIM!
ARGAN, WITH ALL THE STRENGTH HE CAN SUMMON, THROWS THE ORB. UNERRINGLY IT STRIKES THE RIDER'S FOREHEAD! WITH AN AGONIZING SHRIEK THE THING TOPPLES OVER DEAD, ITS BODY DISAPPEARING AMIDST LIGHTINING AND THUNDER. WITH A GRIM SMILE ARGAN GAINS HIS FEET, THEN BENDS TO HELP FAHRID KNOWING, FOR A TIME AT LEAST, HIS WORLD IS SAFE.
THE END
4

MM: So were you drawing much at that point?

CHARLES: All the time. It's the one thing I was good at.

MM: What would you draw?

CHARLES: Well, when I was ten or eleven I drew A-Man, a guy that had glowing hands, glowing feet, and a glowing head, and he went around bashing crooks in the head.

MM: So did you want to do comic books, or mostly just illustration?

CHARLES: Just before high school I did make one friend, Robert Rector, who also was deeply into comic books. It took half an hour to walk over to his house, but it was always a treat. He had more money than I did, so he could order coverless comics from Ken Bald or some other exotic, far-away comic book dealer. We were in a constant detective game of attempting to find out who had drawn or written a particular comic book story. At that time there were no books or a handy Internet Google search to tell you any of these details. So he would order these old, Golden Age comics, and we'd pore through them picking out individual styles.

Robert would also write comic book scripts and I would draw them on onion-skin paper—the only paper I had at the time. We recreated *Spirit* stories or invented new super-heroes on our own. It was fun!

By the early '60s, I'd also found *Creepy* and *Eerie*. I didn't just like super-heroes, I didn't just like science fiction and fantasy in art: I liked storytelling. So if it was told well, drawn well, I liked it. Those two magazines came out and they had those famous Frazetta covers. I couldn't get enough of his art. The *Lord of the Rings* trilogy of novels came out at about the same time, so I was introduced to that fantasy subgenre, which was a perfect off-shoot of reading the "Tales of Asgard" stuff.

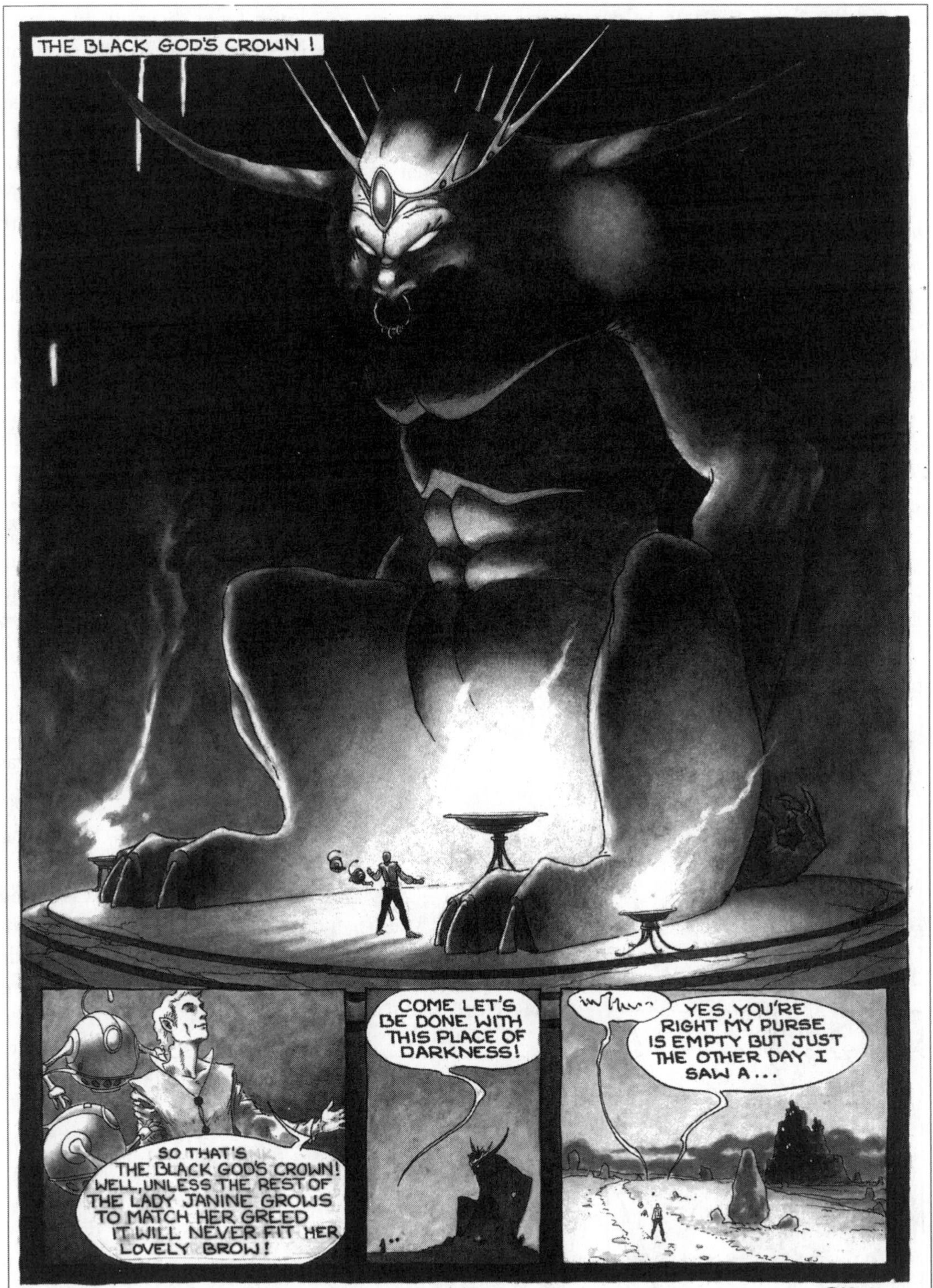
THE BLACK GOD'S CROWN!
SO THAT'S THE BLACK GOD'S CROWN! WELL, UNLESS THE REST OF THE LADY JANINE GROWS TO MATCH HER GREED IT WILL NEVER FIT HER LOVELY BROW!
COME LET'S BE DONE WITH THIS PLACE OF DARKNESS!
YES, YOU'RE RIGHT MY PURSE IS EMPTY BUT JUST THE OTHER DAY I SAW A...
·END·

I kept trying to draw sequential stories, but I'd get bored with my plot or frustrated with my inability to draw something and abandon it before I reached the end. I did finish *The Dark Rider*, a five-page comic strip that I did for my high school literary magazine. It was inked with a watercolor brush that I'd cut down to ten or twelve bristles, because every time I had tried to ink with a dip pen it had spattered everywhere. The story was done on this strange, yellow art paper from Sears, but it was the only kind of art paper that I knew how to get. My parents would buy it for me. The drawing seems pretty crude to me now, but I was sure trying hard! It was my five-page version of *Lord of the Rings*! Maybe if Mort Drucker had drawn a five-page *Lord of the Rings* parody for *Mad*, it would've been better, and I expect a lot funnier too.

Another story that I actually finished was "Tros of Samothrace," my sword-&-sorcery story. I got several pages into it and couldn't for the life of me think of an ending. Hint: *Never* start a story without an ending folks. My friend, Robert, came to my rescue with a great twist-ending. Years later I redid that story for *Epic Illustrated* and called it "Jack Tales." Using that same ending worked out very well.

MM: Were there any cartoonists or even movies that you picked up storytelling tricks from?

CHARLES: Well, Nostalgia Press started putting out *Flash Gordon*, *Popeye the Sailor*, and *Prince Valiant* reprint books. I studied them all looking for some way to unlock their secrets. I read anything and everything that was sequential in nature. Then sometime in my junior year of high school there was an article in the newspaper that featured four young men—Michael Kaluta was one of them—whose comics were being published in *Graphic Showcase*, a magazine out of Richmond, Virginia. The article said nothing about where they actually lived, but I was so excited, that I tried to convince my parents to drive me to Richmond, which was about two hours away from my hometown. I needed to find those guys and talk to them because I wanted to be one of them... be the fifth guy. Eventually, I choose the university that I did, VCU, because it was in Richmond, and I knew that I was going to be able to eventually find those four artists. And I did; I met them all, and years later, after moving to New York City, became roommates with one of them.

MM: I saw Mark Wheatley at a convention, and he said, "Oh, yeah, I went to VCU with Charles." I asked him what made him decide to go to VCU. "Well, Kaluta did." I went, "Really?" "Yeah, Mike Kaluta told me there were two girls for every guy there. So that settled it."

So how much older is Michael than you?

CHARLES: Three years.

MM: So, when you were going in as a freshman...?

CHARLES: He was already out. He just went for two years and then left for New York. But he would come down every once in a while to stay for extended periods of time, and I met him then through Phil Trumbo, a friend. Phil is a gifted artist and a great animator. The opening credits to the old *Pee Wee's Playhouse* are his work, as well as the dinosaur family that lived in the playhouse wall. Now he's out in Seattle directing Playstation games based on *Harry Potter* and Narnia, etc. Through him, I met a whole bunch of local art people; he was sort of the art nexus of Richmond, Virginia.

So, I was attending VCU and was going to major in commercial art in order to, in my mind, learn how to draw comic books. But the Commercial Art department at VCU at that time was all about graphic design and that was it. They were basically teaching you how to do paste-ups, which people don't do anymore, but you'd have four years of that. After about three weeks there, doing paste-ups, I decided that it wasn't for me. I didn't want to really change schools, because I really liked Richmond, so I switched into the Fine Art department. Once I moved into that department, I found the focus was on conceptual art and abstract expressionism, also affectionately called squat and piss painting by those of us who wanted something more.

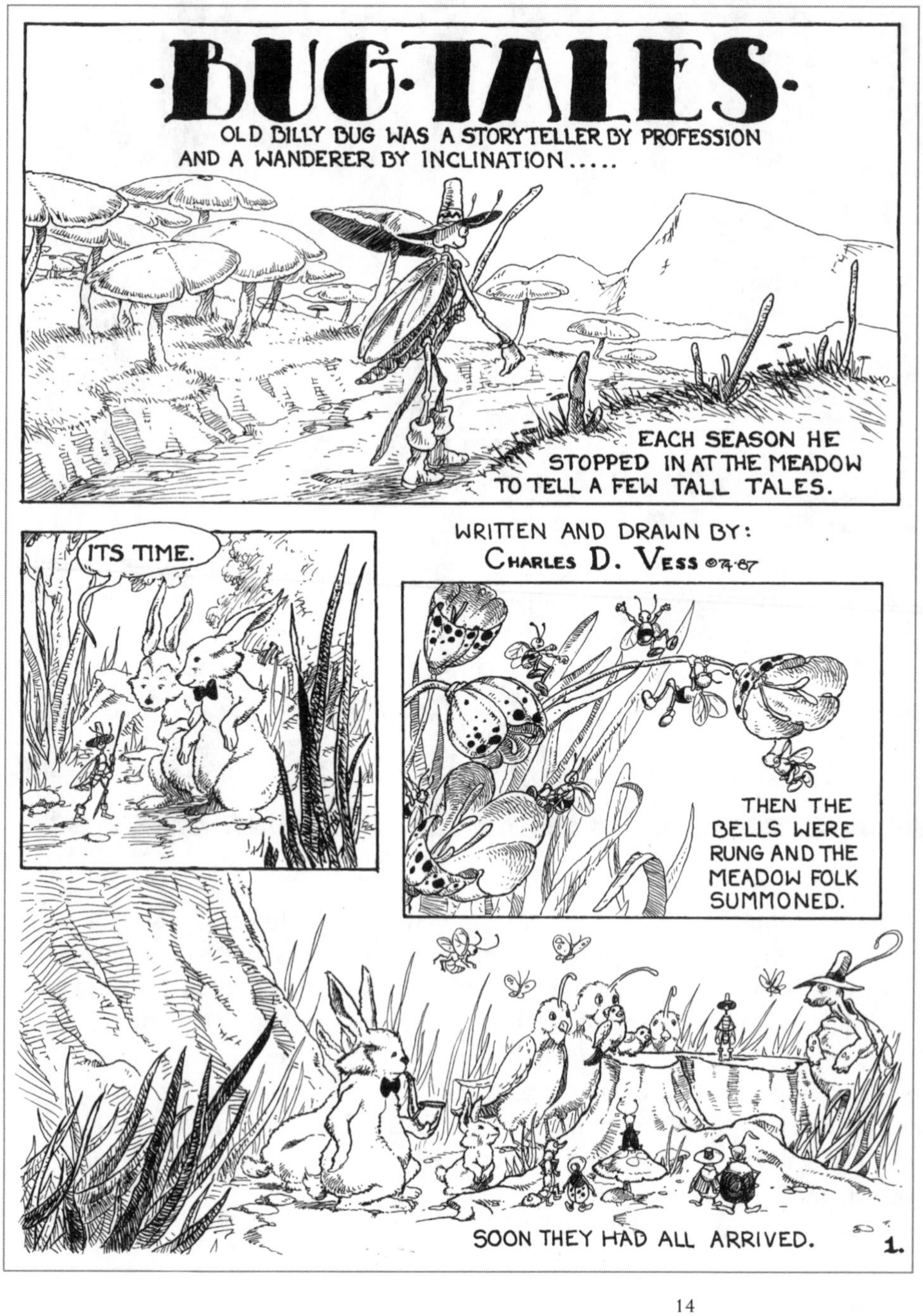

·BUG·TALES·
OLD BILLY BUG WAS A STORYTELLER BY PROFESSION AND A WANDERER BY INCLINATION.....
EACH SEASON HE STOPPED IN AT THE MEADOW TO TELL A FEW TALL TALES.
WRITTEN AND DRAWN BY: CHARLES D. VESS
ITS TIME.
THEN THE BELLS WERE RUNG AND THE MEADOW FOLK SUMMONED.
SOON THEY HAD ALL ARRIVED.
1.

MM: I always thought of VCU as pretty liberal. Was it the same way back then?

CHARLES: It was. I remember going to visit the campus for the first time with my parents in 1969. Every guy had long hair and blue jeans, girls with flowers in their hair and long dresses. It was very hippie. My parents asked, "Are you sure you want to go here?" I'm going, "Yeah. Looks good to me."

MM: How would you describe the approach your teachers gave you to painting?

CHARLES: If I did anything with figures it was considered narrative, and narrative was not art to my teachers. I started fashioning large, semi-surrealistic landscapes—secretly in the vein of *Krazy Kat*—that my teacher's rather liked. There I would be, sitting in a painting studio at school reading Jack Kirby's Fourth World saga or various DC horror titles with art by Wrightson, Neal Adams, and Kaluta, and other students would look at me like I was very weird. I know a lot of people don't like art school, but other than the sometimes overt prejudice against comic books I really enjoyed the atmosphere there; it was really exciting. [It was] another four years of basically not having to worry about making a living, just concentrating on doing art. Cool to me! During the summers I would take all my artwork and make money selling it at Shafer Court.

MM: Did you have a favorite spot?

CHARLES: Yeah, it was in the middle of the campus then, and I'd just lean my art

SUDDENLY IT WAS THE LATE 1960'S AND I WAS ATTENDING ART SCHOOL. THE SHOOTINGS AT KENT STATE MOMENTARILY TOOK MY THOUGHTS AWAY FROM MY DRAWING BOARD AS I MARCHED ON WASHINGTON AND JOINED "PEACE-INS" ON CAMPUS WITH ALL THE RIGHTEOUS FERVER OF THE OTHER HIPPIES AND FREE SPIRITS.

up against a low stone wall and sit and wait for prospective customers to walk by.

MM: So at that point, were you still interested in super-hero comics?

CHARLES: I just wanted to tell stories with my art and somehow make a living from it. It was never that I even really wanted to draw just super-heroes or just horror or just fantasy, I simply wanted to draw for a living. So when I got out of school I had my only nine-to-five job doing animation.

MM: Was it freelance?

CHARLES: It was freelance, but an almost constant source of work. The studio, Candy Apple Productions, did a lot of 30-second TV commercials. I remember one of them being for the Virginia Department of Transportation: "Right Turn on Red." Pretty exciting. [*laughter*]

MM: Sounds pretty action-packed, but a good start.

CHARLES: From the early to mid-'70s on, books about artists that I really responded to began to be published. There was just an explosion of really exciting art books coming out—all sorts of stuff—and it was a constant growing. To buy them all I needed a job.

Previous Page: Charles drew the anthropomorphic strip, "Bug Tales," way back in 1974.
Above: Panel from Charles' "one and only autobiographical strip— done for a local exhibition that was themed around Elvis."
Left: Photo of Shafer Court—one of Charles' favorite hang-out spots during college—taken around the time Charles attended VCU. Courtesy VCU Special Collections.

Bug Tales ™ and ©2007 Charles Vess. Artwork ©2007 Charles Vess. Photo ©2007 Virginia Commonwealth University.

Interlude: Under the Influence

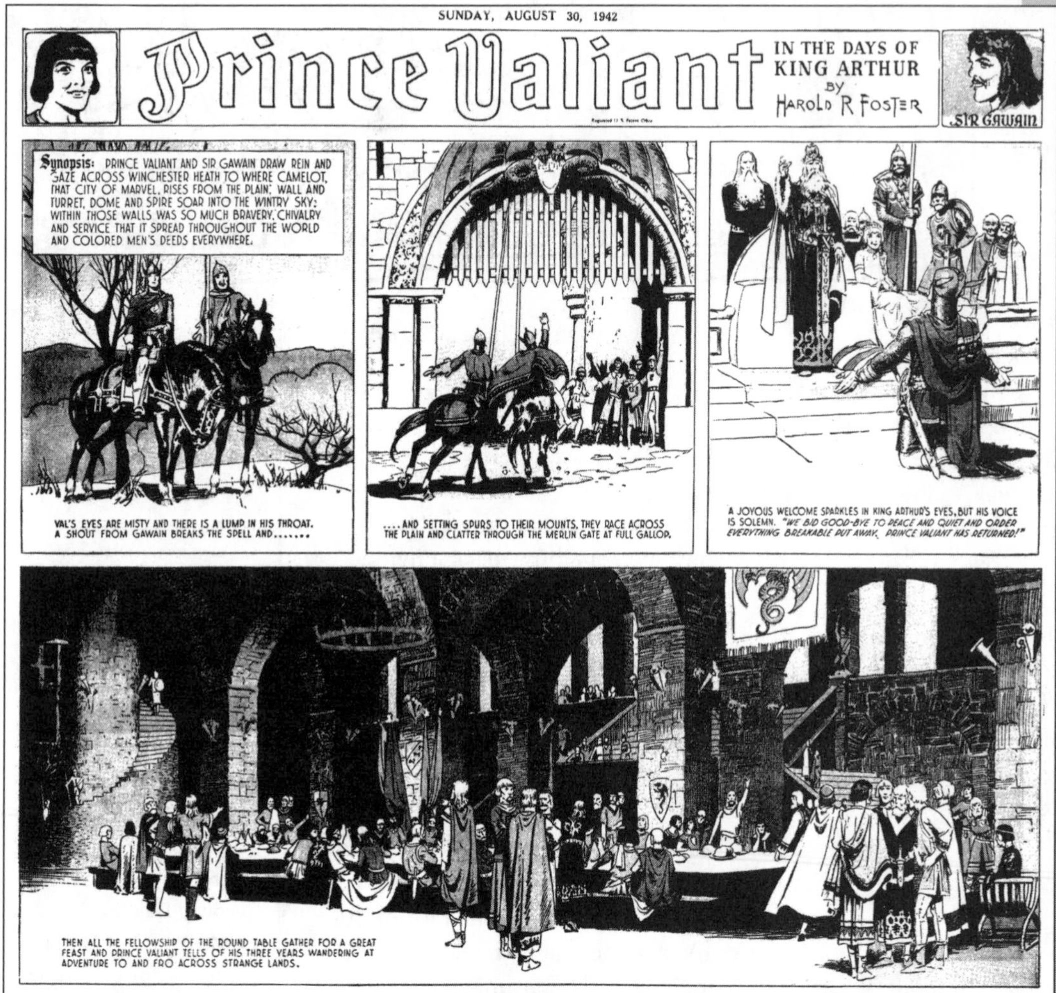

SUNDAY, AUGUST 30, 1942
Prince Valiant
IN THE DAYS OF KING ARTHUR BY HAROLD R FOSTER
SIR GAWAIN
Synopsis: PRINCE VALIANT AND SIR GAWAIN DRAW REIN AND GAZE ACROSS WINCHESTER HEATH TO WHERE CAMELOT, THAT CITY OF MARVEL, RISES FROM THE PLAIN; WALL AND TURRET, DOME AND SPIRE SOAR INTO THE WINTRY SKY: WITHIN THOSE WALLS WAS SO MUCH BRAVERY, CHIVALRY AND SERVICE THAT IT SPREAD THROUGHOUT THE WORLD AND COLORED MEN'S DEEDS EVERYWHERE.
VAL'S EYES ARE MISTY AND THERE IS A LUMP IN HIS THROAT. A SHOUT FROM GAWAIN BREAKS THE SPELL AND.......
....AND SETTING SPURS TO THEIR MOUNTS, THEY RACE ACROSS THE PLAIN AND CLATTER THROUGH THE MERLIN GATE AT FULL GALLOP.
A JOYOUS WELCOME SPARKLES IN KING ARTHUR'S EYES, BUT HIS VOICE IS SOLEMN. "WE BID GOOD-BYE TO PEACE AND QUIET AND ORDER EVERYTHING BREAKABLE PUT AWAY. PRINCE VALIANT HAS RETURNED!"
THEN ALL THE FELLOWSHIP OF THE ROUND TABLE GATHER FOR A GREAT FEAST AND PRINCE VALIANT TELLS OF HIS THREE YEARS WANDERING AT ADVENTURE TO AND FRO ACROSS STRANGE LANDS.
AT LAST KING ARTHUR ARISES AND SILENCE FALLS THROUGHOUT THE GREAT HALL.
"GRAVE TIDINGS HAVE COME FROM THE NORTH. PREPARE YOU ONE AND ALL FOR WAR!"
290 8-30-42
"REST YOU WELL FROM YOUR TRAVELS, SIR VALIANT, FOR SOON WE WILL HAVE A DANGEROUS QUEST THAT ONLY YOU CAN UNDERTAKE."
HAL FOSTER
NEXT WEEK— Preparedness.

Hal Foster

I grew up reading Hal Foster, so I always looked forward to Sunday's big comic strip and disappearing into the world of King Arthur and Prince Valiant. He tells a story, not in visual terms, really, but in tableaus and a more illustrative manner. I love his sense of environment surrounding the people—you feel the world is real. As I've gotten older, I'll notice in crowd scenes of his that every character has an individual personality, which is amazing. The way he spotted blacks, drew horses... there's many an artist nowadays who ought to look at his horses... I found it all fascinating. In the late '60s, I was studying the work of both he and Alex Raymond, who are both on par as my favorite artists. I've sort of gotten bored with Alex Raymond, but I keep learning from Hal Foster.

Arthur Rackham

Arthur Rackham's a British illustrator who worked from about 1895 to 1940. He's one of my very, very major influences: There are lots of fairy tale and fantasy illustrations in a magnificent edition of the Wagner Operas, and he did three editions of *A Midsummer Night's Dream*. I love the line and watercolor feel of the pieces, the beautiful women, the forests that surround them, and the imps and goblins that inhabit it.

It was like coming home, when I first saw his work in 1970. My first or second year in college I saw one or two pieces, and somewhere in the mid-1970s, an art book came out. I have a limited edition book that's vellum-bound with a signature, and someone even gave me a small black-&-white original.

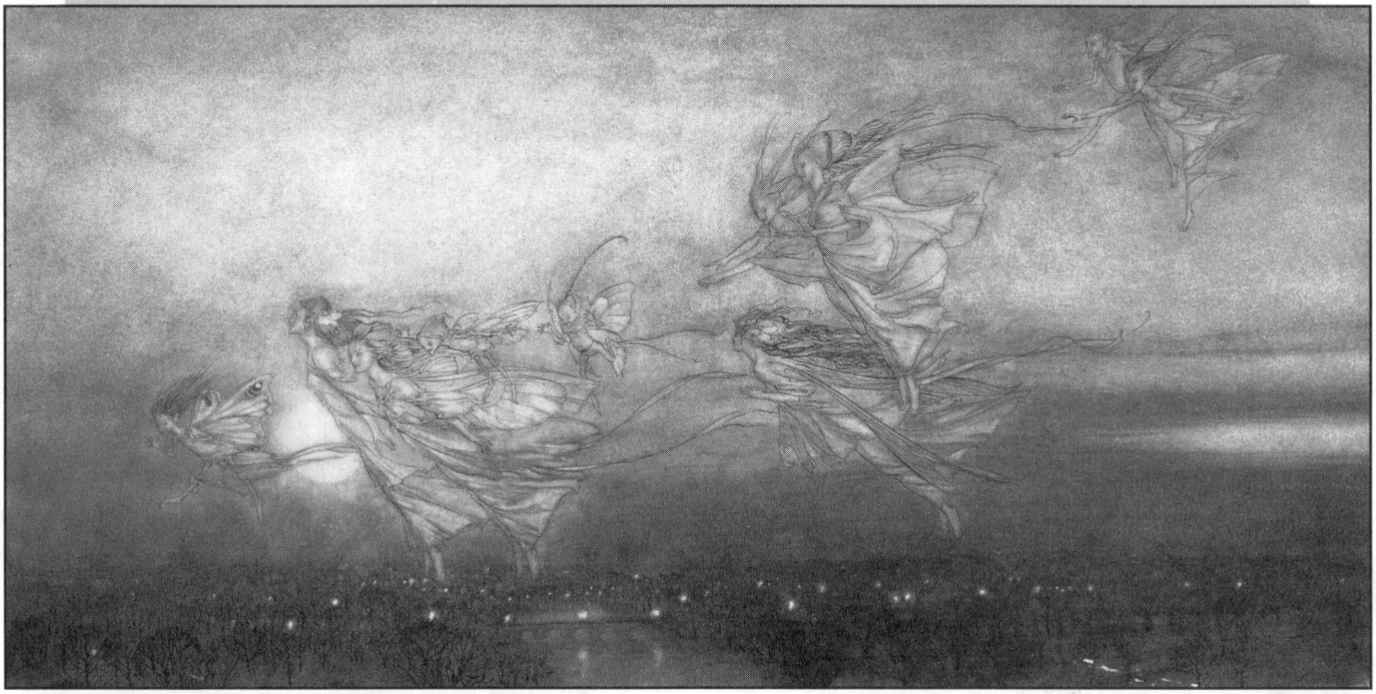

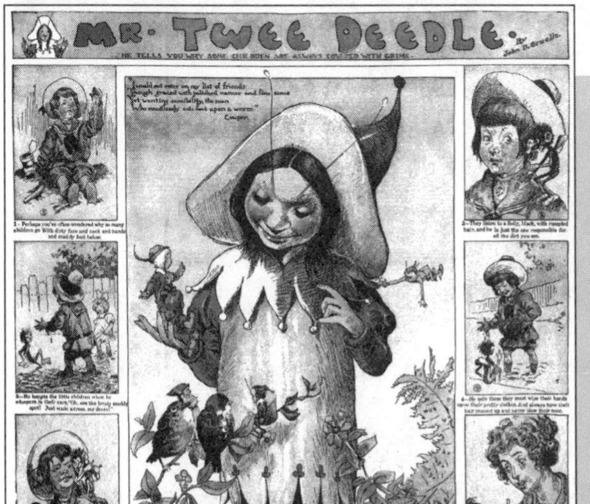
Mr. Twee Deedle.

Johnny Gruelle

I discovered Johnny Gruelle at about the same time as Rackham, from the *Raggedy Ann and Andy* line of books that he wrote and illustrated. I can't read the books because they're too treackly, but I love the drawings—the playfulness and whimsicality of them. I later discovered that he did a newspaper strip, *Mr. Twee Deedle*, for about ten years, before the *Raggedy Ann* books became so enormously popular. He's a really interesting artist to study. The strip ran from 1911 to 1914. When the same newspaper that was running *Little Nemo in Slumberland* lost it to another paper, they ran a contest for a new strip to replace it, and Johnny Gruelle won and got to do a strip for a while. It's certainly not the level of *Little Nemo*, but is gorgeously drawn. I love it.

Hermann

Hermann is a Belgian artist who has been doing graphic albums since the 1960s. He did *Jeremiah*—which Fantagraphics published in English—a post-apocalyptic Western. It's always beautifully drawn, and he's a great storyteller. There's great color in everything he's done. Hermann draws 48- to 64-page graphic albums, about two a year.

They're really lovely strips. I saw a lot of originals when I was over in Europe and have 20 to 25 of his albums. I really enjoy his work, even though the people are kind of ugly.... It's this European realistic approach, but I can look past that. His environments always have the landscape interacting with everyone in it, and the storytelling is magnificent.

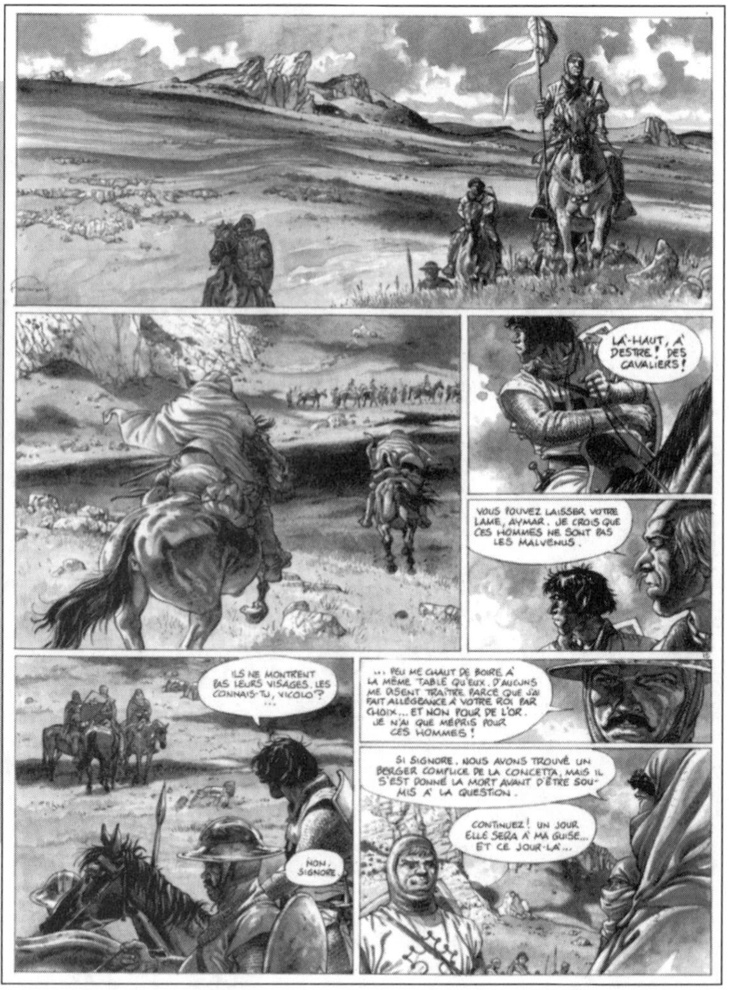
LÀ-HAUT, À DESTRE! DES CAVALIERS!
VOUS POUVEZ LAISSER VOTRE LAME, AYMAR. JE CROIS QUE CES HOMMES NE SONT PAS LES MALVENUS.
ILS NE MONTRENT PAS LEURS VISAGES. LES CONNAIS-TU, VICOLO? ...
NON, SIGNORE.
... PEU ME CHAUT DE BOIRE À LA MÊME TABLE QU'EUX. D'AUCUNS ME DISENT TRAÎTRE PARCE QUE J'AI FAIT ALLÉGEANCE À VOTRE ROI PAR CHOIX... ET NON POUR DE L'OR. JE N'AI QUE MÉPRIS POUR CES HOMMES!
SI SIGNORE. NOUS AVONS TROUVÉ UN BERGER COMPLICE DE LA CONCETTA, MAIS IL S'EST DONNÉ LA MORT AVANT D'ÊTRE SOUMIS À LA QUESTION.
CONTINUEZ! UN JOUR ELLE SERA À MA GUISE... ET CE JOUR-LÀ...

™ and ©2007 respective owner.

Carson of Venus ™ and ©2007 ERB, Inc.

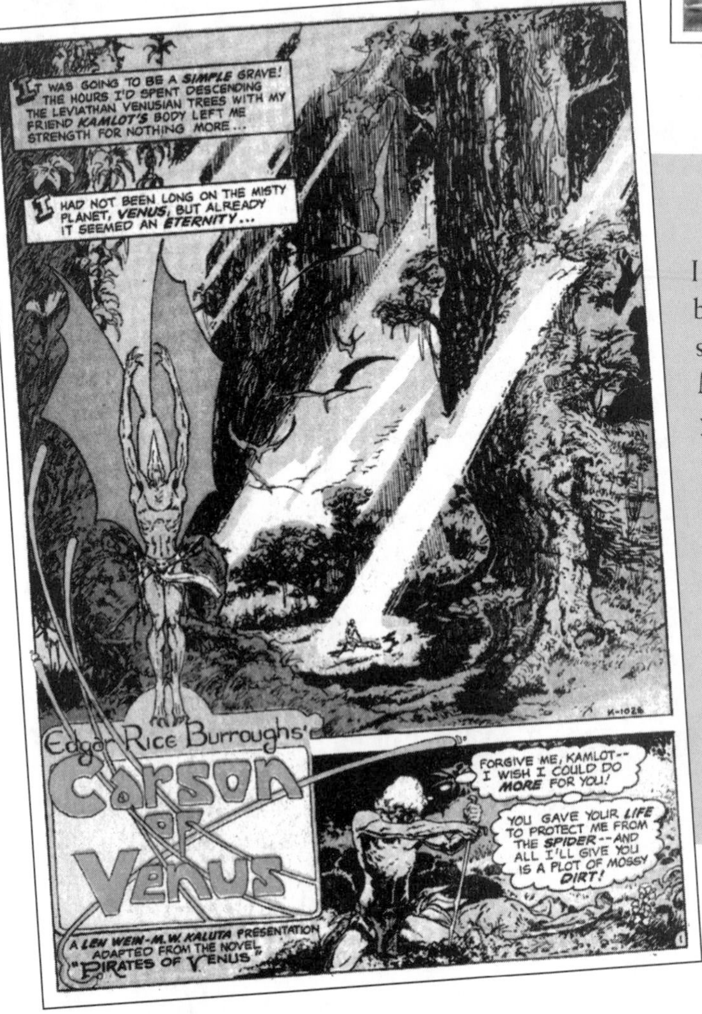
IT WAS GOING TO BE A SIMPLE GRAVE! THE HOURS I'D SPENT DESCENDING THE LEVIATHAN VENUSIAN TREES WITH MY FRIEND KAMLOT'S BODY LEFT ME STRENGTH FOR NOTHING MORE...
I HAD NOT BEEN LONG ON THE MISTY PLANET, VENUS, BUT ALREADY IT SEEMED AN ETERNITY...
Edgar Rice Burroughs'
Carson of Venus
FORGIVE ME, KAMLOT-- I WISH I COULD DO MORE FOR YOU!
YOU GAVE YOUR LIFE TO PROTECT ME FROM THE SPIDER--AND ALL I'LL GIVE YOU IS A PLOT OF MOSSY DIRT!
A LEN WEIN-M.W. KALUTA PRESENTATION ADAPTED FROM THE NOVEL "PIRATES OF VENUS"

Michael W. Kaluta

I went to the school that I did because Kaluta had been there, and years later met him. It took six to seven years to be able to have a conversation with Michael. I shared an apartment with him for twelve years in New York City, in the time of the studio situation with Jeff Jones, Bernie Wrightson, and Barry Smith. We just collaborated on a story for *Fables: 1,001 Nights of Snowfall*. We both have a lot of the same influences, but we think differently from those influences, and it's interesting to see his work and work with him. He's someone that usually doesn't get mentioned a whole lot, as far as influences, because he's not someone who immediately knocks you over the head, but he's brilliant. If you study his work, and see how he thinks, he's an amazing artist.

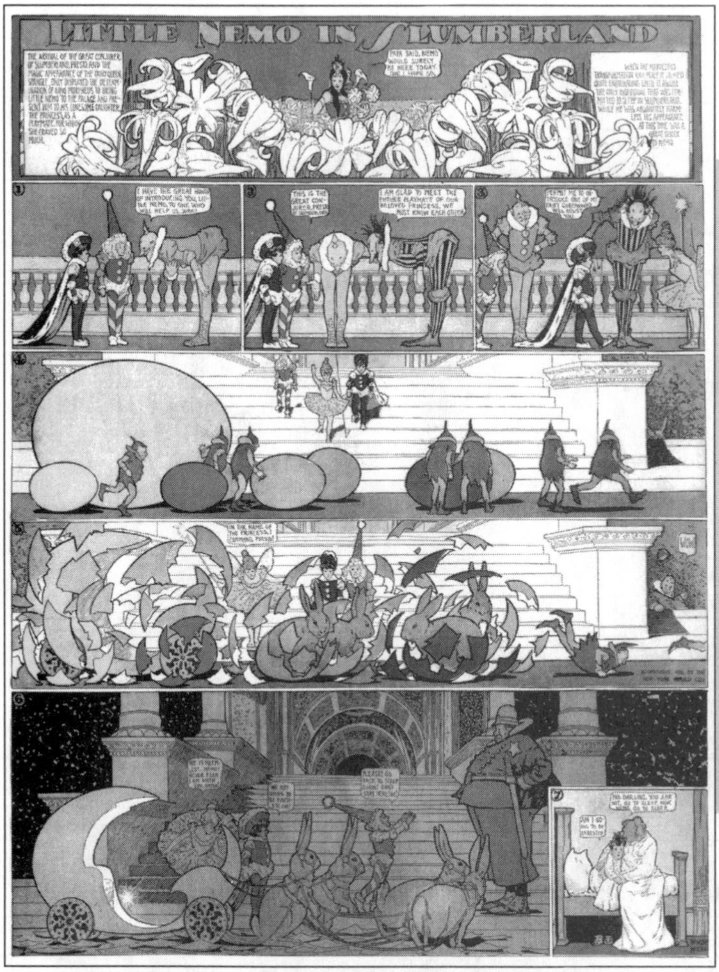
LITTLE NEMO IN SLUMBERLAND

Winsor McKay

The amazing imagination Winsor McKay had, the amazing drawing ability he had, the amazing storytelling ability he had, but he was not a very good letterer! I discovered him in that same burst of finding a multitude of brilliant artists back in the early '70s. At first, there was a small, black-&-white, horizontal book that published a number of *Little Nemos*, then in the late '70s, Nostalgia Press put out a very badly colored *Little Nemo* edition. It was something to die for at the time, but now that So Many Sundays put out their gorgeous, full-sized edition, you can see the strip the way it was always meant to be seen.

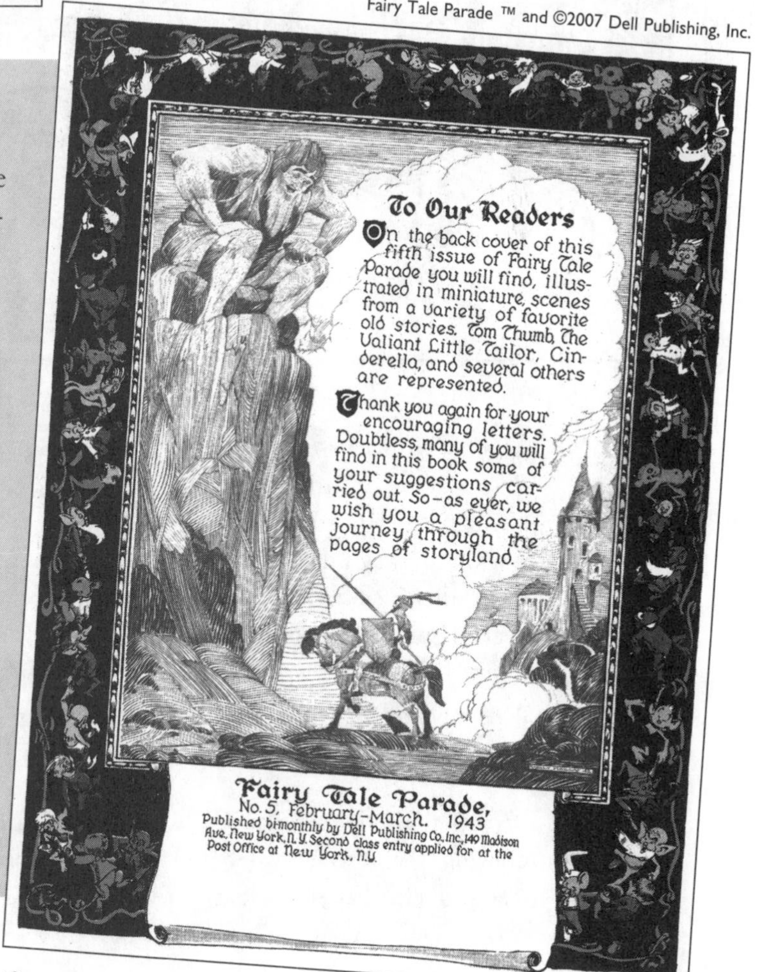
To Our Readers
On the back cover of this fifth issue of Fairy Tale Parade you will find, illustrated in miniature, scenes from a variety of favorite old stories. Tom Thumb, The Valiant Little Tailor, Cinderella, and several others are represented.
Thank you again for your encouraging letters. Doubtless, many of you will find in this book some of your suggestions carried out. So—as ever, we wish you a pleasant journey through the pages of storyland.
Fairy Tale Parade,
No. 5, February–March, 1943
Published bi-monthly by Dell Publishing Co. Inc. 149 Madison Ave. New York, N.Y. Second class entry applied for at the Post Office at New York, N.Y.

Walt Kelly

Walt Kelly's most famous for *Pogo*, but in the late '30s he was working for Disney Studios, animating most specifically on *Dumbo*. There was a strike there, and bad feelings that emerged from it, so he left there to go do comic books for Dell Comics. He did *Our Gang* and started doing a crude version of "Pogo" in *Animal Comics*. At that time he also wrote and drew several of the first issues of *Fairy Tale Parade*. Some of them are new stories, some are adaptations of older fairy tales. There are about twelve issues of the book, and various excellent artists came in to replace Kelly after a while. I've always been very enamored of a humorous drawing style with a naturalistic rendering, and he's a prime example of that. I have a large *Pogo* original on my wall that I stare at, every once in a while, and go "Gee, he sure could use a brush."

He's aping Franklin Booth, another illustrator, but in his own whimsical style, which is interesting.

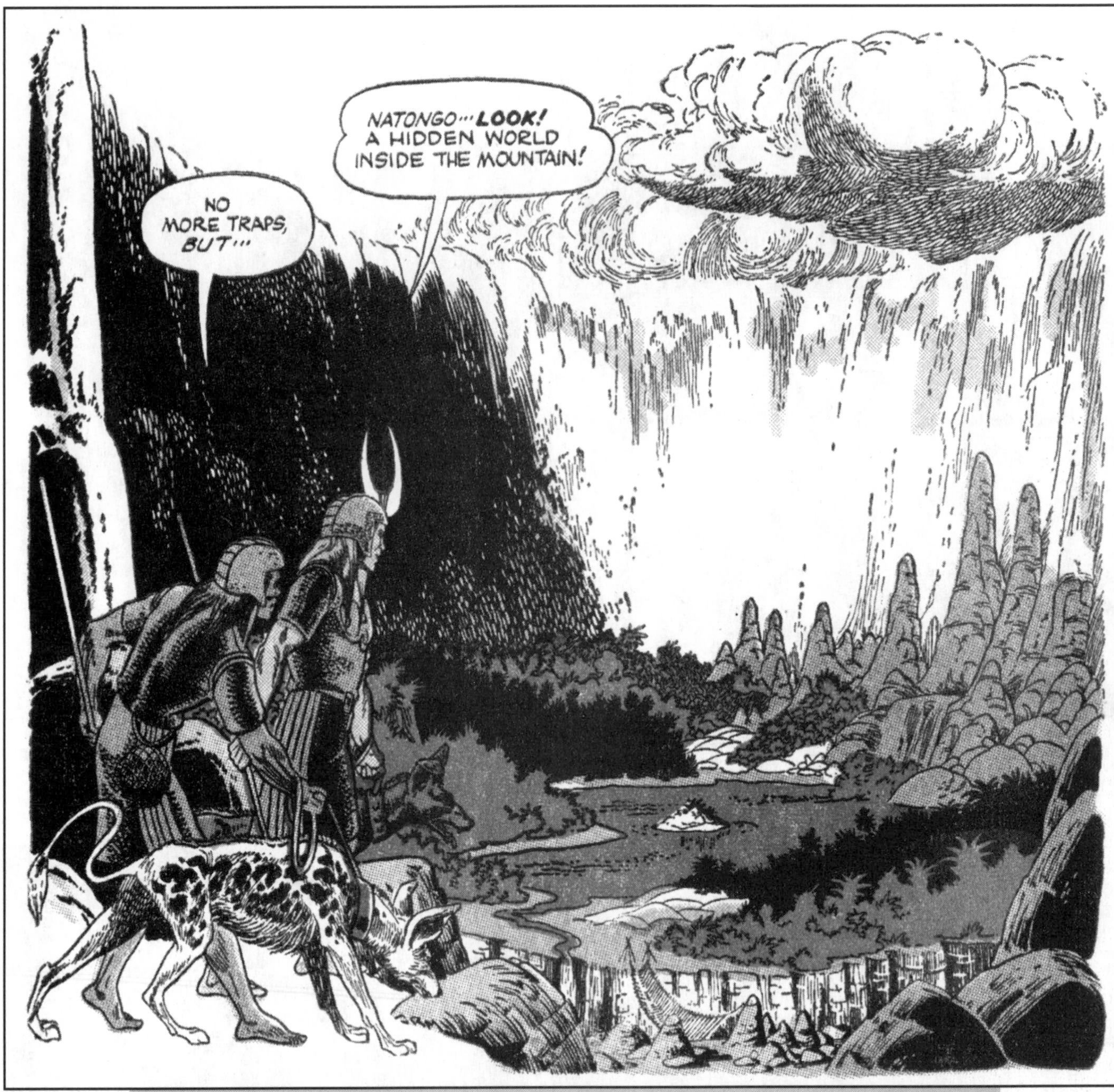
NO MORE TRAPS, BUT...
NATONGO... LOOK! A HIDDEN WORLD INSIDE THE MOUNTAIN!

Russ Manning's "Brothers of the Spear"

Russ Manning's "Brothers of the Spear".... When I went back and found this page, after having remembered it for some 20 years, I was amazed at how much of an influence it was on the way I draw comics. I liked Manning's later work, but I loved the line quality of this earlier time period, which is not quite as slick as what he produced during the next 20 years. It's a shame we can't show the storytelling that preceded it. The two brothers are in a very claustrophobic, underground cavern—it's very tight and dark. Then, you turn the page and you're in this big valley. The shadows of the clouds are cast down the rocky cliffs... it's really beautiful in both the drawing and storytelling.

When I draw my own comics, I want all of those elements: good storytelling and beautiful drawing. I want to know where I am, and to know that the world around the characters is real. It doesn't have to be drawn realistically, but it has to at least feel real.

Jack Kirby

Jack Kirby influenced me quite a bit in my earlier years, and his "Tales of Asgard" back-ups in the monthly *Thor* were a revelation. Really great stories where everyone's going to die—perfect for the pre-adolescent mind. I quickly started reading all the Norse mythology I could find, which led me into Celtic mythology, a really exciting mythology that I've worked with ever since. I could always spot a Jack Kirby page from across the room. It was always disappointing when he'd lay out just the splash page of a particular Marvel comic, and then turn the rest of the story over to another artist that was never quite as good.

I love his sense of epic grandeur, but he got too stylized for me towards the end of his career. There's a really cool *Yellow Claw* comic book from the '50s that John Severin inked that is also a favorite.

TALES OF... ...ASGARD!
HOME OF THE MIGHTY NORSE GODS
BEFORE MAN COULD READ OR WRITE, HE HAD HIS LEGENDS! AND NO LEGENDS WERE MORE THRILLING, MORE COLORFUL, MORE FILLED WITH FANTASY AND HIGH ADVENTURE THAN THE LEGENDS OF ASGARD, HOME OF THE GODS! THUS, WITH GREAT PRIDE, WE PRESENT THIS NEW, TREND-SETTING SERIES, BASED UPON HIGHLIGHTS OF NORSE MYTHOLOGY-- TALES OF ASGARD, THE BIRTHPLACE OF THE MIGHTY THOR!!
WRITTEN BY: STAN LEE
DRAWN BY: JACK KIRBY
INKED BY: G. BELL
LETTERED BY: ART SIMEK

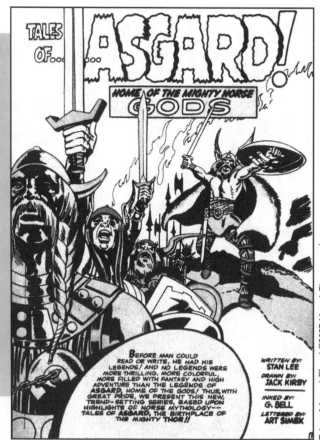

W.H. Robinson

W.H. Robinson is another British illustrator who was working at the same time as Arthur Rackham, and had the ability to do both finely rendered pieces, but was also very adaptable to humor. He's most famous now for his illustrations of how to stop the Axis war machines in the 1910s. He could invent and draw the most elaborate pre-Rube Goldberg contraptions. W.H. also wrote and illustrated many of his own books.

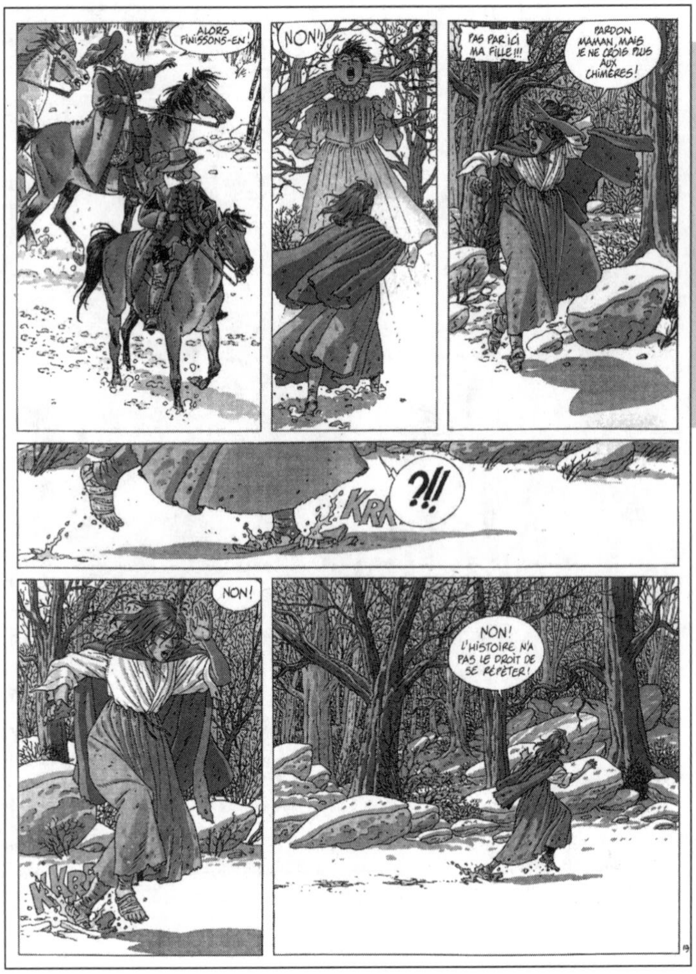
ALORS FINISSONS-EN!
NON!!
PAS PAR ICI MA FILLE!!!
PARDON MAMAN, MAIS JE NE CROIS PLUS AUX CHIMÈRES!
?!!
NON!
NON! L'HISTOIRE N'A PAS LE DROIT DE SE RÉPÉTER!

Andre Juilliard

Andre Juilliard is another French graphic novelist who has done 20 to 30 albums. He has a clear line with a harder edge than Hermann, and has beautiful story-telling and a sense of place.

I spoke about him elsewhere in the interview, so I won't repeat myself here.

Alfred Bestall

Alfred Bestall's *Rupert* is an English comic strip that's been running since about 1915. It was originated by a woman named Mary Tourtel. When her eyesight got bad, they looked for another artist and found Alfred Bestall, who'd been a prolific newspaper artist up until that time. He started writing and drawing the strip and continued up until the 1970s. It was black-&-white in the newspaper, but then they'd reprint them in albums every year and color them up. Alfred would paint these gorgeous endpapers which became incredibly famous to those who followed the adventures of the little bear. The books are worth a fortune now. There's even a society called The Friends of Rupert. Paul McCartney's a huge fan and produced an animated short, "Rupert and the Frog Song."

He also draws a lovely landscape that becomes just as important to the overall story as the characters themselves. There's a whimsicality in his work that I respond to far more than the fire, brimstone, and murder in others'. That one panel is such an influence on the way I draw comics.

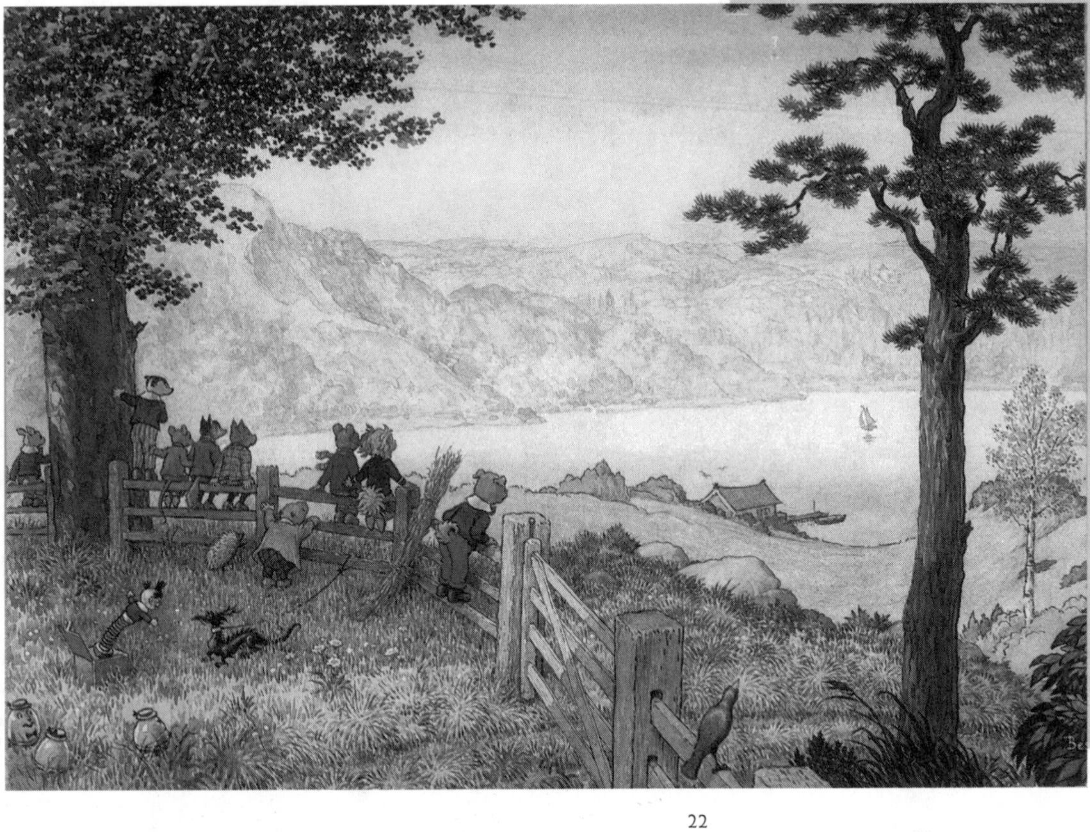

Part 2: "Your Work Is Just Too Nice for Us"

MM: How long did you stick around in Richmond?

CHARLES: I graduated with my BFA and hung around for about three years, and then Kaluta asked me if I wanted to move to New York. That would have been '76.

MM: So how would you describe Kaluta?

CHARLES: Well, he was mysterious, because he seemed 20 years older than I was, as he was an already established comics pro whose work I'd been buying for years. But in reality he was only about two or three years older. I was a huge fan before I ever met him and then suddenly I was introduced to his studio mates: Bernie Wrightson, Barry Windsor-Smith, Jeff Jones.... They were all art gods to me. Every one of them was very well known in the comics field and were exploiting their status by doing prints and posters, and selling them at conventions to make gobs of money. Bernie and Michael were drawing monthly, fully painted posters for Christopher Enterprise's Land of Enchantment Press. Barry was doing prints for his own Goreblimey Press. Jeff was working on *Blind Narcissus*, which is one of his masterpieces, a very large oil painting. They'd all quit comics at that point, being fed up with the low page rates and the non-return of their artwork, which was a common practice in the field at that time. Over the course of two to three years, the studio book that Dragon Stream published was released. The process of the design and layout of the art that the four of them put into that landmark book produced a lot of bruised egos.... Bernie, who had already begun his illustrations for his amazing *Frankenstein* book, actually moved to Florida to escape the turmoil, and finished it there.

But the upside to all this was that I was dropped into an incredibly creative environment that centered around those four artists, who were working really hard at what they wanted to do, and that was a big eye-opener. I learned about artists' rights from them, and how to keep your originals and keep your printing rights, all that stuff. Also, you could walk out the door and go to the Metropolitan Museum of Art, or the Natural History Museum, and see all this art. It was amazing, absolutely amazing, to be exposed to so much energy, art, and people. It really influenced everything I did and made me want to keep drawing.

Below: Charles has collaborated with Michael Kaluta many times over the years, including "The Adventures of Brucilla the Muscle, Galactic Girl Guide" in the late '80s, which Charles inked over Michael's pencils.

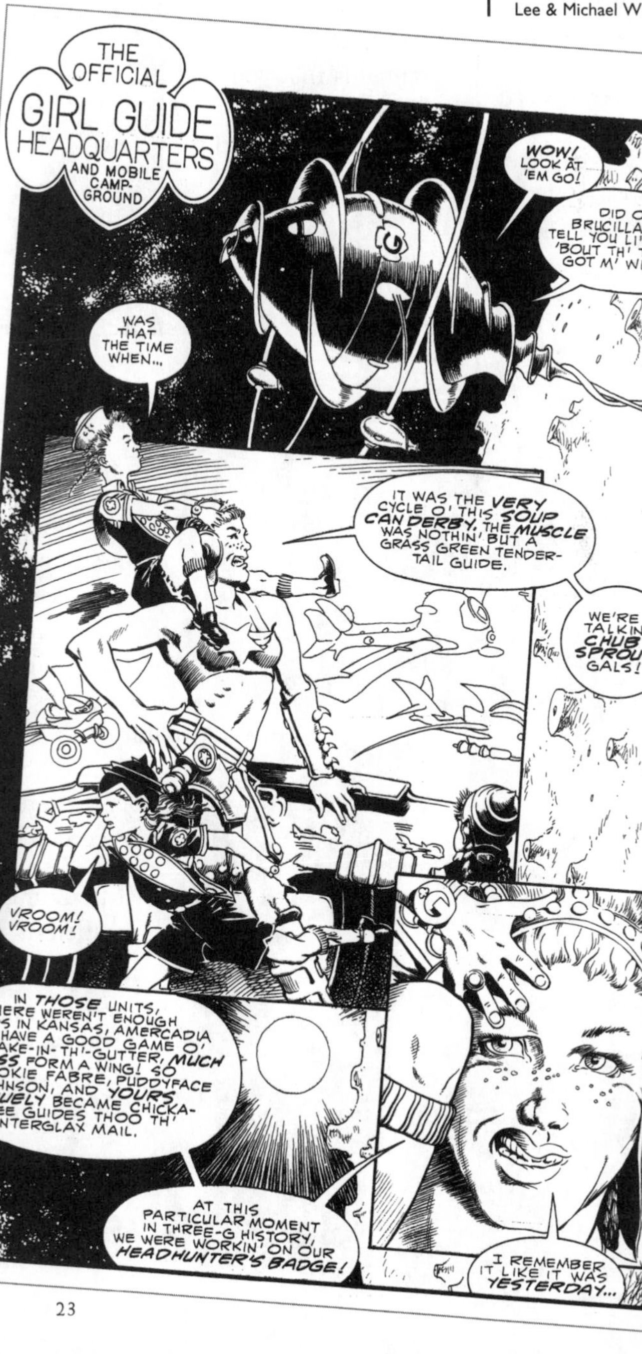
THE OFFICIAL GIRL GUIDE HEADQUARTERS AND MOBILE CAMP-GROUND
WOW! LOOK AT 'EM GO!
DID OLE BRUCILLA EVER TELL YOU LI'L GALS 'BOUT TH' TIME I GOT M' WINGS?
WAS THAT THE TIME WHEN...
IT WAS THE VERY CYCLE O' THIS SOUP CAN DERBY. THE MUSCLE WAS NOTHIN' BUT A GRASS GREEN TENDER-TAIL GUIDE.
WE'RE TALKIN' CHUB SPROUT, GALS!
VROOM! VROOM!
IN THOSE UNITS, THERE WEREN'T ENOUGH KIDS IN KANSAS, AMERCADIA TO HAVE A GOOD GAME O' SNAKE-IN-TH'-GUTTER, MUCH LESS FORM A WING! SO COOKIE FABRE, PUDDYFACE JOHNSON, AND YOURS TRUELY BECAME CHICKA-DEE GUIDES THOO TH' INTERGLAX MAIL.
AT THIS PARTICULAR MOMENT IN THREE-G HISTORY, WE WERE WORKIN' ON OUR HEADHUNTER'S BADGE!
I REMEMBER IT LIKE IT WAS YESTERDAY...

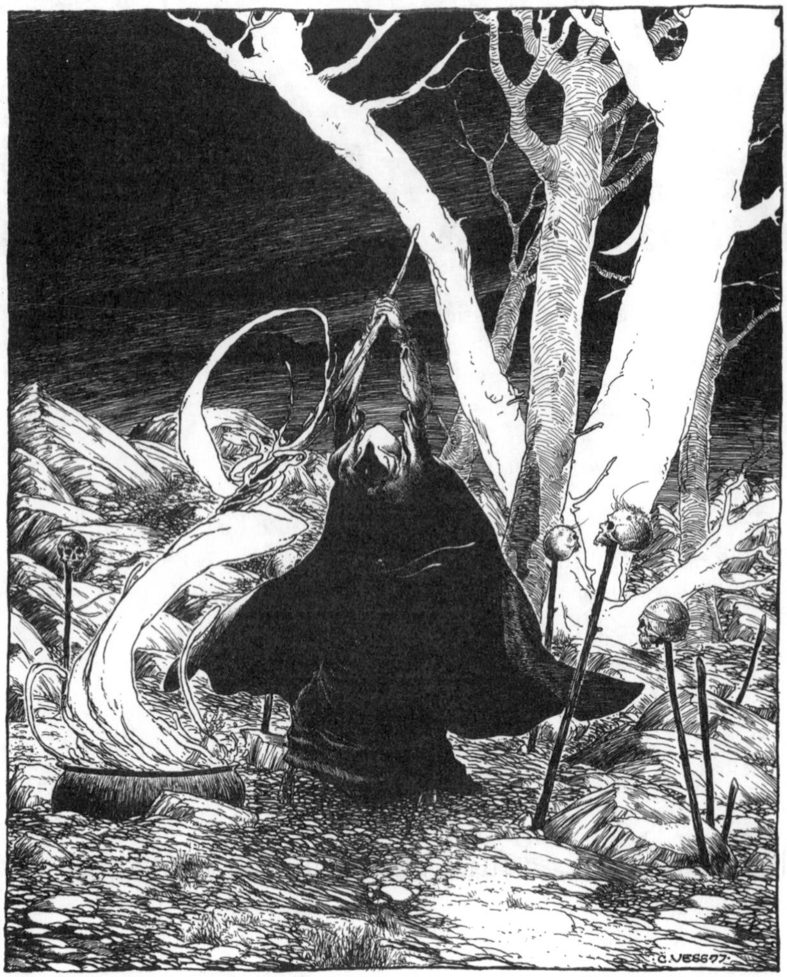

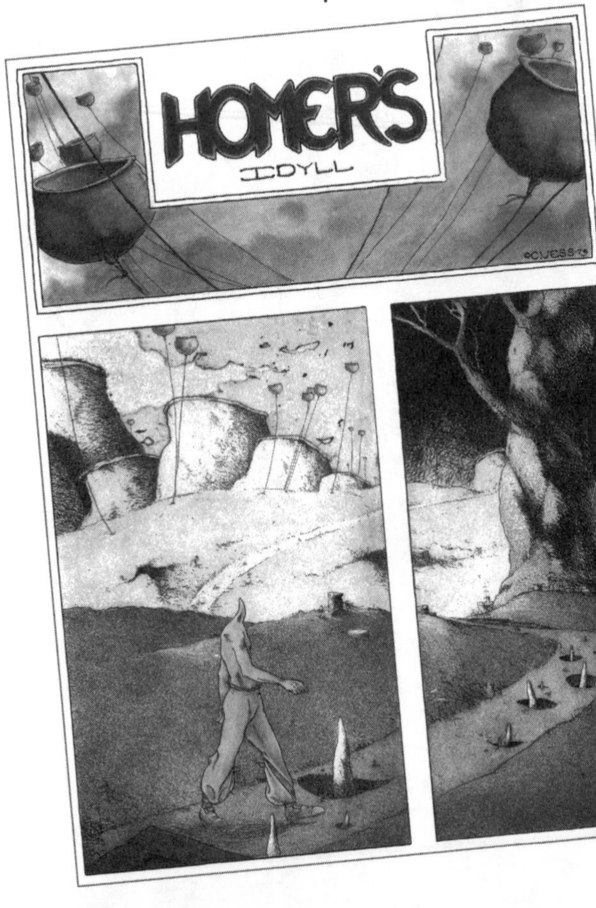

HOMER'S
IDYLL

Right: 1977 illustration which ran in the fanzine, *Vertigo*.
Below: The 5-page wordless story, "Homer's Idyll," appeared in the October 1979 issue of *Heavy Metal*. Charles incorporated etchings from his years in college as backgrounds.
Next Page Top: An illustration from the third story in *The Horns of Elfland*, "The Fiddler and the Swan."
Next Page Bottom: A panel from "Zealot's Lake," a back-up in *Sabre* #2. Charles: "This panel shows my attempt at a big Hal Foster type crowd scene. I was also consciously emulating Foster's ink work at that point."

MM: Where in New York were you living?

CHARLES: Upper West Side, the same place Michael has been living at since 1971. It's rent-controlled. I didn't have any money for a cab or subway, and was walking 70-some blocks down to the studio. I was hanging out with three or four artists that had just quit comics. One of the things most younger artists just seem to take for granted is that you get your artwork back. At that point in the '70s they were maybe getting $25 a page, but you didn't get the artwork back. You never saw the artwork again, and you were only in it if you really, really wanted to be.

It was just in that time period, the late '70s, that the artwork started to be returned. The '80s, then, were sort of the rise of the independents... independent companies that were hiring, managing to get artists that might have worked for bigger DC and Marvel with the promise of better page rates. So Marvel, in the early '80s, decided to launched a graphic novel line. They started with Jim Starlin [*The Death of Captain Marvel*], who was working with [Marvel Editor-in-Chief Jim] Shooter on developing a standardized contract for these graphic novel projects. These contracts were including royalties and ownership of the characters by each artist who had developed them. This was really the start of our modern system of creator-friendly contracts. There are many things Shooter may be scorned for, but that was certainly a beneficial landmark for all artists and writers!

MM: Going back to the studio, were you considered a full-fledged member?

CHARLES: No, are you kidding? I was just hanging out.

MM: So you were a kid sidekick?

CHARLES: I was not quite Jimmy Olsen. [*laughter*]

MM: At least you didn't get mutated every month. [*laughter*]

CHARLES: When I had the energy, I would walk down there. It was really exciting.

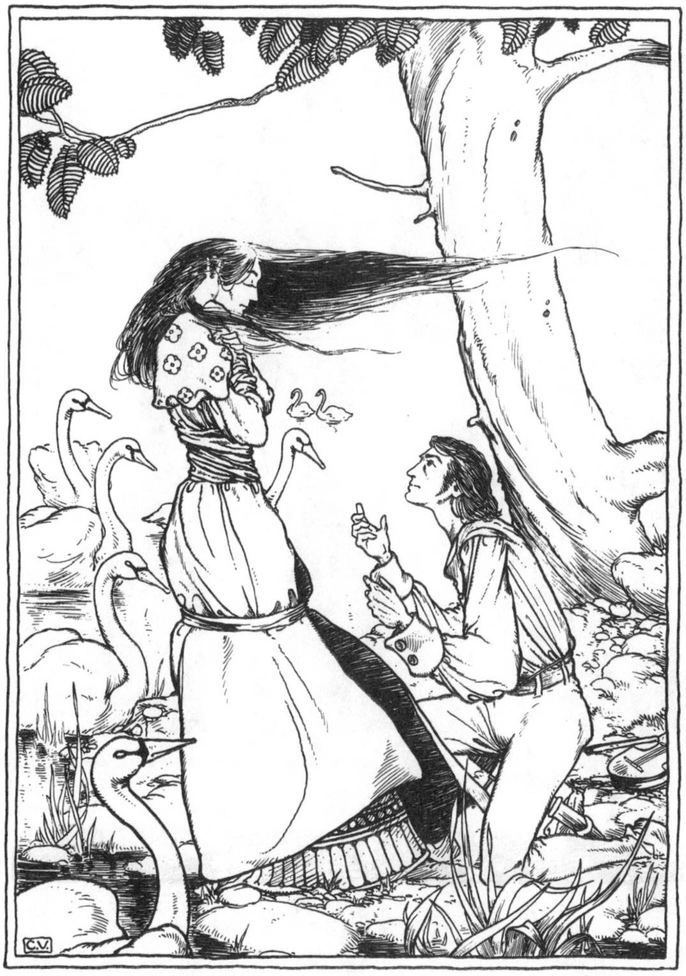
C.V.

MM: What was the vibe like?

CHARLES: There were those warring egos but there was also a lot of fun to be had, a lot of excitement, all sorts of interesting discussions and games. I remember sitting in the dark, on a high stool, then suddenly flipping the lights on in order to shoot at the mice that were scurrying about nibbling at various bits of paper—one set of nibbles was down an entire stack of Barry's signed and numbered prints which then had to be tossed out.

The entire building was mostly commercial offices and would be well heated during the day, but after 5:30 they'd cut the heat off. And it got very, very cold. It was an interesting period. Michael, who usually worked late at night, got the brunt of cold. Jeff would come in early morning, and Barry would just come in on the weekends and play his electric guitar.

And they all had horror stories about comics. They'd also have these giant parties, and all these people would show up, all the editors, writers, and other artists. So at a certain point, instead of being some stranger walking in off the street looking for a job, I'd be someone the editors knew. I'd known Archie Goodwin for about two years. He sort of was aware of my art and aware of my character when he asked me to do a story for *Epic Illustrated*.

MM: We do need to talk about those *Heavy Metal* stories you did, as well, but I'd like to go back to *The Horns of Elfland*, from 1978. How'd this come about?

CHARLES: $750 was what I was paid to do that entire book. Robert Wiener was a publisher that did lots of limited edition prints and a scattering of books. I guess he liked art, and just said, "I'd like you to do a book that would be so many pages at this amount of money." And I spent about a year or so working on it, drawing and writing the stories. I designed the book, as well.

MM: There were certain aspects of these stories, where you can tell you were learning—

CHARLES: There's some really bad drawing in there!

MM: Yeah, but your first story's pretty well cross-hatched and everything. It's this last story with Jack, "The Fiddler and the Swan." It looks more like today's Charles Vess than the other stories do.

CHARLES: Well, "The Shadow Witch" was the first story

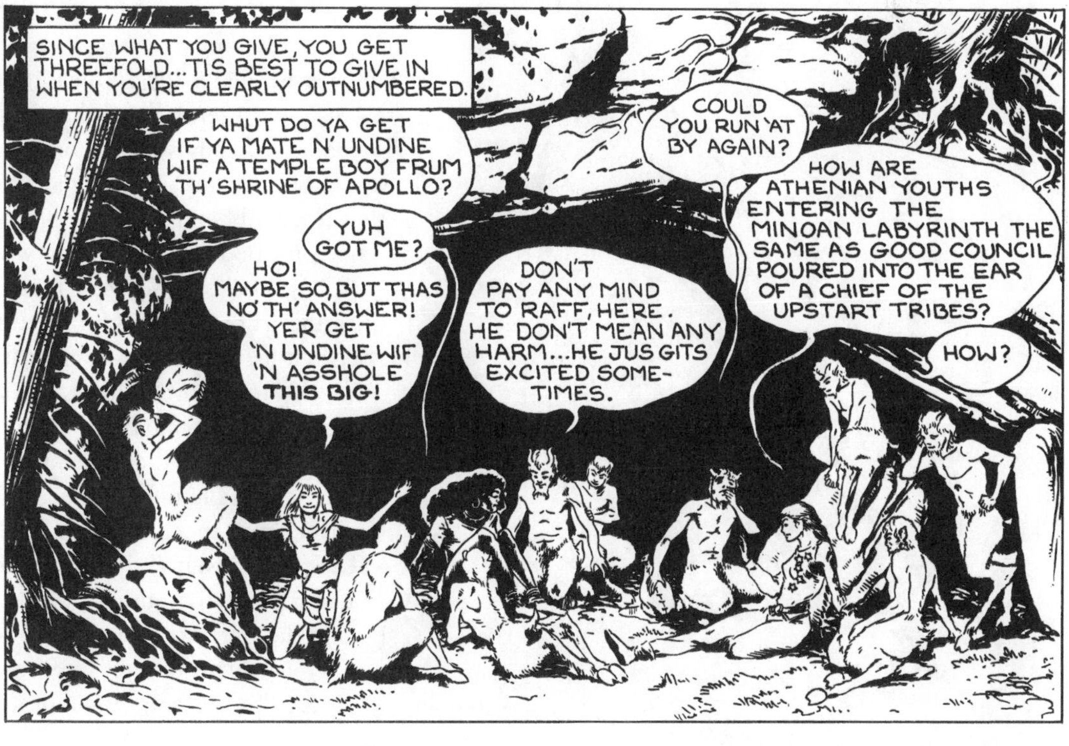
SINCE WHAT YOU GIVE, YOU GET THREEFOLD...TIS BEST TO GIVE IN WHEN YOU'RE CLEARLY OUTNUMBERED.
WHUT DO YA GET IF YA MATE N' UNDINE WIF A TEMPLE BOY FRUM TH' SHRINE OF APOLLO?
YUH GOT ME?
HO! MAYBE SO, BUT THAS NO TH' ANSWER! YER GET 'N UNDINE WIF 'N ASSHOLE THIS BIG!
DON'T PAY ANY MIND TO RAFF, HERE. HE DON'T MEAN ANY HARM...HE JUS GITS EXCITED SOME-TIMES.
COULD YOU RUN 'AT BY AGAIN?
HOW ARE ATHENIAN YOUTHS ENTERING THE MINOAN LABYRINTH THE SAME AS GOOD COUNCIL POURED INTO THE EAR OF A CHIEF OF THE UPSTART TRIBES?
HOW?

Right and Next Page: Pages 4 and 5 of "Morrigan Tales," as it appeared in *Taboo #4*. This story stirred up a bit of controversy when it was first presented in the pages of *Sabre #1*, and it's one of Charles' favorites.
Below: Pencils for the opening page of the 4-page "Age of the Dragon." This story was originally meant to appear in *Heavy Metal*, but was eventually published in *Epic Illustrated #21*.

that was actually done, in about 1971. It was before I moved to New York and just wanted to draw a story. The comic book story in there I completely choked on. I would say there's some really bad drawing in that.

MM: A lot of straight shots.

CHARLES: I didn't really know what I was doing, but all in all it was a great experience, and it's a graphic novel from 1978.

MM: Yes, it is a graphic novel. It's not a trade paperback.

There was also your story, "Morrigan Tales," that had been done at Eclipse, right?

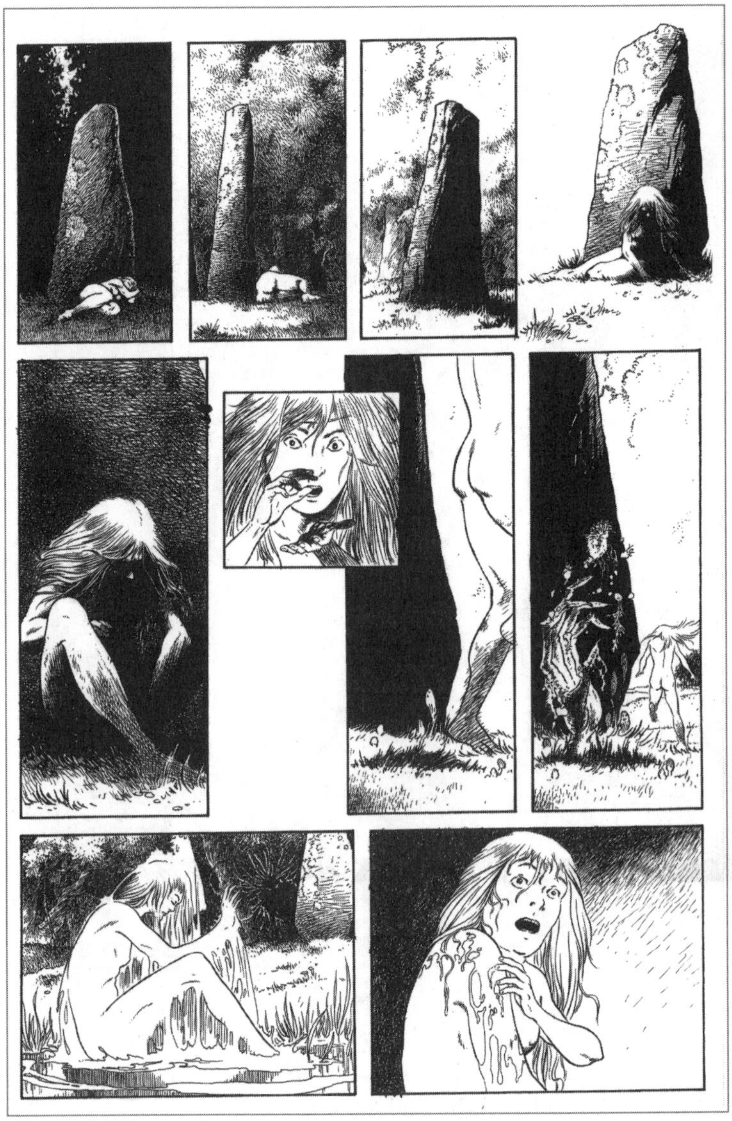

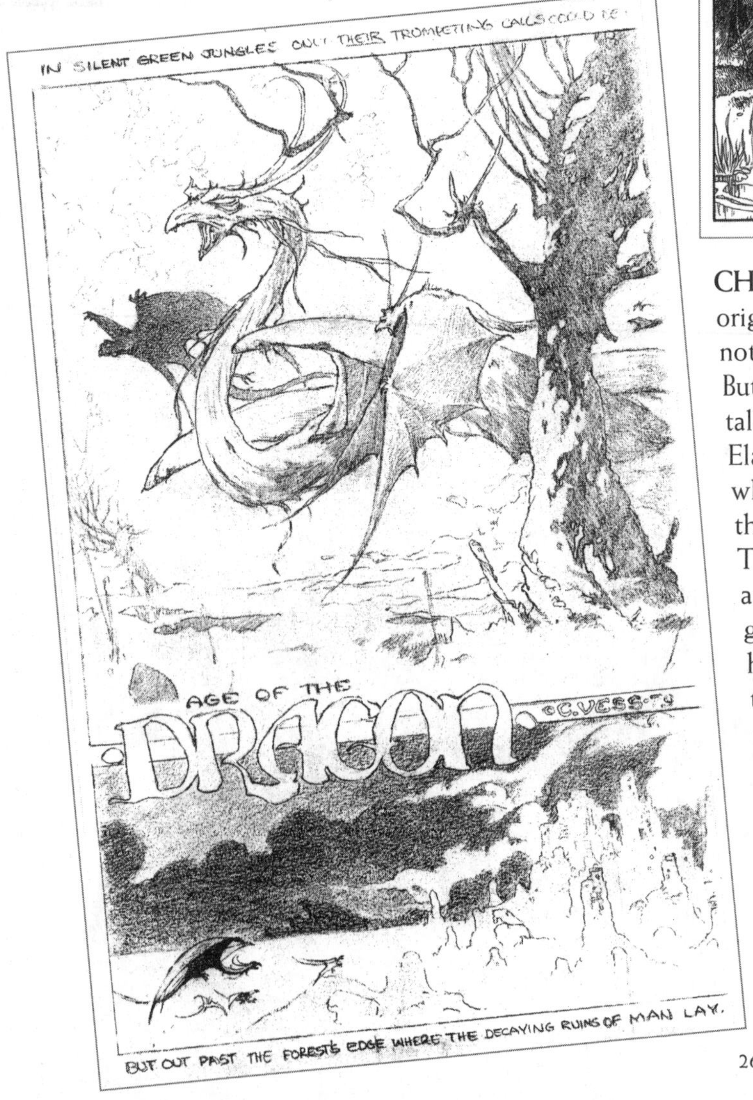
IN SILENT GREEN JUNGLES
THEIR TRUMPETING CALLS
AGE OF THE DRAGON
BUT OUT PAST THE FOREST'S EDGE WHERE THE DECAYING RUINS OF MAN LAY.

CHARLES: Don McGregor wrote and Paul Gulacy drew the original black-&-white *Sabre* graphic novel. Eclipse had the notion of dividing and serializing the story as a color comic. But they needed a back-up feature to fill out the comic, so I talked to my friend, Elaine Lee, and we came up with a story. Elaine had already written some snippets about a young girl who would eventually become a powerful witch. I thought that it would be fun to draw her story as a comic, so I did. The color on that first version was done by Lynn Varley and was, I believe, her very first coloring job. In it the little girl doesn't begin to attain her true power until she's had her first menstruation. Apparently this was the first time that this recurrent biological function had ever been mentioned in the comic book world and it resulted in a huge controversy. I read commentary about it in letter column after letter column. People got very upset about this simple act that appeared in a book whose major plot line concerned itself with rape and dismemberment. No one cared about that more typical violence. We went ahead and did one more short story for the second issue.

Many years later, *Taboo* magazine was being edited by Steve Bissette, and I thought it would be really interesting

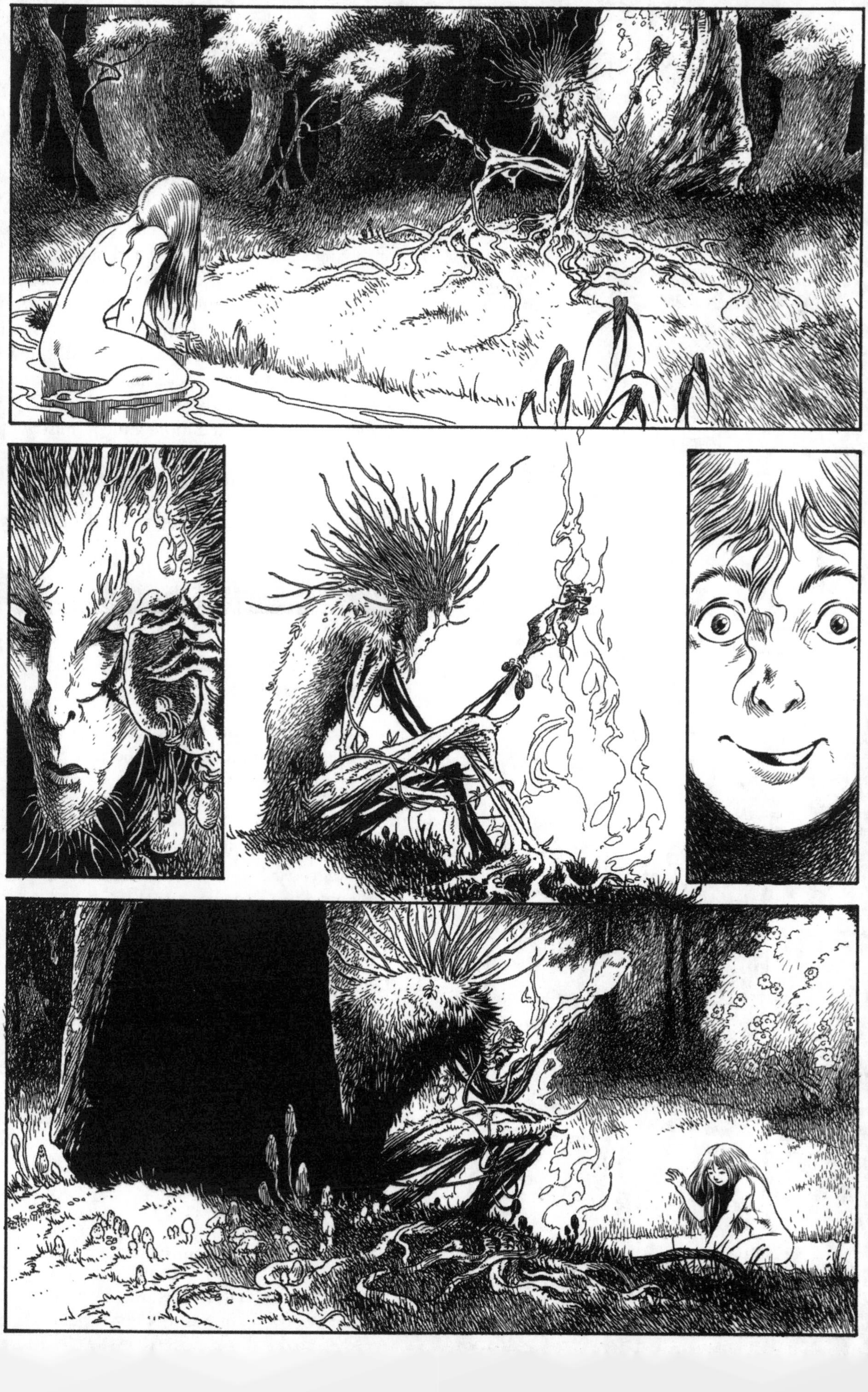

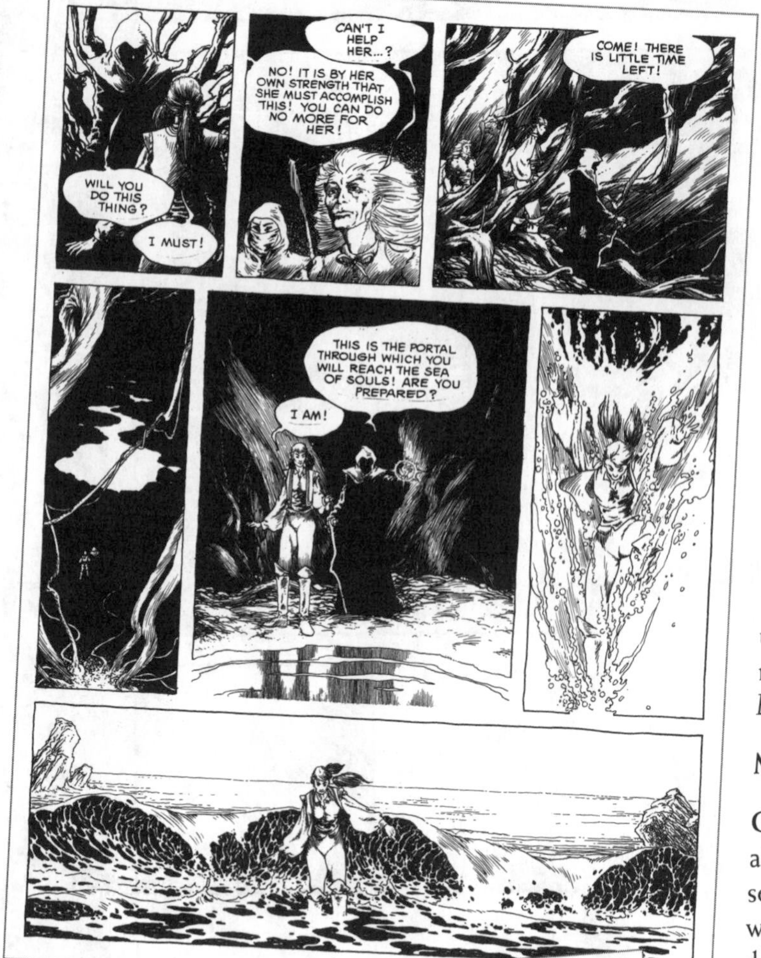
WILL YOU DO THIS THING?
I MUST!
CAN'T I HELP HER...?
NO! IT IS BY HER OWN STRENGTH THAT SHE MUST ACCOMPLISH THIS! YOU CAN DO NO MORE FOR HER!
COME! THERE IS LITTLE TIME LEFT!
THIS IS THE PORTAL THROUGH WHICH YOU WILL REACH THE SEA OF SOULS! ARE YOU PREPARED?
I AM!

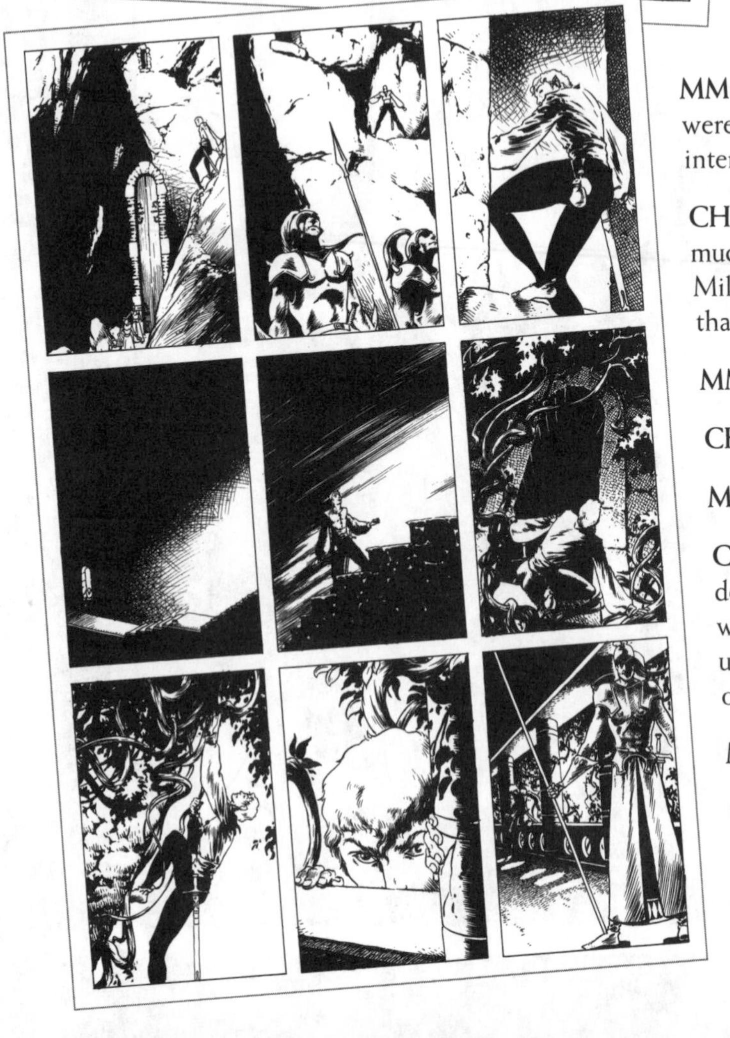

to redraw the story and do it the way it should have been done. So I redrew many panels and then we extended the story from eight pages to 18 pages. It's still one of my most favorite works of comic art.

MM: You had worked on breaking in with *Heavy Metal* at one point?

CHARLES: It was, again, back in the late '70s. I had approached the editors about working for them, and they bought a couple pieces. But they were notorious for buying a story from France and not bothering to do the translation right, or dropping the last page on purpose. They actually wanted that sense of dislocation or hallucination that comes from a totally non-sensical plot so, being much more of a traditionalist, I wasn't really a great fit for the magazine. Finally, I remember the editor saying, "Charles, your work is just too nice for us," meaning they wanted more violent, misogynist stories. I wasn't a good fit for that. I was a much better fit at *Epic Magazine*, and working with Archie Goodwin.

MM: I've heard nothing but great stories about Archie.

CHARLES: You can't think of anything you can say bad about him. He is the editor that put his ego away and served the story, and you never felt threatened by him. It was like your very best friend in the world was sitting down giving you advice. That went for "Jack Tales," or any number of stories I did for him.

MM: Epic was pretty separate from Marvel at that time? If you were able to get away with a lot, was it because Shooter didn't interfere with Epic?

CHARLES: It was a side project, so Shooter didn't have that much sway. But it's sort of like when I started working for Al Milgrom for *Marvel Fanfare*. Al was one of the very few editors that Shooter would back down from.

MM: Did he respect him?

CHARLES: He just backed off. [*laughter*]

MM: So what was the vibe like?

CHARLES: It was an expanding market, and they were doing this graphic novel line, and then there was Epic, which was creator-owned. It wasn't until four or five years later that, under a lot of outside pressures, Jim Shooter started handing out the weirdest rules. They really didn't make any sense.

MM: What was the strangest?

CHARLES: It's not even important.

MM: So, going in, was it kind of just, "Man, I'm working with Archie Goodwin," or was it, "I finally get to do comics!"?

CHARLES: It was very exciting that I was getting paid to do work, and it didn't even occur to me that I would have to draw super-heroes. My style was and is not a typical super-hero style, but it was Al Milgrom who, at *Marvel Fanfare*, asked me if I wanted to a Doctor Strange story. That sort of brought me into that genre. It's the only time I've ever actually drawn a script by a writer I'd never talked to before.

MM: Who was the writer?

CHARLES: It was Roger Stern. And it's got some atrociously bad drawing. Some of it was awkward. It was really awkward; my work really, really bothered me.

MM: Why was it—?

CHARLES: I just couldn't draw that well.

MM: Did you feel that way with "Jack Tales"?

CHARLES: No, there was some good drawing in that. But with this particular story, there was this sort of choking at drawing a character that I'd essentially grown up with. But because I did that one story, I think a couple months later, Al said "I've got another writer, Alan Zelenetz, who's got a Warriors Three story that you might want to do." Alan was coming from a teaching background and had a really good sense of humor.

I think that was at the point where, really, you could do just about anything you wanted to at Marvel. Everything they produced was selling. So one day Alan and I just tracked down Shooter in the hall and said, "We've got this idea for this graphic novel. It's called *The Raven Banner*, and it's a story of Asgard without Thor." "Yeah, go ahead. Do it." "Cool." So, at that point, it was "whatever you want to do."

MM: Going back to "Warriors Three," you'd mentioned that Kirby's "Tales of Asgard" was a big influence on you. What was it like to be drawing "Ballad of the Warriors Three"?

CHARLES: Well, it was a little intimidating. But also, I was trying to mix Jack Kirby and Hal Foster, from his work on the *Prince Valiant* newspaper strip. Of course, Kirby has a huge Foster influence, especially with

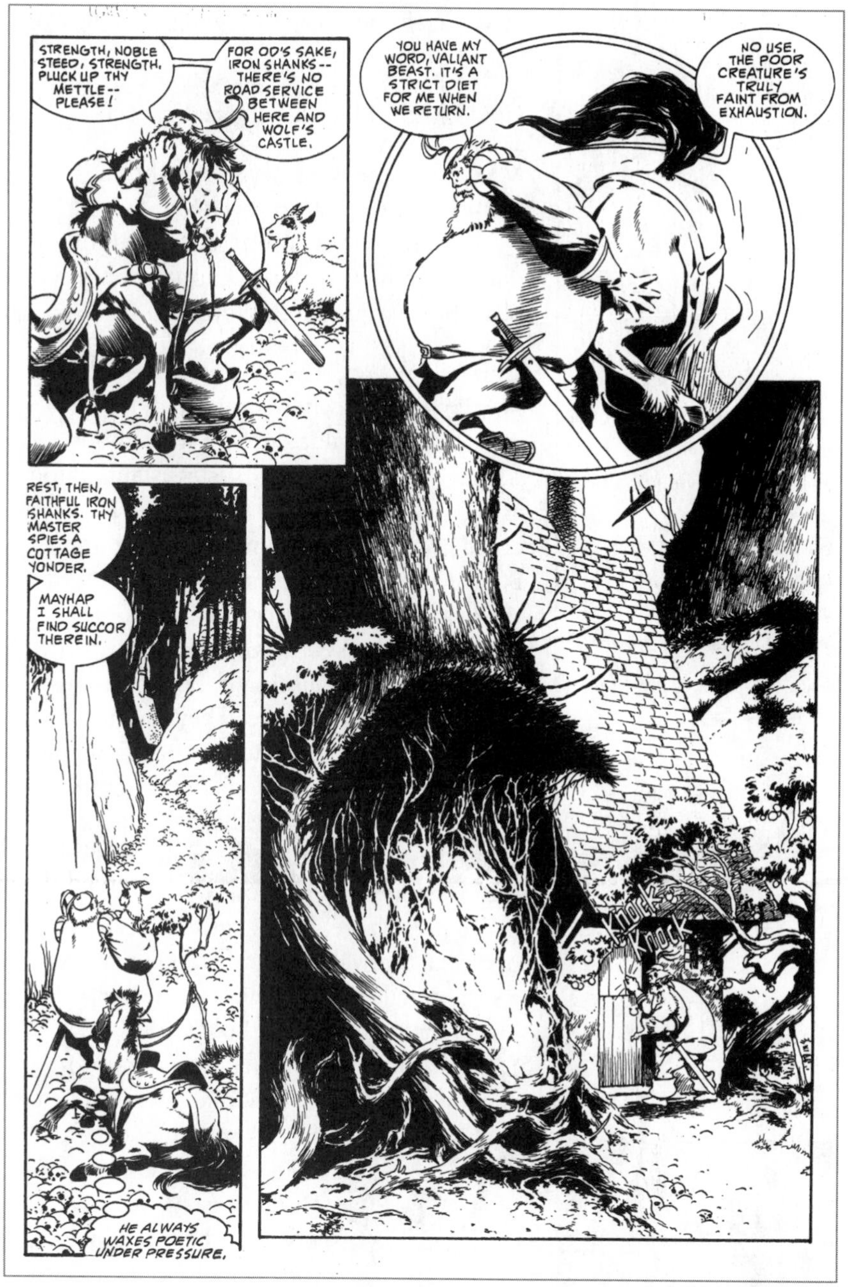
STRENGTH, NOBLE STEED, STRENGTH. PLUCK UP THY METTLE-- PLEASE!
FOR OD'S SAKE, IRON SHANKS-- THERE'S NO ROAD SERVICE BETWEEN HERE AND WOLF'S CASTLE.
YOU HAVE MY WORD, VALIANT BEAST. IT'S A STRICT DIET FOR ME WHEN WE RETURN.
NO USE. THE POOR CREATURE'S TRULY FAINT FROM EXHAUSTION.
REST, THEN, FAITHFUL IRON SHANKS. THY MASTER SPIES A COTTAGE YONDER.
MAYHAP I SHALL FIND SUCCOR THEREIN.
HE ALWAYS WAXES POETIC UNDER PRESSURE.

The Demon. Again, I didn't have quite the drawing skills for it. It wasn't until I was doing the four-issue mini-series with the Warriors Three [also for *Marvel Fanfare*, in 1987] that I realized how to actually draw Volstagg. One day I was watching a Warner Brothers cartoon, "King-Sized Canary"—a Tex Avery cartoon about a cat and bird who keep drinking a magic formula that makes them get bigger and bigger. I just looked at them and went, "Volstagg! He's a cartoon character. There's no bones in him!" And that's when I could finally draw him.

MM: Rather than a real—

CHARLES: Rather than trying to figure out how this thing would actually work.

Previous Page: (left) A page from "Children of the Stars," Charles' first extended story, which ran in *Epic Illustrated* #8-10. (right) About this page from "Two Sisters" (*Epic Illustrated* #16), Charles says, "[I was] trying to apply what I'd learned from *years* of studying Will Eisner's *Spirit*. **Above:** The cartoonish Volstagg from *Marvel Fanfare* #34.

Below: *Web of Spider-Man #1*—sporting one of the most recognizable Spider-Man covers of all time.
Next Page: Another iconic pose of the wall-crawler. Cover art for *Web of Spider-Man #8.*

MM: Yeah, he's very exaggerated, a very bottom-heavy character.

CHARLES: He's a king-sized canary!

MM: Yeah, he is! He even has those feathers sticking out of his head.

Raven Banner was pretty dark; the color's duller than how your work usually appears. Was that just production messing it up?

CHARLES: Yes, it was. I spent a long time penciling it, and when I got around to inking it, I was intimidated. So I went to my friend, Jim Owsley, who was assistant editor at the time, and asked if there was a book I could ink, and he gave me an issue of John Buscema's *Conan the Barbarian* [#163]. I inked the whole issue, and that sort of got me ready. Then I inked *Raven Banner* and spent six months or so painting it, being careful with each and every page. They sent it off to the color separators, brought it back, had me go through all the colors and make corrections to all the pages. The head of production came in and laughed at my suggested corrections and just sent it off as is.

To me, Marvel has never had any sense of production values, and DC will really go the extra mile in that department. Marvel just wants it out. I lucked out with the Spider-Man graphic novel. The then-production manager—a new one—really loved my art on the book, and made sure it went through okay—overseeing it—which is why it looks much better.

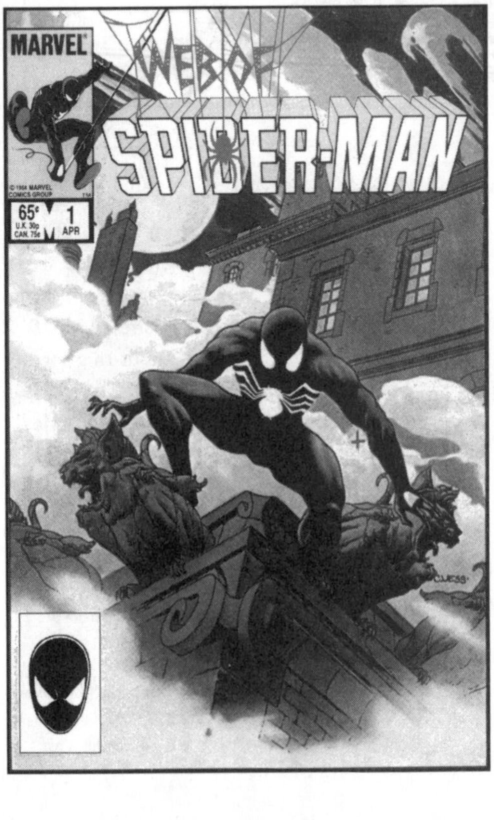
MARVEL
WEB OF
SPIDER-MAN
65¢
1
APR

Another problem with *The Raven Banner* is, I was having trouble really keeping my interest up to produce thumbnail layouts for all 64 pages. It was just *so* boring to me that I just start drawing straight onto the pages. We got near the end of the book, and I had to cram our very complex story into a far too abbreviated space. The last three pages should have been spread out over at least ten.

MM: It's Asgard really without Thor.

CHARLES: Everyone was excited about the idea of graphic novels. All of the stuff that's happening now is what we wanted to do with *The Raven Banner*. But Marvel decided that since there was no connection to their on-going continuity in *Thor* they were going to ignore our odd, little book. So there was no PR, no advertisements, and then, of course, no one knew that it had even been published.

When I did one of my first signing tours, I was out in California, and the only advertising the store had done was the interior of their front door, which was open all day long, with the sign facing into a wall so that no one could see it. People came into the shop and kept asking me, "Did Marvel really publish this?"

MM: Back to inking over John Buscema's work: What did you get from his pencils? Were they very tight?

CHARLES: Intimidation. [*laughter*] His pencils were very tight and beautifully drawn. My favorite John Buscema work was when he drew "Sir Lancelot" for Dell Comics and he was doing sort of a Hal Foster take in his work. I think he's an incredible storyteller, but his work just doesn't excite me too much.

MM: It's interesting that the two artists that were most influential to people like Buscema were Foster and Alex Raymond, who were not so much storytellers as illustrators.

CHARLES: Especially Foster.

MM: Do you feel yourself channeling your Raymond and Foster stuff more when you do illustrations?

CHARLES: No, I actually got bored with Alex Raymond. It doesn't really excite me anymore, but with Hal Foster, I continually return to his work and learn something more. There's a sense of visual reality to his work that I love; it's something Michael Kaluta puts into his work, too.

MM: And right around this time you started doing Spider-Man covers, including *Web of Spider-Man #1*, that iconic shot of him in the black costume.

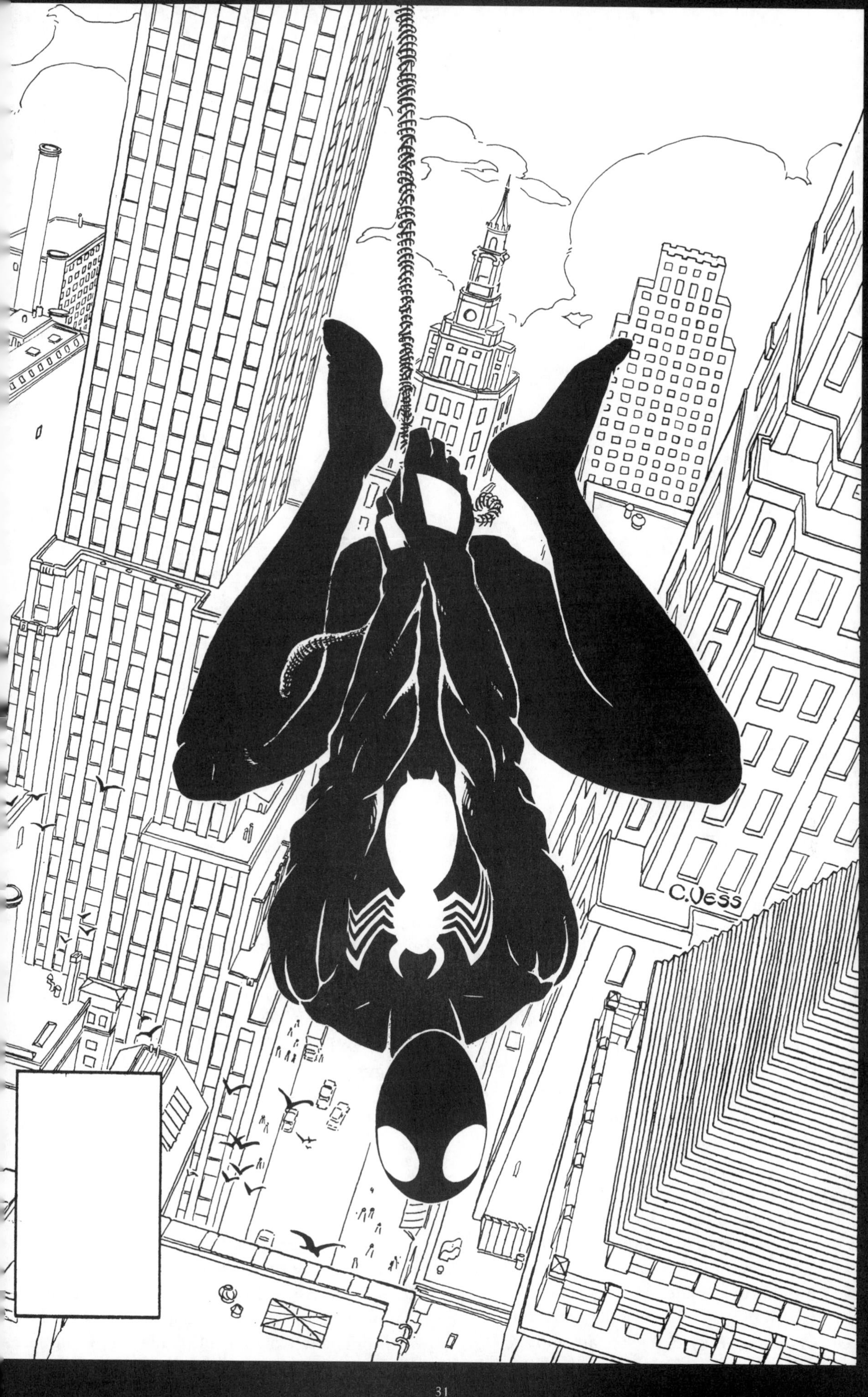
C.Vess

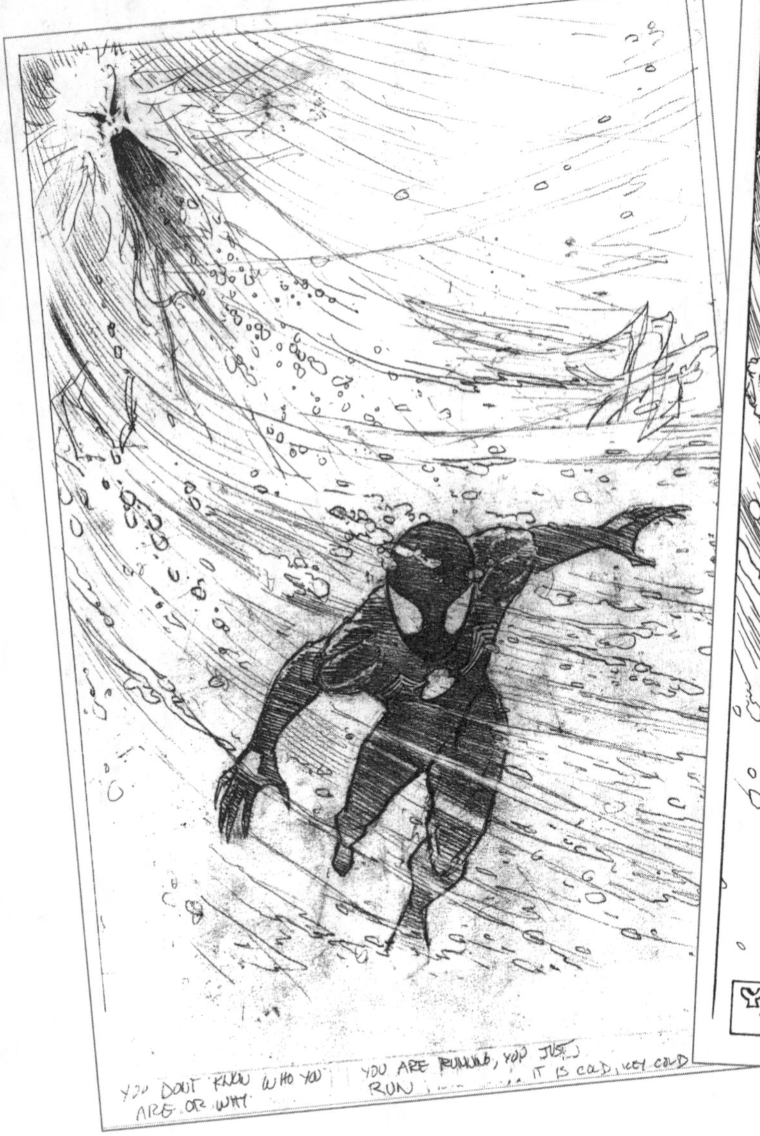
YOU ARE RUNNING, YOU JUST RUN
IT IS COLD, VERY COLD

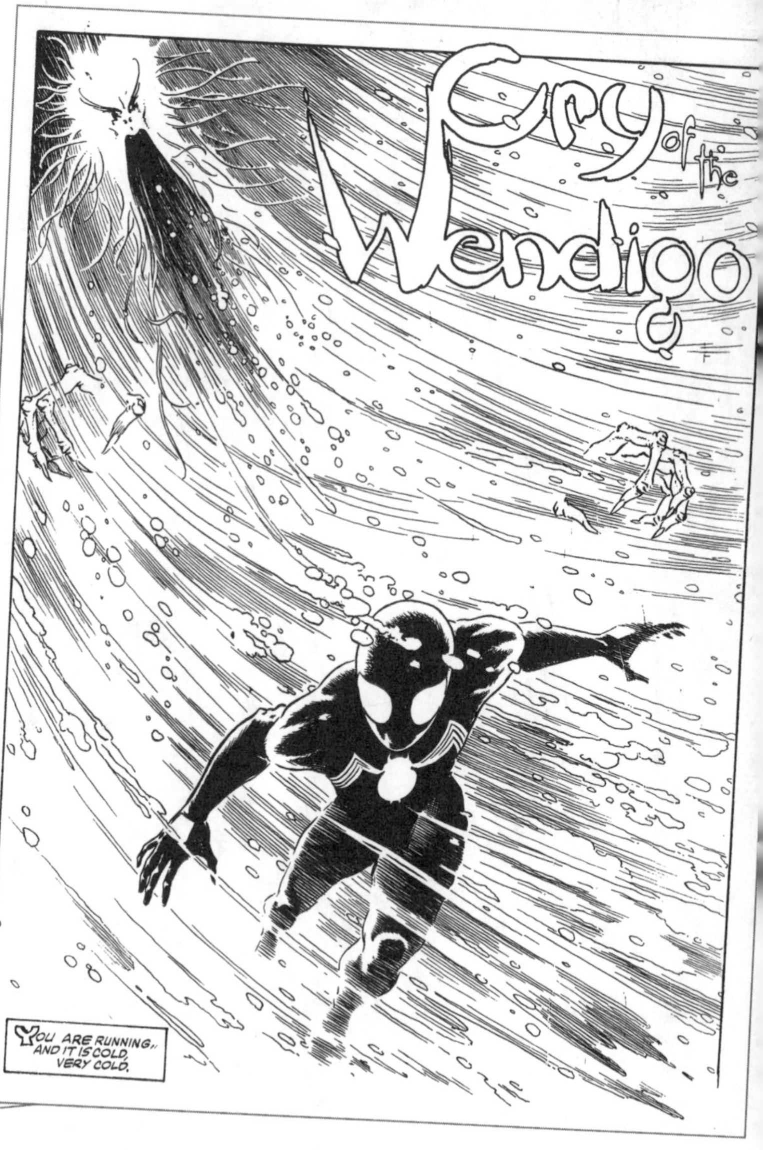
Cry of the Wendigo
YOU ARE RUNNING, AND IT IS COLD, VERY COLD.

CHARLES: Marvel even did a wall hanging of it.

MM: Yeah, the image seemed to be everywhere. Everyone I've mentioned this interview to, when talking about Spider-Man, they go "Oh, man, there's this one Spider-Man cover!"

CHARLES: Jim Owsley, the then-editor of the Spider-Man family of comics, asked if I wanted to do anything for him. One morning I woke up with a Spider-Man story idea, which eventually turned into "The Cry of the Wendigo" [*Amazing Spider-Man* #277]. I guess it was at the same time. I told him about the story, and he liked it and said, "Do it." I also had some cover ideas, and at that time at Marvel every editor was buying two or three stock covers. These cover images weren't story-oriented so that they could be used wherever needed. They'd put those covers in a file drawer and would have them ready if a too-tight deadline came up. At that time they were starting this new Spider-Man series, *Web of Spider-Man*. Apparently they had the whole book done, then Shooter read it and really didn't like any of it. They decided to rewrite the whole comic, and they needed a new cover in a hurry. So they took my painted cover and slapped it on the book, and suddenly they said the sales went up 200,000 copies. "Oh, cool!"

Then I did that single story. I'd done these covers, and I'd done a single issue, and Jo Duffy, who was a friend and an assistant editor, said, "Charles, what you should do is one of the major Marvel characters as a graphic novel, so everyone"—meaning retailers and fans—"will know who you are."

Because I'd loved Spider-Man as a kid, because I'd done gymnastics in high school—I was too short to play basketball—I thought, "Okay, I'll somehow combine Spider-Man with the landscape of Scotland," which I loved to paint. Spider-Man is always such a city character, and I wanted to put him in a totally rural environment so he couldn't just swing away from a problem—there's no place to swing to—and see what would happen.

During that time, I was going to Scotland as often as I could to this beautiful village near the west coast. On one of those visits I found out that if you talked to the locals you could stay as late as you wanted at the pub, which officially closed at 11 p.m. They would just shut the windows, lock the door, and keep on drinking. Well, one of these nights, at about two or three in the morning, I walked outside and stumbled over something. When I looked around, there were a dozen cows sleeping on the street. Now, they were free-range cattle, and they were there sleeping because the pavement was still warm, but if you've had a bit to drink you have to ask, "Well, are they real or are they Memorex?" I did end up using that experience in my story.

MM: Back to the "Wendigo" story, I just love the visual of Spider-Man fighting in the snow, and you've got the obvious contrast with his black costume. I noticed through reading it, or I should say reading it again, that this really doesn't fit into continuity.

CHARLES: No. I didn't know any continuity to fit it into, as I wasn't reading the regular comic at the time.

MM: There are maybe two or three word balloons that actually relate to continuity.

CHARLES: Probably the editor put those in there.

MM: So you just went ahead and did it and they made those changes?

CHARLES: Yeah, I woke up one morning and the story was there, so I sat down and wrote it out. Then I decided where I wanted it in New York, and went to the street and drew all the landmarks and Central Park and stuff. But then I put it in a snowstorm, so you didn't see many of those actual details, but it's at the Bethesda fountain on East 70th Street.

MM: You printed a map in the letters column.

CHARLES: But you couldn't really tell any of it in the story. And then, of course, the Wendigo was thrown in.

MM: It's very unusual Spider-Man material.

CHARLES: Yeah, a lot of people hated it.

MM: He's in the black costume. Was that your choice?

CHARLES: That's what he was wearing at the time I wrote it.

MM: Right. They're using the red one in the main story, but at that point, they tended to switch back and forth.

Previous Page: Pencils and inks to the opening splash page of "Cry of the Wendigo," the back-up story in *Amazing Spider-Man* #277.
Above: Charles' cover for *Mighty Mouse* #11, based on the iconic Jack Kirby *Amazing Fantasy* #15 cover. Unfortunately, *Mighty Mouse* was cancelled with issue #10, and the cover was never published.
Left: Spider-Man's black costume really stood out against the snow-covered backgrounds. Page 10 of "Cry of the Wendigo."

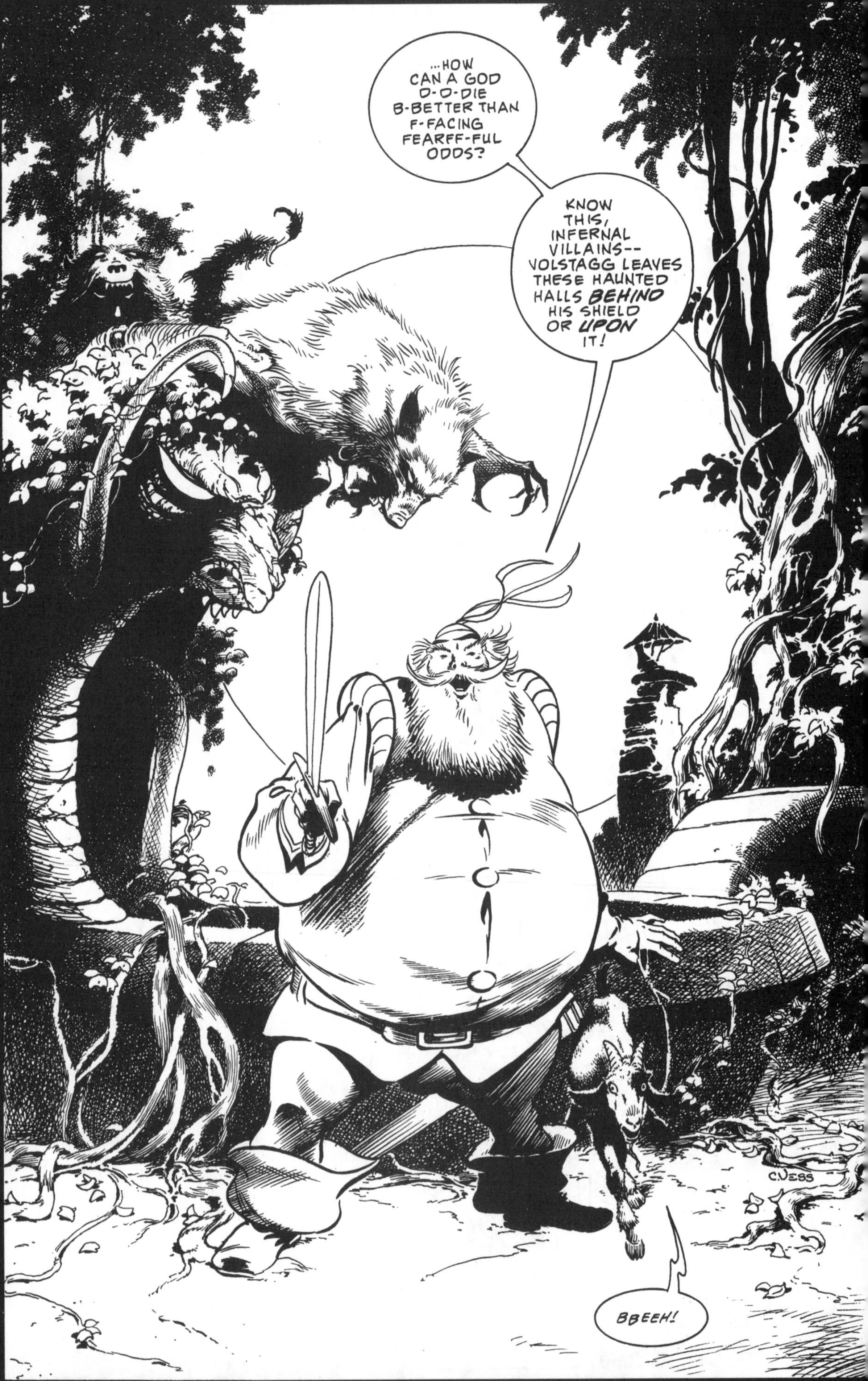
...HOW CAN A GOD D-D-DIE B-BETTER THAN F-FACING FEARFF-FUL ODDS?
KNOW THIS, INFERNAL VILLAINS-- VOLSTAGG LEAVES THESE HAUNTED HALLS BEHIND HIS SHIELD OR UPON IT!
BBEEH!
C.VESS

CHARLES: That costume works beautifully. It's just a great graphic design.

MM: I think, hands-down, it's one of the better costume designs out there. I mean, I love the red and blue, but that black one was such a great design, and this costume funded your first Scotland trip! So, why Scotland?

CHARLES: I'd seen a movie, *Dragonslayer*, loved the landscapes, and sat through the credits to see where it was shot, and part of it was shot in Scotland—on the Isle of Skye. So, I finished a story for *Epic Illustrated*, took the check, and headed for Scotland.

MM: How often do you go?

CHARLES: Not enough, it's a really crazy, beautiful landscape.

MM: And that "Warriors Three" miniseries came out shortly after. It's funny, because I was looking at your earlier work, and what it reminded me of was "The Shining Knight" by Frazetta, especially in the faces.

CHARLES: I was also looking at a lot of European graphic novels at that point, in particular a Belgian artist named Hermann, who does the comics *Les Tours de Bois-Maury* and *Jeremiah*. It was a huge influence on my storytelling and color.

MM: Your work did remind me a lot of Frazetta, the eyes especially.

CHARLES: In the first part the wolfmen are straight out of Frazetta's "Loathsome Lore" one-page strip in *Creepy* or *Eerie*. I had a lot of fun with it; it was a gloriously silly story.

MM: Oh, yeah. I also like your inclusion of the Katzenjammer Kids as Volstagg's children.

CHARLES: Yes, well, that was Alan's idea.

MM: Oh, yeah?

CHARLES: I went, "Oh, cool! Sure!" Not many people noticed that.

MM: Few people know who they are, really. The whole story's very Monty Python-esque. What really alerted me was in the Hogun chapter. There's this toad troll [*Charles laughs*] on a bridge. I don't know why, but when I turn the page, that's where it's just like you just turn into "Charles Vess" from there on out. I mean the Charles Vess that guys like me were introduced to in the early '90s. But what's really interesting to me is, the inking is very different on pages 37 and 38; it's a bit more heavy-handed.

CHARLES: It was P. Craig Russell inking for me.

Previous Page and Below: Pages 19 and 20 of "Life with Volstagg," the first chapter of the Warriors Three saga, from *Marvel Fanfare* #34—complete with Frazetta-esque wolfmen.

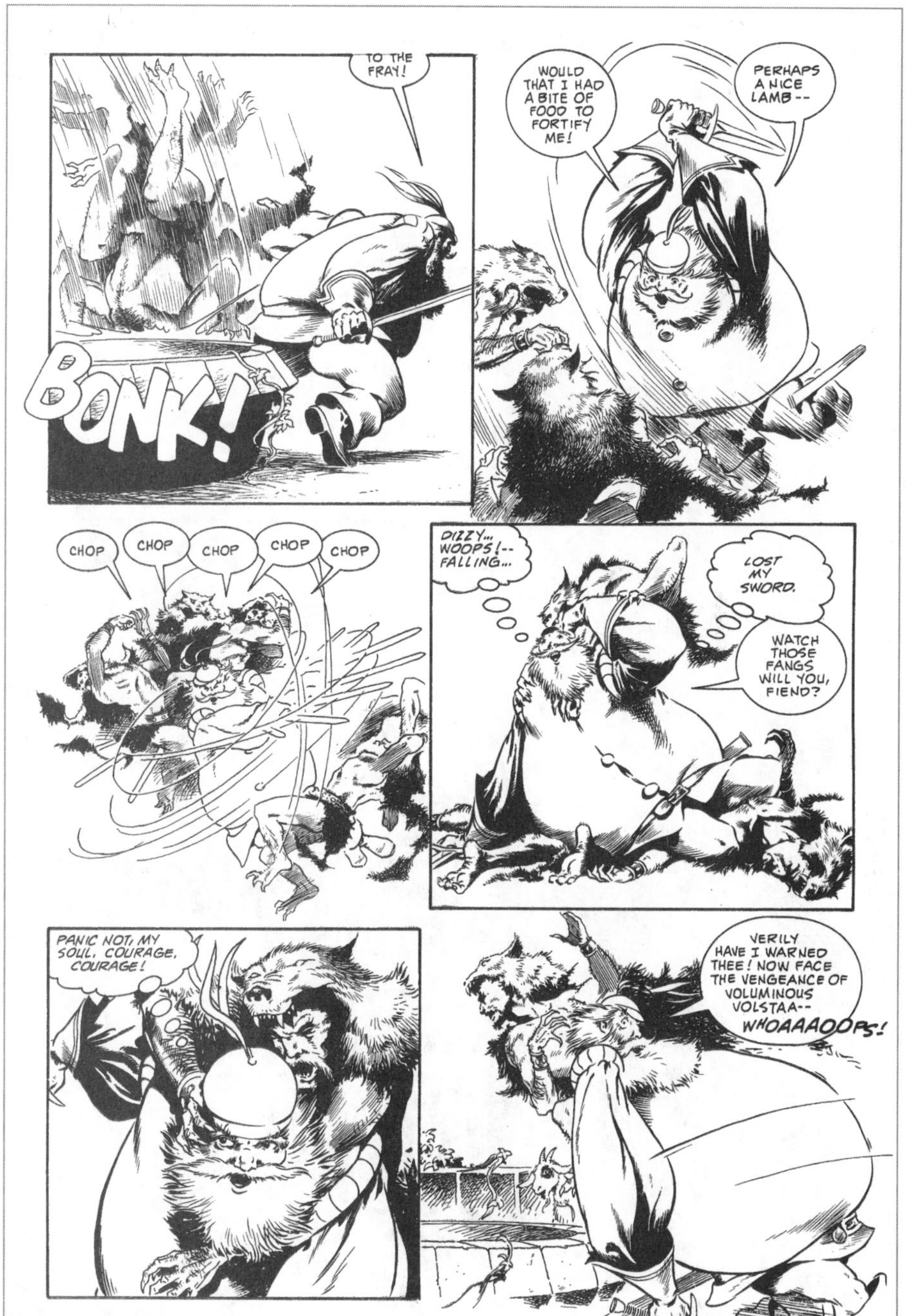
TO THE FRAY!
BONK!
WOULD THAT I HAD A BITE OF FOOD TO FORTIFY ME!
PERHAPS A NICE LAMB --
CHOP
CHOP
CHOP
CHOP
CHOP
DIZZY... WOOPS!-- FALLING...
LOST MY SWORD.
WATCH THOSE FANGS WILL YOU, FIEND?
PANIC NOT, MY SOUL. COURAGE, COURAGE!
VERILY HAVE I WARNED THEE! NOW FACE THE VENGEANCE OF VOLUMINOUS VOLSTAA--
WHOAAAOOPS!

Right and Next Page: Hogun—lighten up, fella. Panel and page from "Hogun's Goat" [*Marvel Fanfare* #35].
Below: Fandral takes the stage in *Marvel Fanfare* #36, doing what he does best—saving the damsel in distress.

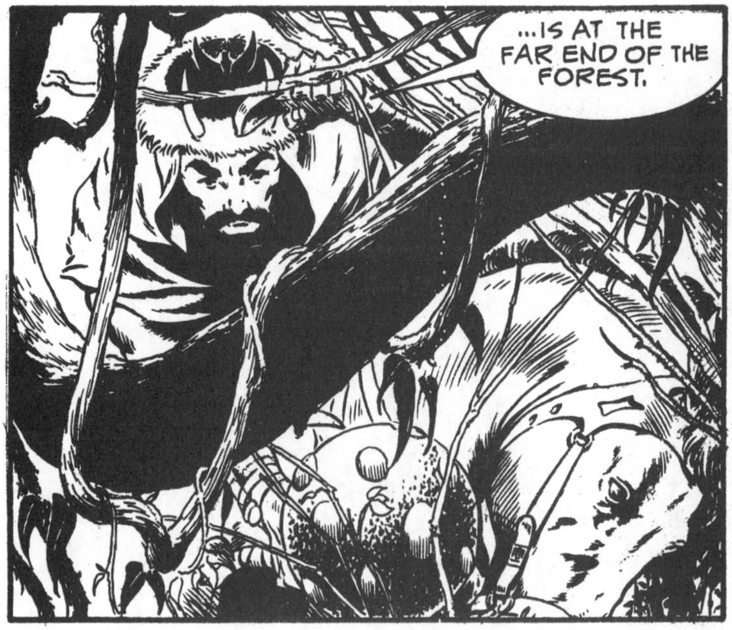
...IS AT THE FAR END OF THE FOREST.

MM: Yeah, it looks like P. Craig Russell's linework.

CHARLES: I was going off to Scotland and I couldn't finish, so I gave him a couple pages to ink for me.

MM: You've got this distinctive, thin linework in your inking. So, even though you were inking your own stuff, how did you go about drawing it? Did you loosely pencil it or did you tightly pencil it?

CHARLES: Tight-ass.

MM: Why tight-ass?

CHARLES: Because that's just the way I draw. As I've gotten older I've gotten more confident, and I tend to do backgrounds as just implied. But there's still so many possibilities that happen. Just a slip of a pencil that leads to a better drawing can happen when drawing tight-ass.

MM: What is it about this story arc in *Marvel Fanfare* that really—?

CHARLES: Well, we wanted to come up with a story that would be making fun of heroic-ness. We actually went to two or three editors who simply did not get what we were trying to say, and finally went back to Al Milgrom, who completely understood the story. He knew what we were trying to do. A lot of the other editors kept saying, "Make it serious—some giant, epic thing." "No, no, no, we're make fun of all these very grim people—grim and grimmer."

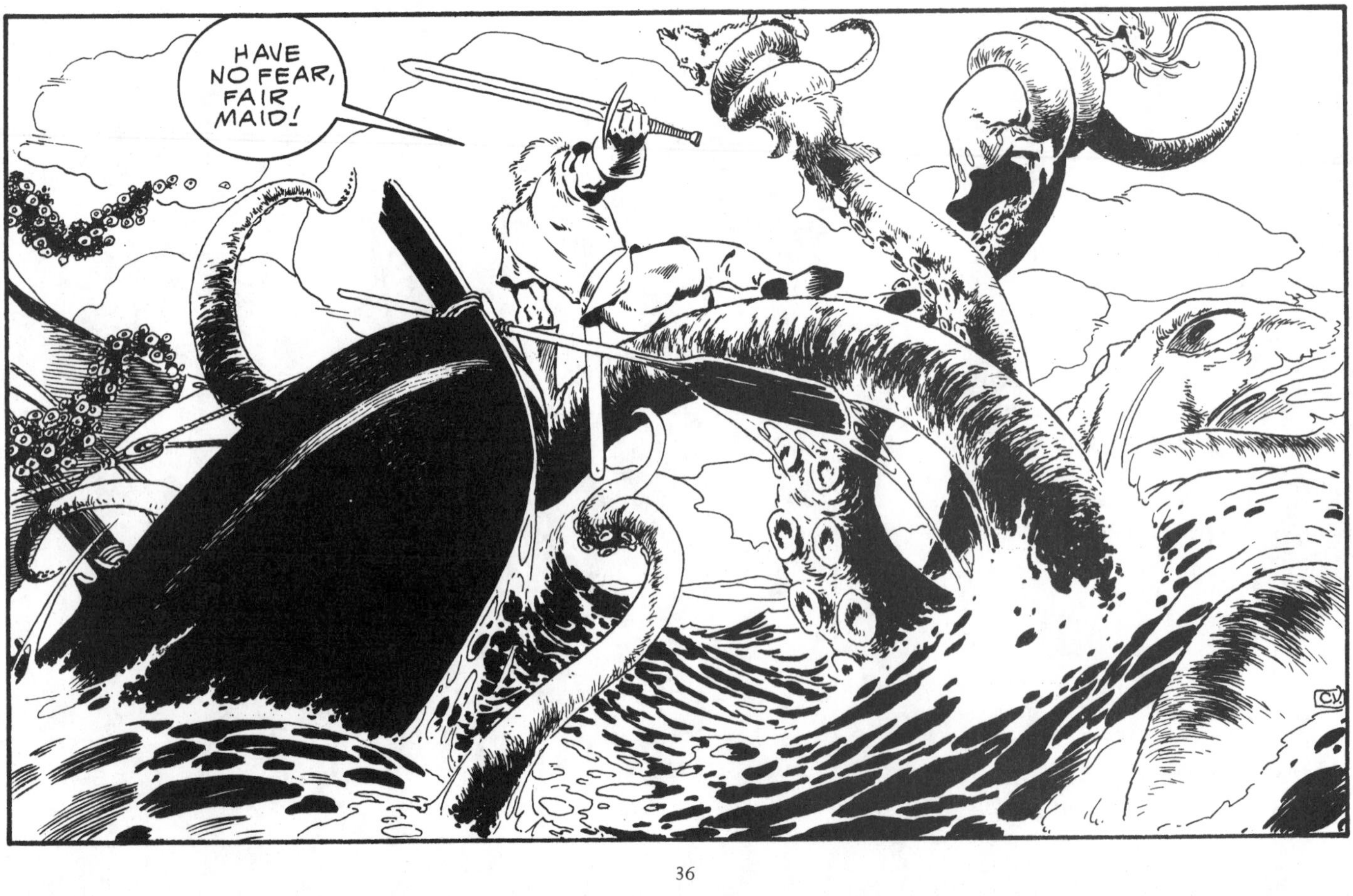
HAVE NO FEAR, FAIR MAID!

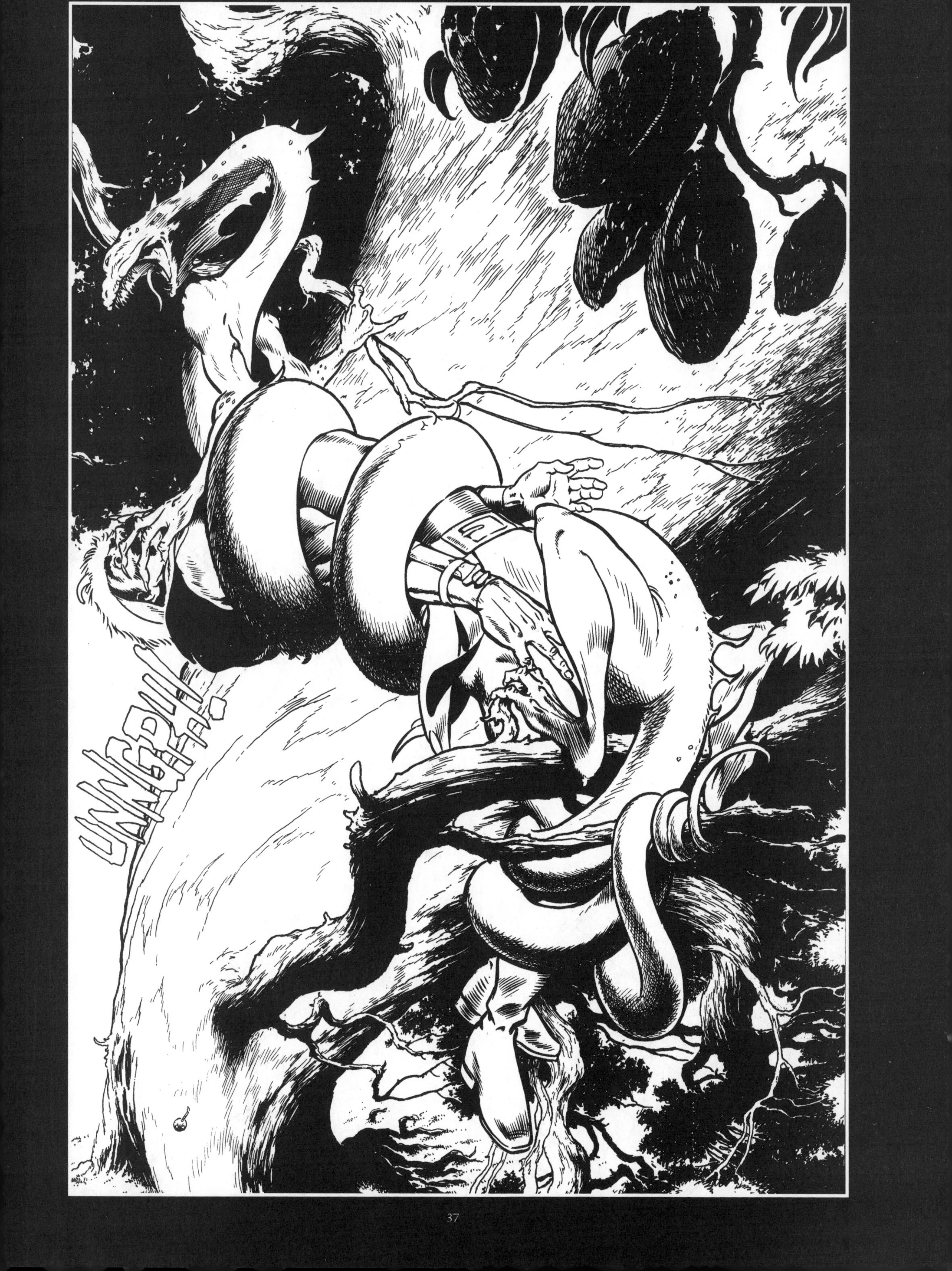
UNNGRH!!

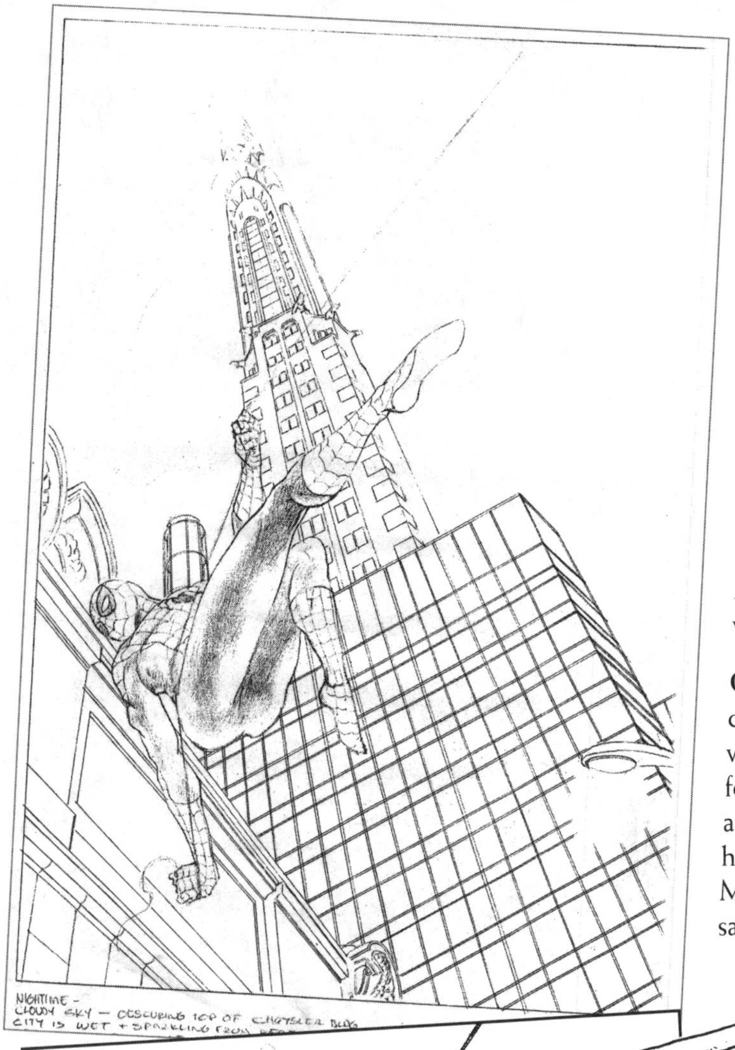
NIGHTIME -
CLOUDY SKY — OBSCURING TOP OF CHRYSLER BLDG
CITY IS WET + SPARKLING FROM

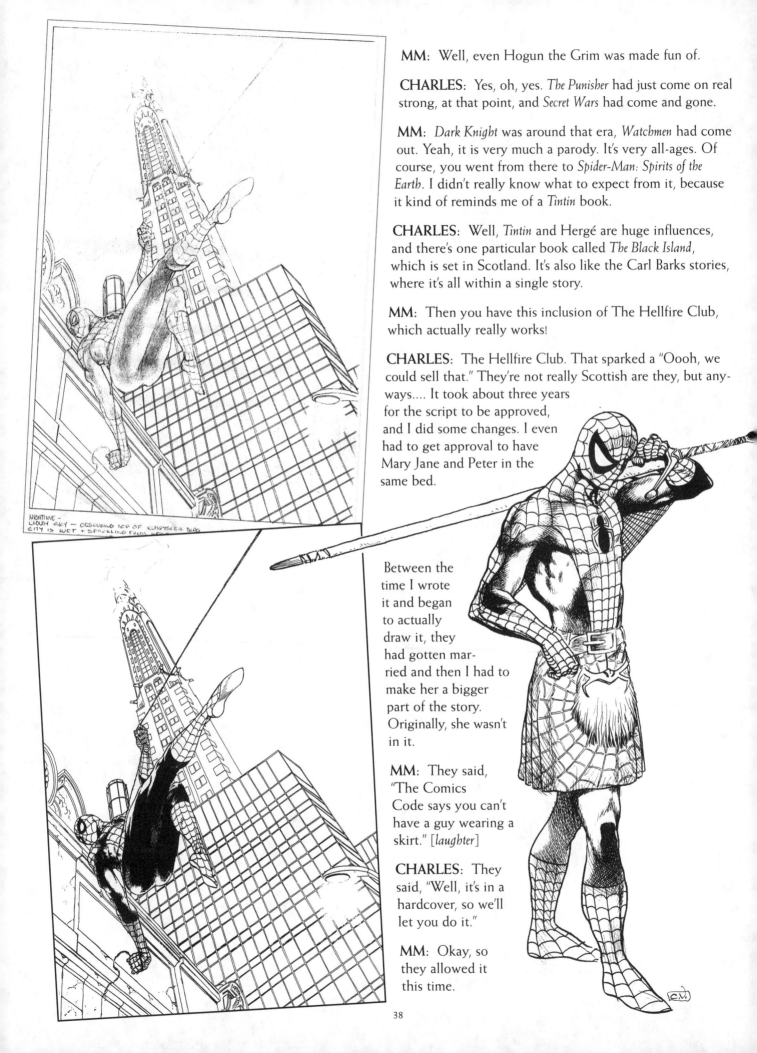

MM: Well, even Hogun the Grim was made fun of.

CHARLES: Yes, oh, yes. *The Punisher* had just come on real strong, at that point, and *Secret Wars* had come and gone.

MM: *Dark Knight* was around that era, *Watchmen* had come out. Yeah, it is very much a parody. It's very all-ages. Of course, you went from there to *Spider-Man: Spirits of the Earth*. I didn't really know what to expect from it, because it kind of reminds me of a *Tintin* book.

CHARLES: Well, *Tintin* and Hergé are huge influences, and there's one particular book called *The Black Island*, which is set in Scotland. It's also like the Carl Barks stories, where it's all within a single story.

MM: Then you have this inclusion of The Hellfire Club, which actually really works!

CHARLES: The Hellfire Club. That sparked a "Oooh, we could sell that." They're not really Scottish are they, but anyways.... It took about three years for the script to be approved, and I did some changes. I even had to get approval to have Mary Jane and Peter in the same bed.

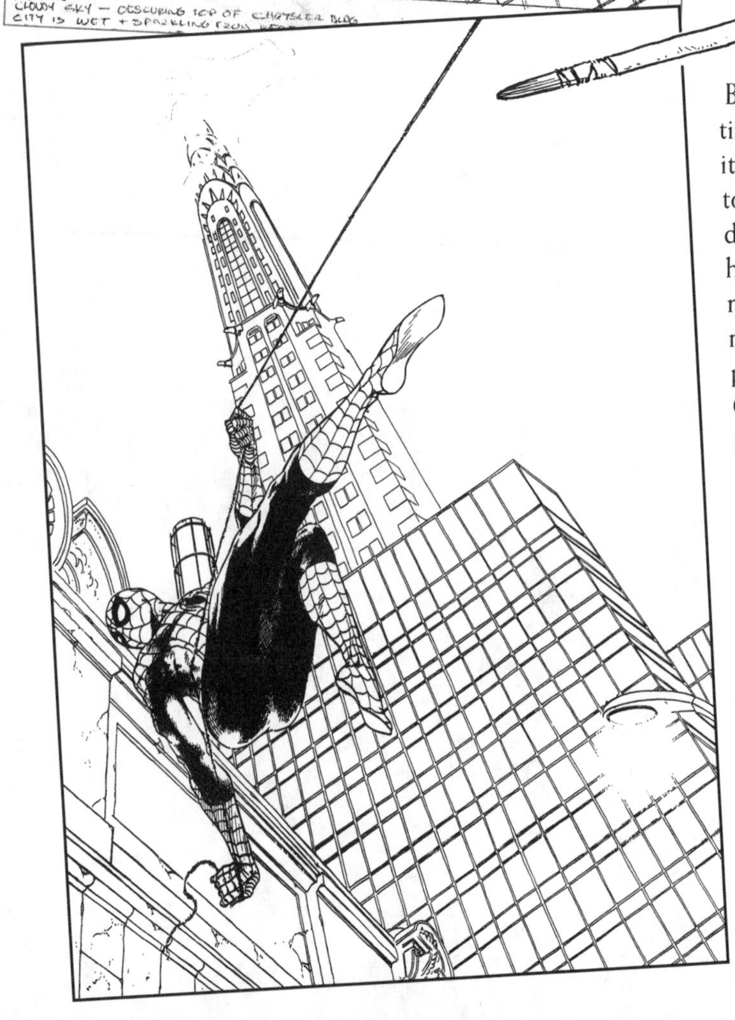

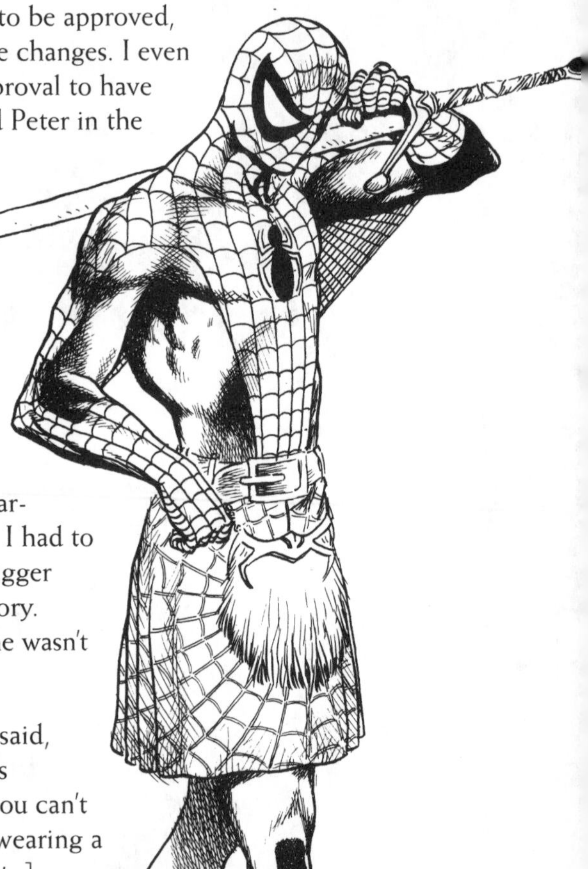

Between the time I wrote it and began to actually draw it, they had gotten married and then I had to make her a bigger part of the story. Originally, she wasn't in it.

MM: They said, "The Comics Code says you can't have a guy wearing a skirt." [*laughter*]

CHARLES: They said, "Well, it's in a hardcover, so we'll let you do it."

MM: Okay, so they allowed it this time.

CHARLES: So I spent a long time writing it. I went through a couple of editors, and Jim Salicrup, who edited Spider-Man at the time, said, "Let's do it." So then I went out and photographed all these scenes in New York. I'm not really that comfortable drawing buildings and cars.

MM: It's kind of ironic, because I read your father was an architect.

CHARLES: Yeah, all those windows.

MM: But I notice you used a lot of blacks and shadows. There's something very Ditko about it.

CHARLES: Well, I loved Ditko's art. I lost interest in *Spider-Man* after he quit drawing it. I won't say that Steve Ditko's the best artist in the world, but there's an incredible amount of personality to his run.

MM: Well, I liked the fact that Peter Parker was an everyman who didn't have any money and had bad luck in general. I can relate.

CHARLES: I mean, is anyone normal?

MM: Exactly. But, relatively speaking, he's a good-looking guy, but not too handsome; he's got horrible luck with the girls. You had a very Ditko feel to your fights, too.

CHARLES: I don't think I've talked about this yet, but I don't like how the final decision in super-hero comics always has to be made by whoever has the bigger fists. I don't think or react to people that way, so it's very difficult to draw fight scenes. If I had to draw a brawl issue after issue, I'd go crazy, but I had this one story and I said, "Okay, I'm gonna do a big fistfight—do a James Bond movie—and be done with it, but I'll do it my way." I knew that I'd only do this once, and it was a lot of fun.

MM: You might as well have fun with it.

CHARLES: Yeah.

MM: What was the response to the book?

CHARLES: It bought our house.

Previous Page: Pencils and inks from the opening splash page of *Spider-Man: Spirits of the Earth*—in the background is the Chrysler Building—and a commission piece of Spidey in a dress... er... kilt.
Above: A fight scene from *Spirits of the Earth*—Vess style!

Spider-Man ™ and ©2007 Marvel Characters, Inc.

MM: That's usually a very—

CHARLES: A very good response.

MM: Critically there was a good response, too.

CHARLES: I believe so. There are very few times in my life when I feel like my work is a big enough event to make enough of an impression on enough people to win any awards. So this had come out, and I felt really good about it, but then two weeks before the end of the year, Frank Miller's *Elektra* came out. "There goes any chance for awards!" [*laughter*] And I was right.

MM: I noticed the embossed Spider-Man on the actual hardcover... it has a very art deco feel to it.

CHARLES: Yes, anytime I'm doing a full book, I approach it all around, and I love putting a cover stamping on these kinds of things, because 90% of the people don't notice these things, but I will.

MM: Then there's this endsheet illustration of the Scottish village and, if you look close enough... there's Spider-Man!

CHARLES: The funny thing about the one in the *Spider-Man* book is that the man who bought the original asked me to take Spider-Man out of it.

MM: Yeah?

CHARLES: Hey, it was his drawing!

Right: Charles' design for the embossing for the *Spirits of the Earth* cover. The woodcut feel of the drawing adds a nice touch of class to the overall appearance of the book.
Below: And what hardcover book would be complete without endpapers? You may have to hunt for Spidey, but he's in there.
Next Page: Sandman trading card art, featuring Oberon, Titania, and good Will Shakespeare.

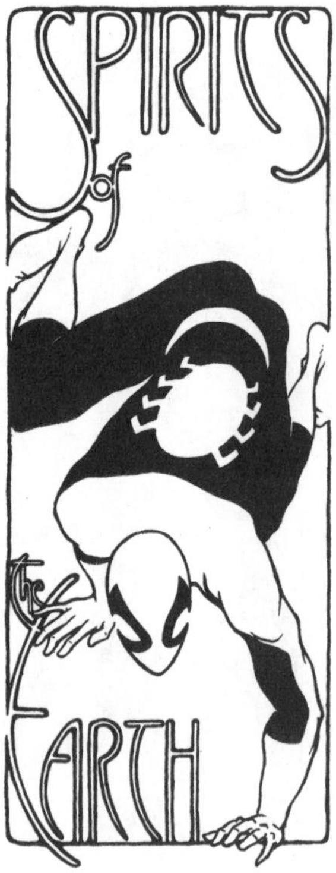
SPIRITS
of
The
EARTH

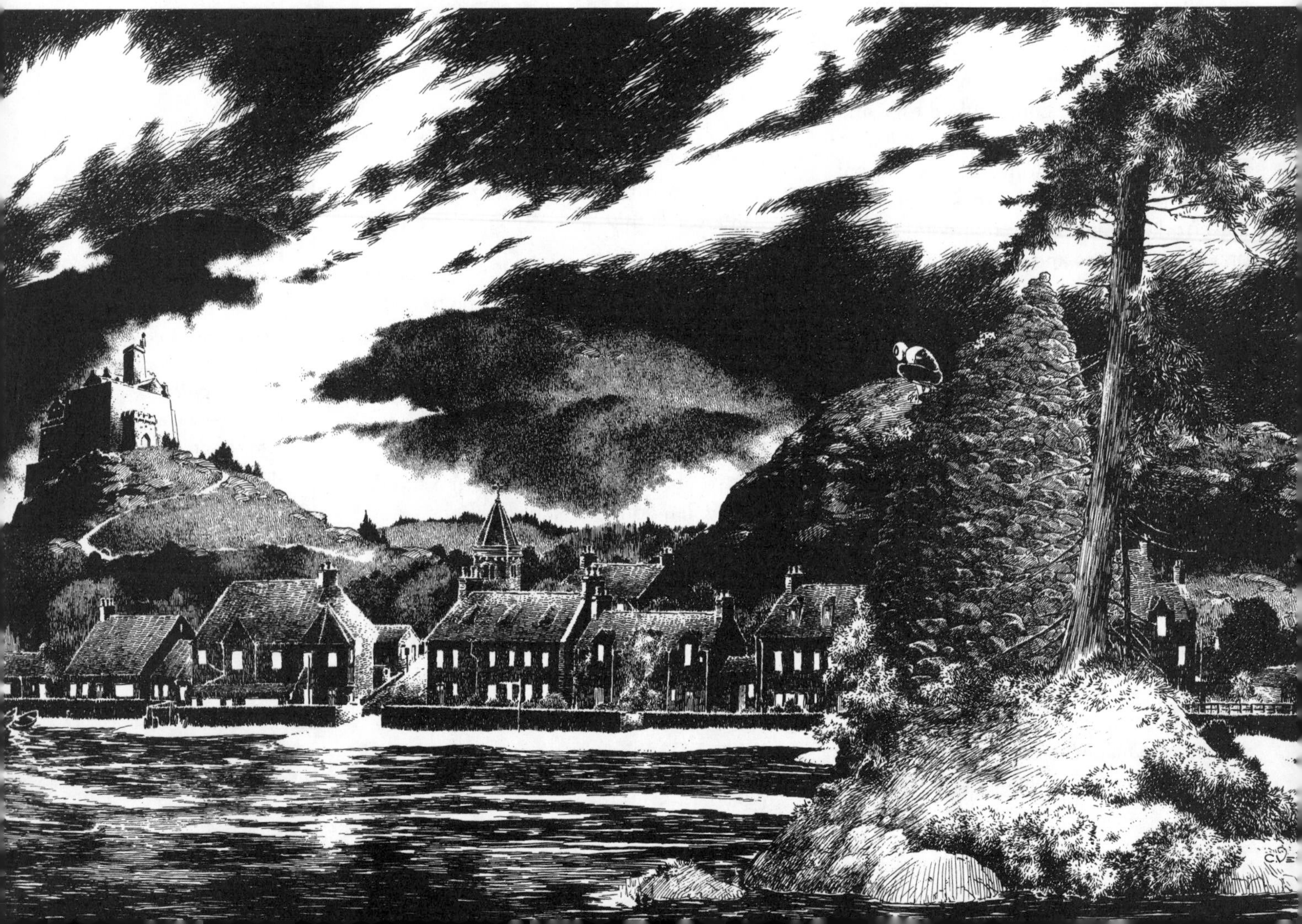

Part 3: The Good Old One-Two Punch

MM: *Sandman* #19 was straight after the *Spider-Man* book?

CHARLES: Yeah. *Spider-Man* should have come out about nine months before it did. I finished it and actually got it in before it was due, which is pretty amazing with me. It sat on Jim Salicrup's desk, and on the top of his file cabinets, for nine months. I'd go in and comment, "You know, you really need to start production on that." Jim would always reply, "Oh, I will, I will."

That summer, Marvel had arranged a signing tour that was to kick off at San Diego Comic-Con and my editor just didn't get into production in time. So I was told that it would be released that fall instead. I had finished the Spider-Man graphic novel around Christmas of the year before, and then taken on the *Sandman* job, and I got that one in on time, too. Those are the only two times in my life I've ever done that.

My issue of *Sandman* was also released about three months late. Karen Berger was having a lot of problems with it in production as they were transitioning from one colorist to Steve Oliff's computer color. So by pure happenstance both projects came out at almost the same time. That made for a great one-two punch for the retailers to go, "Oh! Now I know who Charles Vess is. He just did these two books." And, of course, they both rack up very good sales which also made both the retailers and the fans take notice.

One of the sort of funny, surreal moments of that eventual signing tour for the *Spider-Man* book was when I was appearing at a mall in New Jersey. The store had gone all out in its presentation as well as hiring someone to be Spider-Man, so everyone was pretty excited about the event. In route to the store we'd gotten into a traffic jam and arrived quite late. There were 20 or 30 people in line, all holding the hardcover graphic novel which were all in shrinkwraps. I came in the door, everyone recognized I was there, and started walking to the table. I sat down, took my coat off, got my pen out, and looked up, and all the way down the line, every one of those people has the shrinkwrap in their teeth trying to rip it off so that I could sign their books. Each book was at a wild angle, jerking about as its owner struggled to "uncover" the book. There was something very Monty Python about the sight and I just started laughing.

C. Vess 93
©AND TM D.C. COMICS, INC.

MM: Okay, so *Sandman* and *Spider-Man* came out at roughly the same time.

CHARLES: *Sandman* came out and everyone seemed really happy with it. About a year before that, at San Diego Comic-Con, was the first time I ran into Neil. This was before he was a phenomenon, so he was able to walk around and enjoy himself, and he just stopped and we talked for a while. We had an instant sort of connection with fantasy writers and books we enjoyed. When Neil got ready to leave he said, "Well, if you ever want to draw an issue of *Sandman*, let me know. I'll write you something." Which was very flattering, but at that time maybe the first four or five issues had come out, and the storylines had all featured modern day horror. In my mind, I was thinking "I'd never want to draw that type of story."

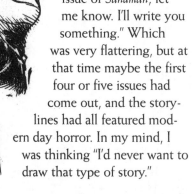

About two months later, I'm reading through my packet of comp comics that had arrived from DC and there in the latest issue of *Sandman* is the African folk tale [Sandman #9], and I went, "Oooh, I could have drawn that story!" And then I had this light bulb going off: "Neil can write any story he wants." I immediately called Neil up to follow up on his offer. By this time he had found a copy of the edition of *A Midsummer Night's Dream* that I'd illustrated for the Donning Company. Neil asked, "Well, would you like to try a different interpretation of *A Midsummer Night's Dream*?" Not being a fool I said, "Sure!" So he sent me the script and it was just a really gorgeous story. It was very exciting to draw it.

MM: It works on so many levels. It was so cool rereading everything, because it's been a few years. I reread *Books of Magic* #3 right after it.

CHARLES: Did you know that *Books of Magic* had gone through four prospective artists before it got to me? I read the script and thought, "Well, didn't he write it for me?" It certainly seemed like it.

MM: Yeah! I mean, it seems like it's just the realm of faerie, which is right up your alley.

CHARLES: But everyone including Ted McKeever and Dave McKean, Kent Williams, all these different people. Tom Yeates.

MM: Why did it go through four artists?

CHARLES: I don't know. It just did. I'm not privy to those mysteries; I'm just happy it ended up on me.

MM: Yeah, definitely. So the "Midsummer Night's Dream" story was your first mainstream non-super-hero work, at least in a while. In the letter column, they mentioned you as an unusual choice. Do you remember anything about the reactions towards the guy who just did *Spider-Man* drawing an issue of *Sandman*?

CHARLES: People really liked our story. I was really pleased with it myself, and was really pleased with my drawing. It had gone a lot easier than usual for me. Like I said, I got it in on time, which surprised everyone all the way down the board. I was also incredibly happy that Steve Oliff was going to do the color, as opposed to the person who had been coloring *Sandman*, who colored pages as a piece of abstract art and not for the story it was telling. And he

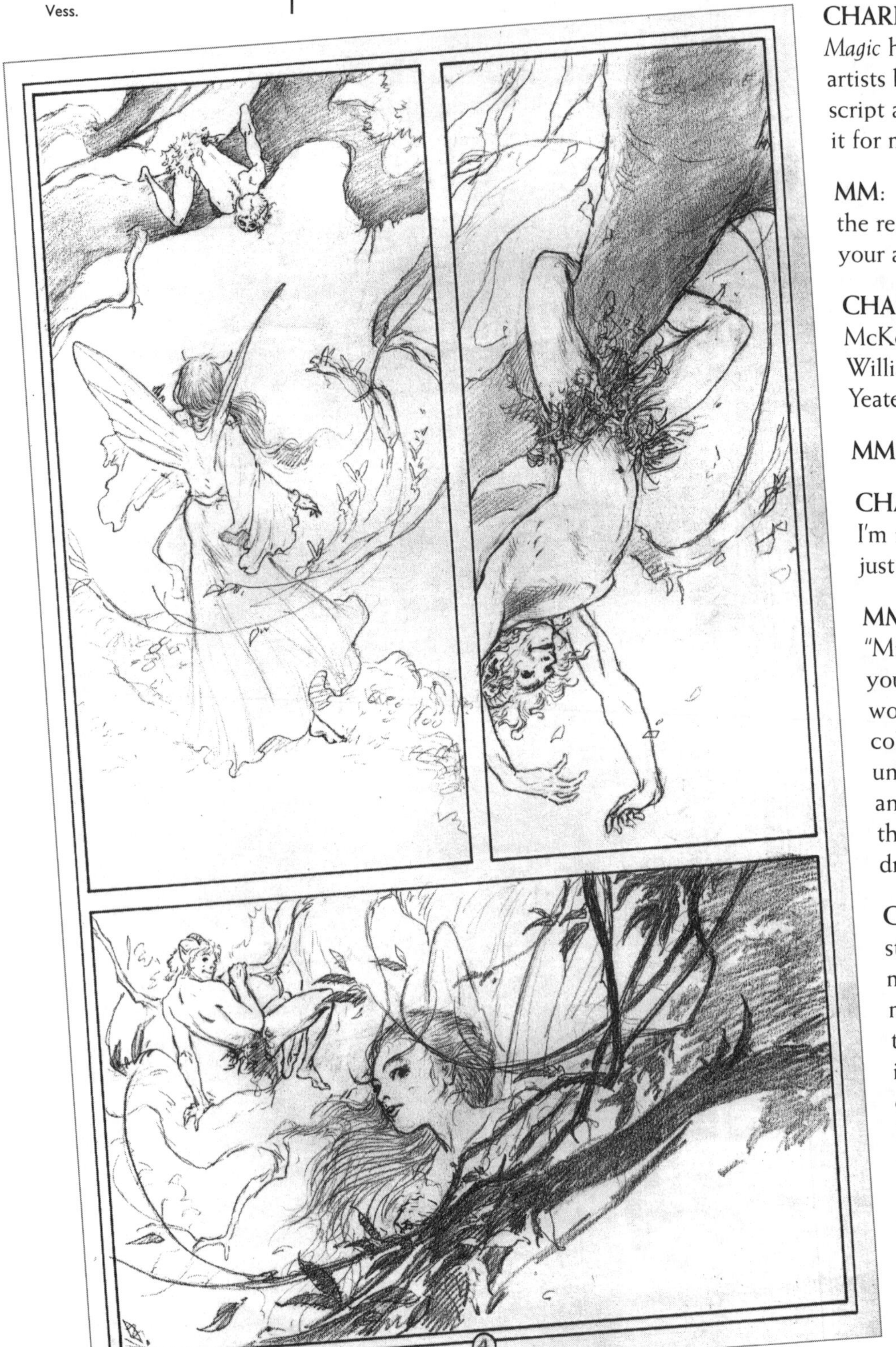
4

Below and Next Page: Charles: "Pages [4 and 5] from my attempt to adapt Shakespeare's *A Midsummer Night's Dream* into graphic novel format for The Donning Company. I later talked them out of the graphic novel format and into an illustrated book edition.

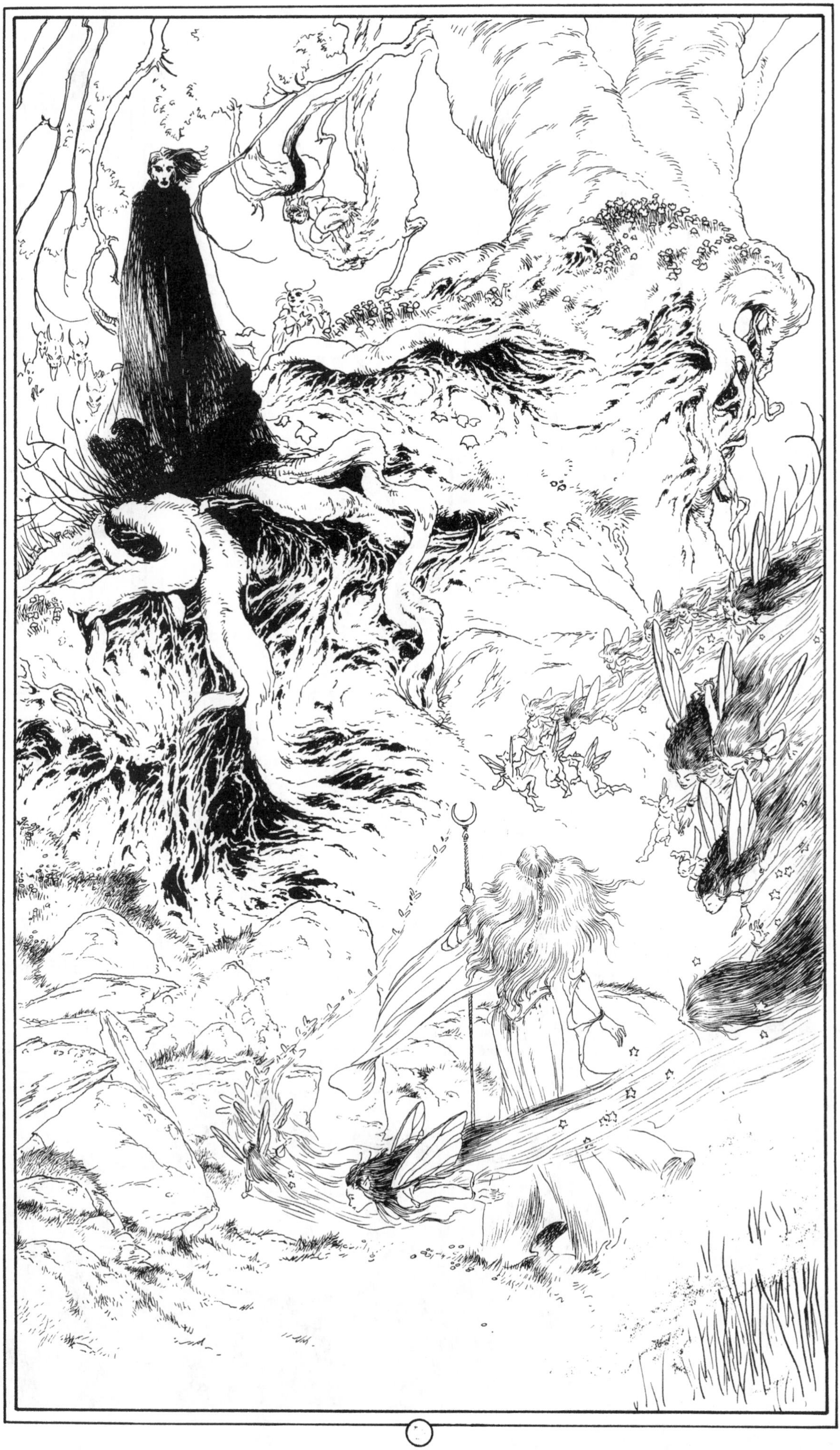

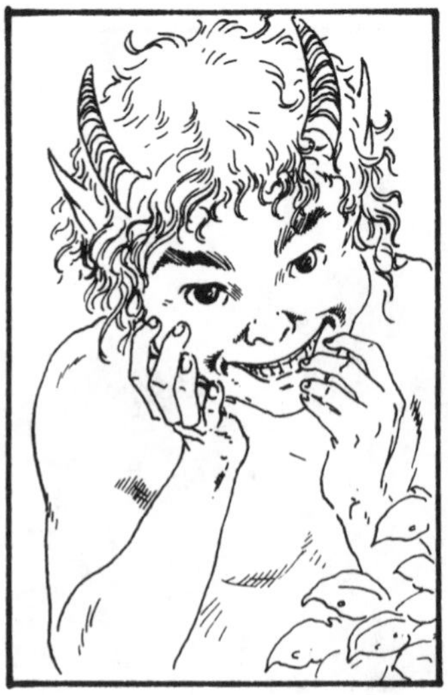

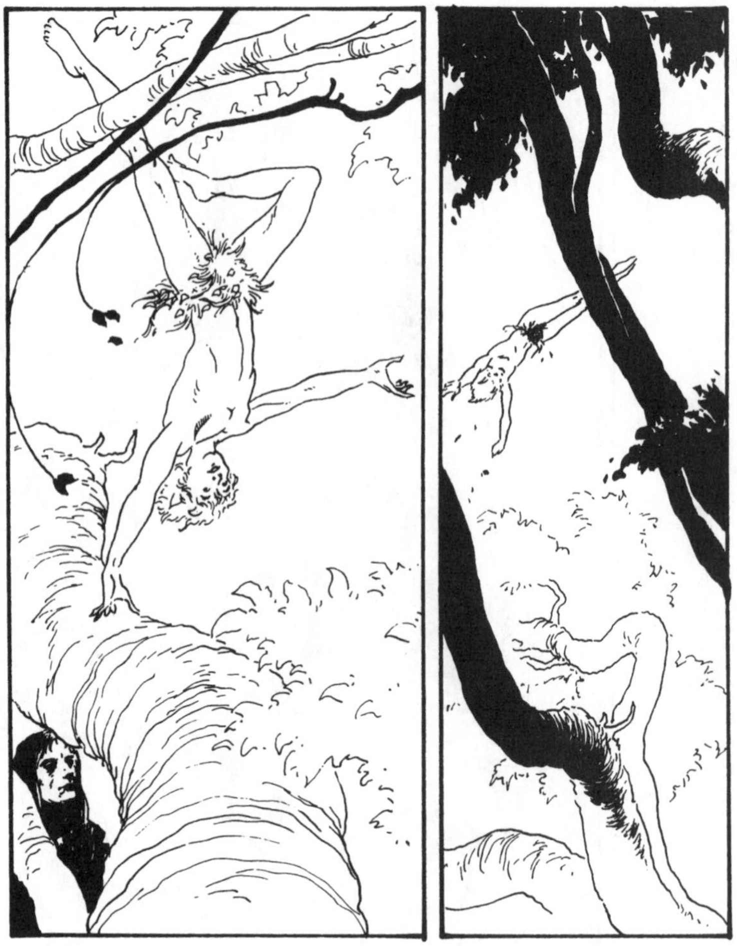

This Page: Puck, as he appeared in Charles' original adaptation of *A Midsummer Night's Dream*. In this version, Puck is rather like a small boy with an impish attitude—very different from the more malevolent look and feel Charles gave him and the other goblins in the pages of *Sandman*. **Next Page:** Charles also contributed drawings to a sequence in *Sandman* #62, though he feels the coloring in the issue obscured his linework too much.

would actually admit to that bizarre idea. He wasn't trying to make it make sense, he was just trying to make a nice, abstract piece of color; he would color explosions as the darkest color on the page, and all the like.

MM: Yeah, I remember a lot of monochromatic—

CHARLES: Oh, it didn't really work.

MM: Yeah. It was over early Sam Kieth artwork, too, which was not his best work.

CHARLES: It wasn't quite a match made in heaven.

MM: Something I noticed about your designs, especially in "A Midsummer Night's Dream," is, especially for Puck, they almost looked like they could be puppets. There's something very Henson-esque about your designs.

CHARLES: That's interesting. Neil had the idea for Puck as a monkey.

MM: A monkey?

CHARLES: An insane, rabid monkey. We agreed that Titania would be pretty much

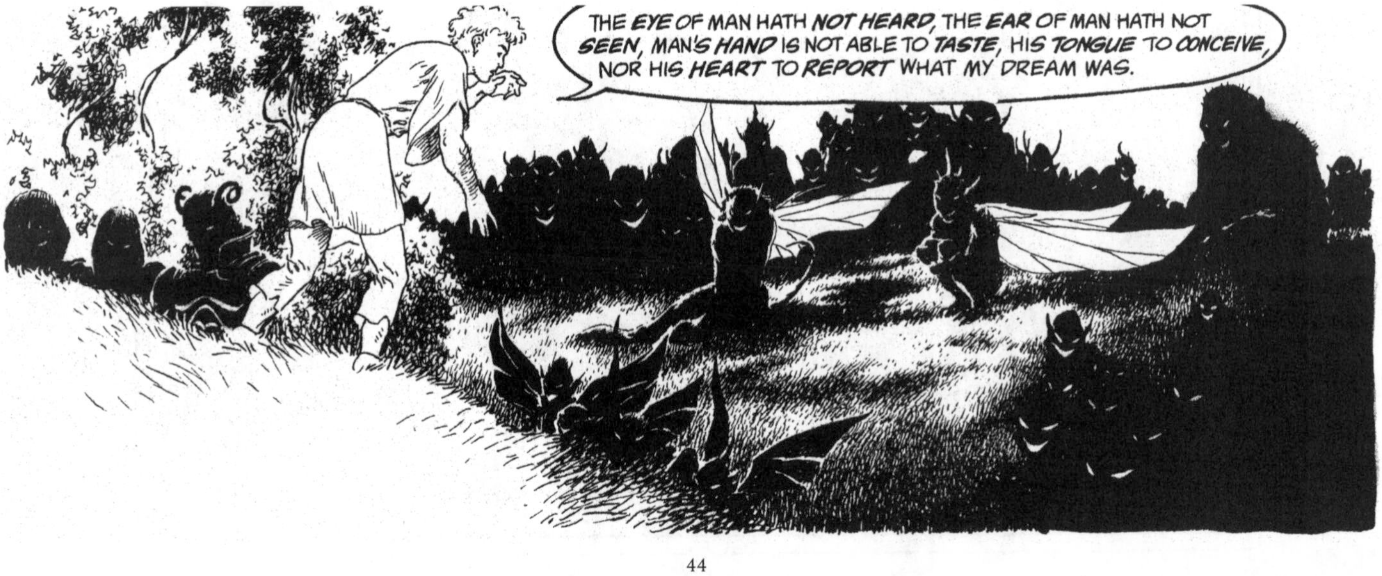
THE EYE OF MAN HATH NOT HEARD, THE EAR OF MAN HATH NOT SEEN, MAN'S HAND IS NOT ABLE TO TASTE, HIS TONGUE TO CONCEIVE, NOR HIS HEART TO REPORT WHAT MY DREAM WAS.

sort of a typical Titania, but I had the idea that Oberon would be a nine-foot guy with antlers and red armor. I remember the long conversations over the phone when we were trying to settle on the visual aspects of the story. This was way before e-mail. All the sketches had to be faxed back and forth. Primitive! [*laughter*]

MM: There was something with them; I look at them and I'm picturing how they would be constructed in real life. It just made me wonder, where do you look, as far as your influences for character design when it comes to Puck, as opposed to designing him as a rabid monkey, or does it just happen?

CHARLES: I just looked at weird, vicious goblin characters, Frazetta....

MM: [Brian] Froud?

CHARLES: Froud would definitely be there, Alan Lee, Kaluta. All those things. It's not particularly pulling out books by them, but all that stuff floats around in your head.

MM: It collects.

CHARLES: And it'll shoot out there hopefully at the right time. I'm looking forward to the *Absolute Sandman* edition [with "A Midsummer Night's Dream"], because

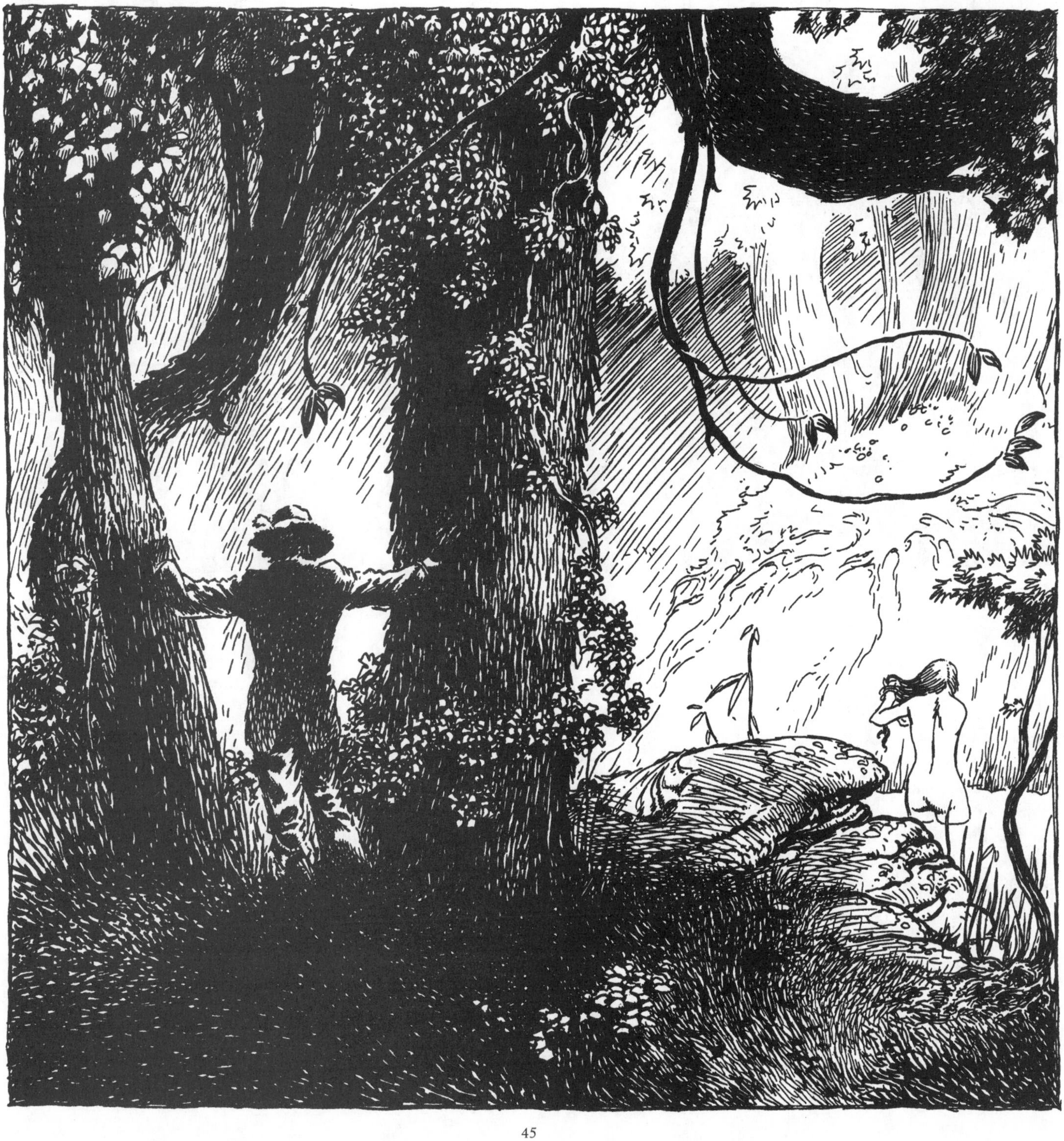

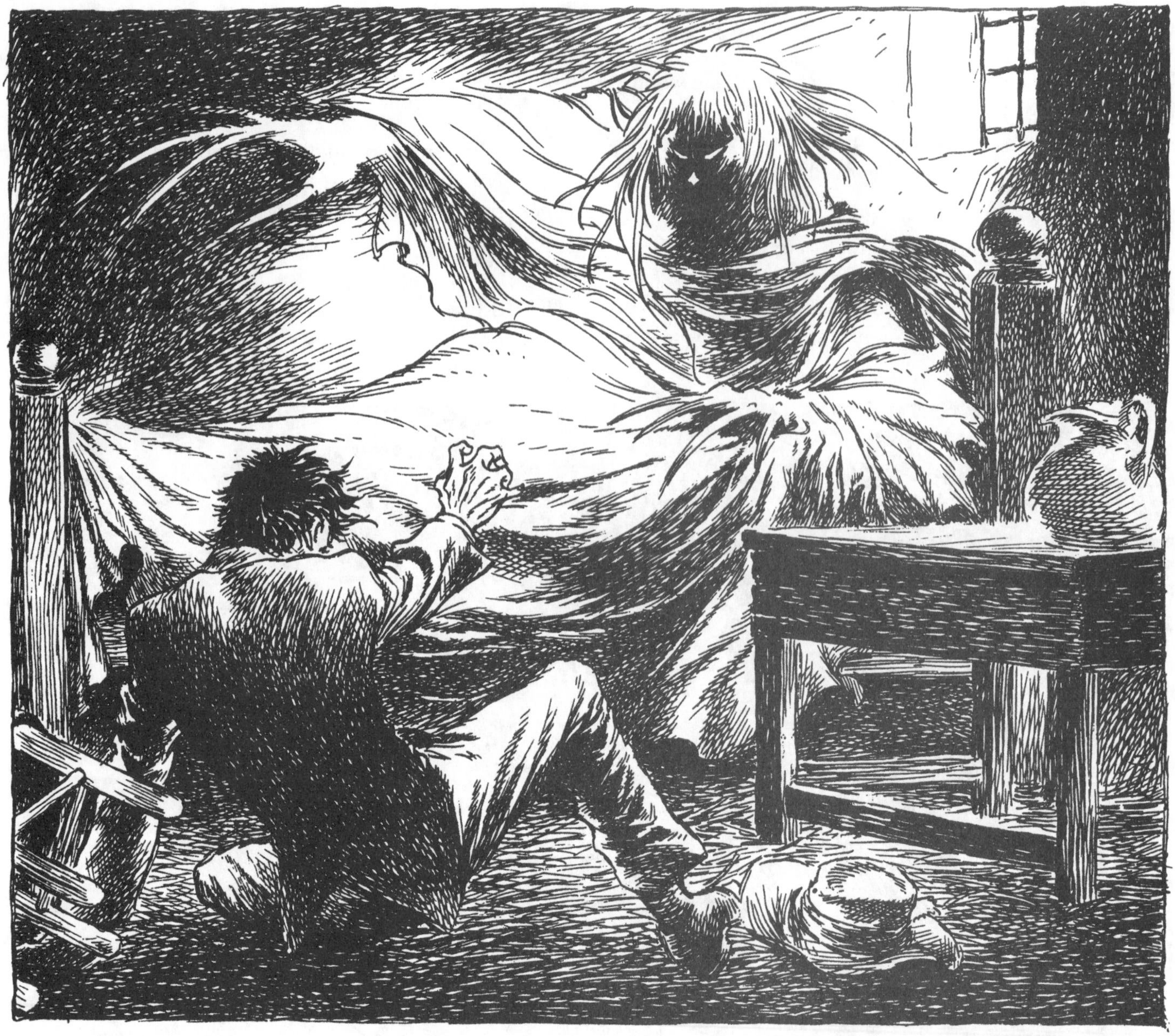

Above: Another illustration from *Sandman* #62. **Next Page:** A painted version of this illustration, featuring the key players of *Sandman* #75, appeared in *Sandman Gallery* #1.

there are a couple of panels where the ink really clogged up [in the printing process]. The pages were reshot, so I'm hoping it will work right. Although I think it's going to be on slick paper, and that's too bad.

MM: Now, this was written with some obvious narrative hooks that Neil put in there. Was there a plan to bookend this later?

CHARLES: Well, we knew we were going to do *The Tempest*. Those were the two stories Neil chose, because those are the two really original stories that Shakespeare made up out of whole cloth, but it was just going to be later on. It wasn't until, I think, our friend Mark Askwith said, "You know, *The Tempest* should really be the last issue because it's Shakespeare's last play."

MM: Yeah! It's fitting. Was Karen Berger the editor at the time?

CHARLES: Yes. Karen asked that one small scene be redrawn. It was a really interesting scene, but the focus of the story needed to stay on Shakespeare's son, Hamnet, and that was being lost, so he was given a soliloquy that reveals the heart of the story's theme. But to do that we had to take out a cool bit of business on the part of some of the other actors.

MM: Interesting. I'm surprised you mentioned *Books of Magic* #3 wasn't done for you originally. That was, what, a year or two after, perhaps?

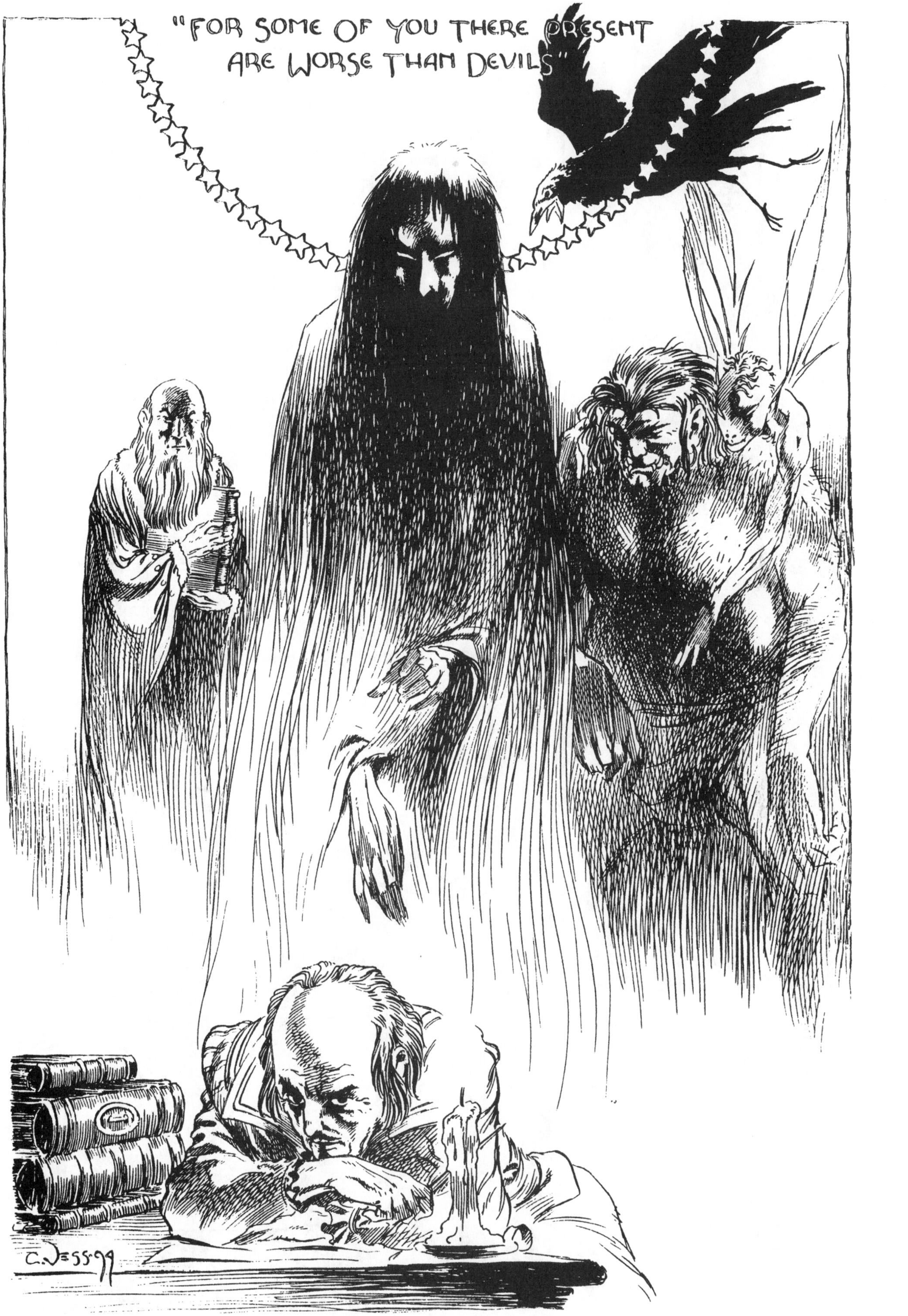
"FOR SOME OF YOU THERE PRESENT
ARE WORSE THAN DEVILS"
C. VESS 99

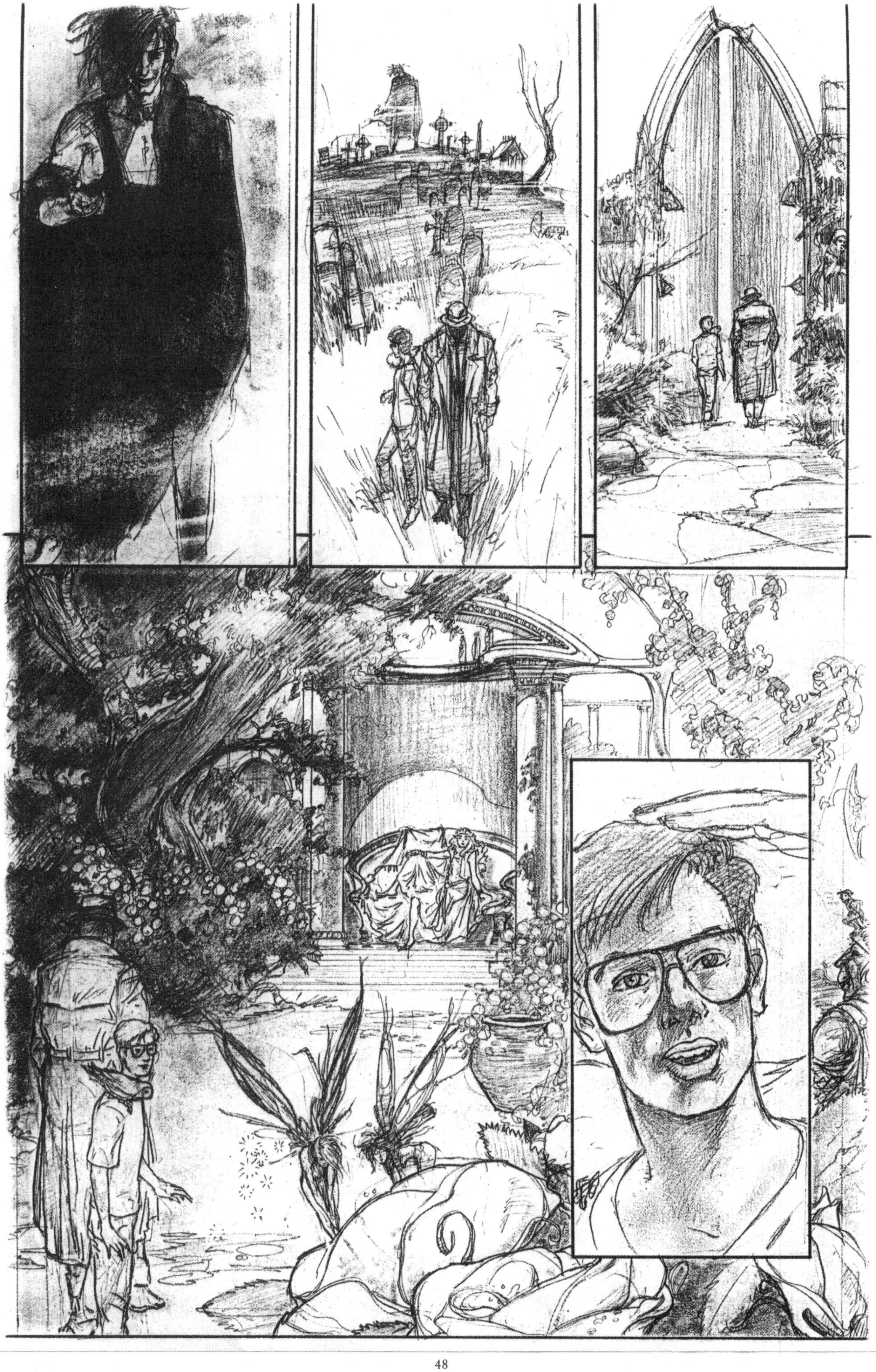

CHARLES: Yes. Well, it was basically right after I did *Sandman* #19. Neil asked if I'd be interested in working on the *Books of Magic* mini-series. "Yes," is what I said!

MM: What amazed me about it is, I read all your stuff in chronological order, and there are things in *Books of Magic* that allude to *Sandman* #19, because Hamnet's in there.

CHARLES: Yes.

MM: Was there any real discussion that Neil was going to kind of pick up a couple of strands with that?

CHARLES: No, most of the plot was already written by the time I received it. But that was when I was over in the UK with the *Spider-Man* signing tour. Neil was still living there at the time and we were able to get together and discuss the story. We spent an afternoon walking through the actual Hundred-acre Wood—home to Winnie the Pooh—and discussed story possibilities. Because he knew I liked ballads and that kind of narrative music, he asked me to send him a mixed-tape of songs whose imagery I'd like to draw.

As I was almost constantly on the road doing these *Spider-Man* signings and the deadline for the *Books of Magic* story got closer, I realized that I would never be able complete the work on it anywhere near on time. So I approached Karen Berger with an idea: If I were to very tightly thumbnail the pages, we could then get a number of artists to pencil from my layouts. Then, after my tour, I could ink and paint them, smoothing the transition from one artist to another. She said, "Good idea," so we did that, with Bryan Talbot, Ron Randall, John Ridgway, Mike Dringenberg, and Tom Yeates producing some lovely pencils for me. In the course of inking and painting those pages I did make a few changes to even the style of the art.

MM: Is there any reference for Tim Hunter?

CHARLES: Well, it was John Bolton's son, and he provided many photographs to use.

MM: So right after that, the *Hook* adaptation came out in '91. [*Vess laughs*] Was that your first time working on a film adaptation?

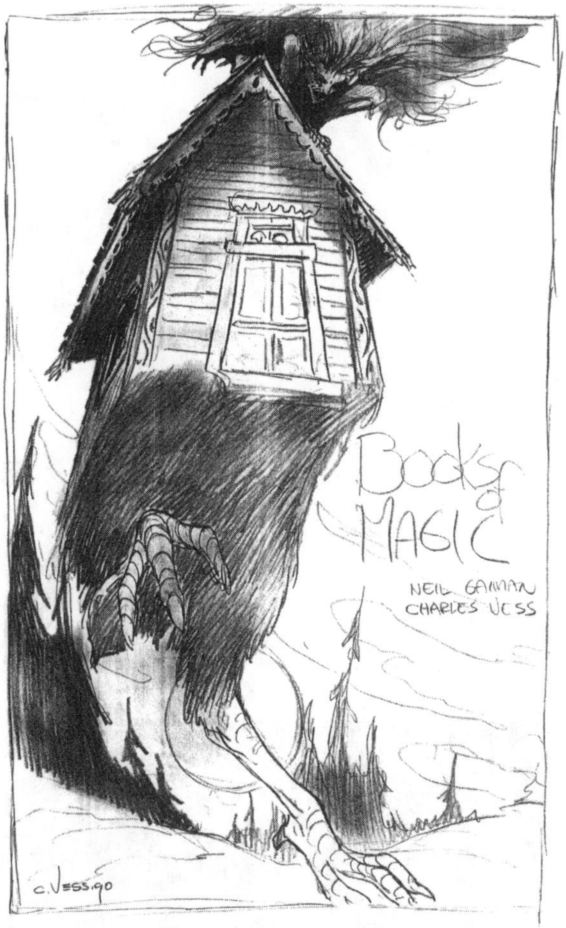

Books of MAGIC
NEIL GAIMAN
CHARLES VESS
C.VESS.90

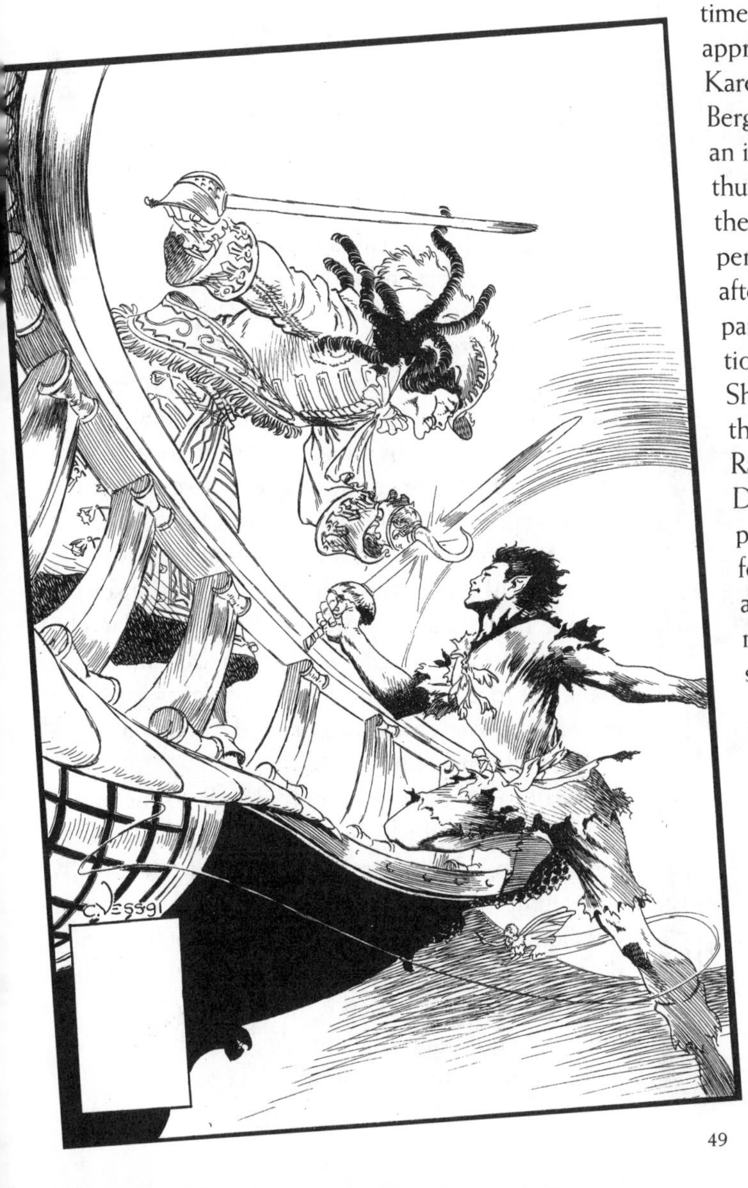

C.VESS91

Previous Page: Tim Hunter meets the Sandman and Queen Titania on his journey through the unseen worlds. *Books of Magic* #3, page 40.
Above: An unused cover sketch idea for *Books of Magic #3*.
Left: Unretouched cover for *Hook* #4. All of the covers for the mini-series adaptation were touched up in the Marvel Bullpen at the request—read "demands"—of the movie's licensors.

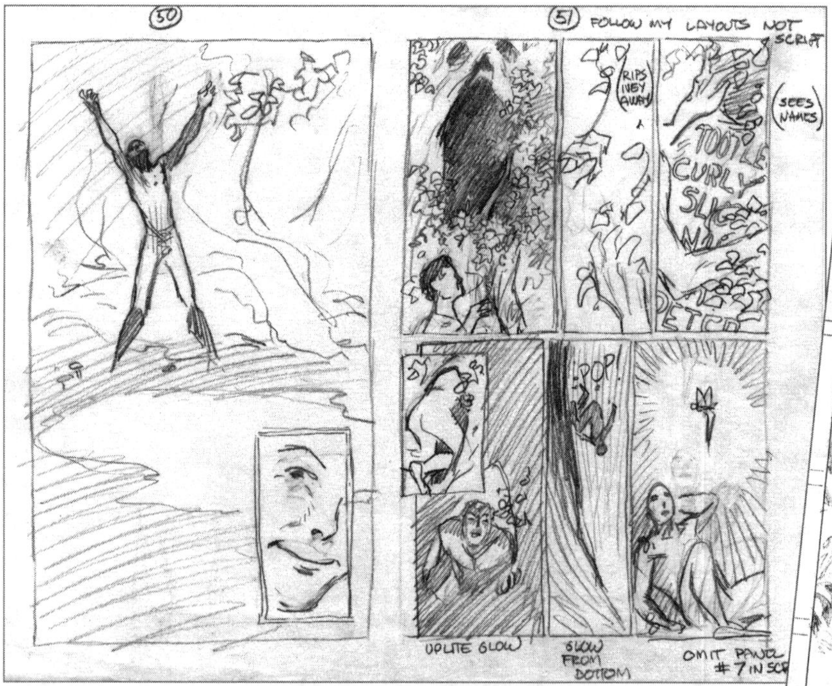

50
51 FOLLOW MY LAYOUTS NOT SCRIPT
RIPS IVEY AWAY
SEES NAMES
POP!
UPLITE GLOW
GLOW FROM BOTTOM
OMIT PANEL

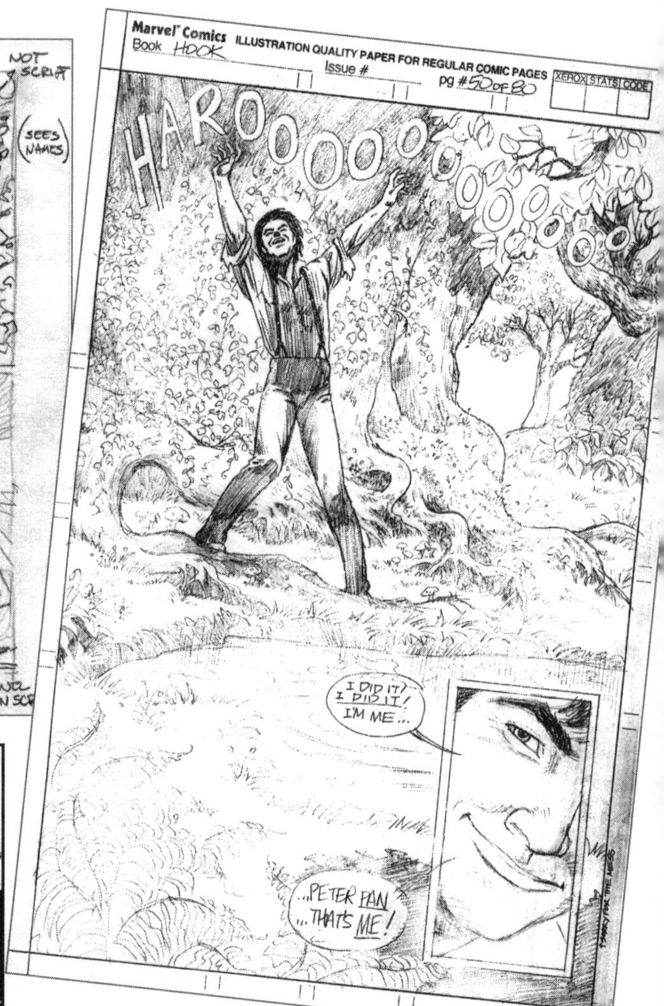

Marvel Comics ILLUSTRATION QUALITY PAPER FOR REGULAR COMIC PAGES
Book HOOK
Issue #
pg #50 OF 80
XEROX STATS CODE
HAROOOOOOOOOOOOO
I DID IT! I DID IT! I'M ME...
...PETER PAN ...THAT'S ME!

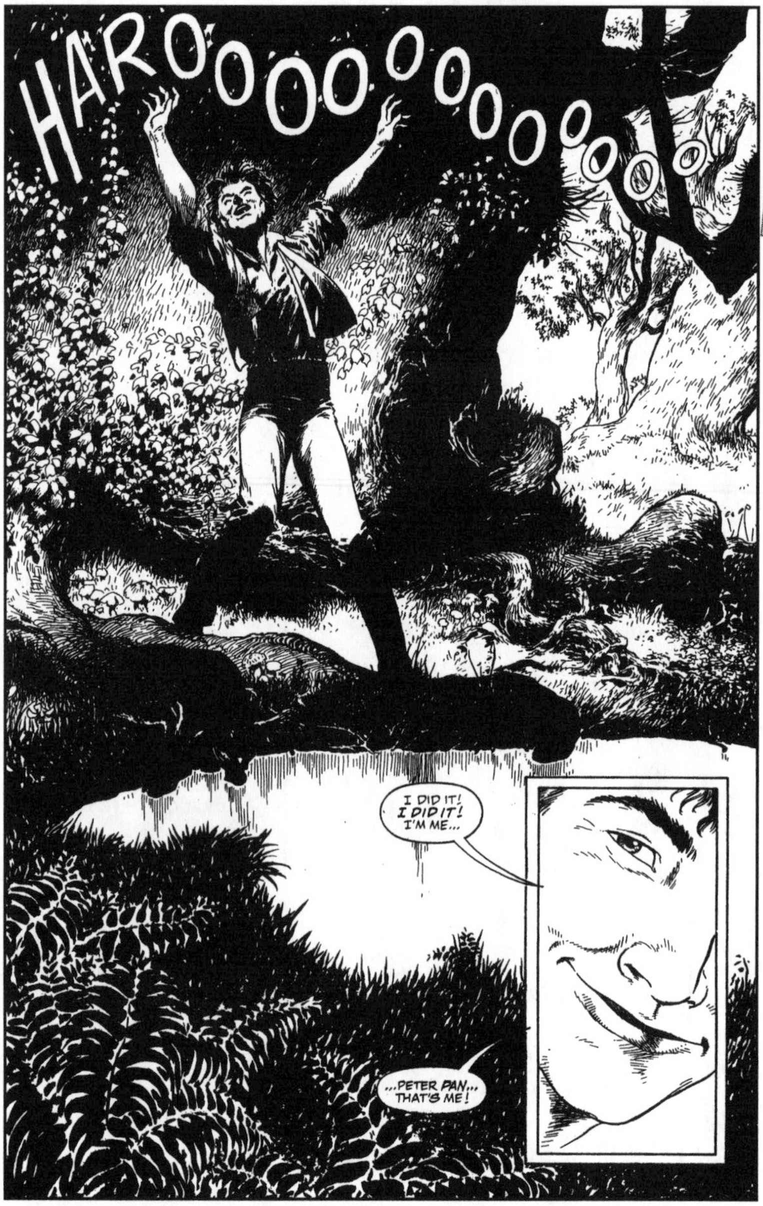

HAROOOOOOOOOOOOO
I DID IT! I DID IT! I'M ME...
...PETER PAN... THAT'S ME!

CHARLES: It was. Fabian Nicieza was the editor and, for some reason he thought I would be perfect for it. This was right at the point that my wife and I were moving down here to Bristol/Abingdon. It was a crazy, crazy project. I was writing the script in a room in our new house, surrounded by boxes, or at the local library. At first, the studio lawyers were telling me that I wouldn't even be able to read the script. Then they relaxed a bit and said that I could come into the licensing office and read the script for one hour. [*laughter*] And everybody at Marvel were rolling their eyes. Finally someone at Marvel managed to contact one of the publicists for the movie who knew what we needed. "You want scripts? I'll send you scripts."

Really, in the end, the only upside to the entire process was that I was flown out to Hollywood to see the sets, which were gorgeous, but never really showed up on the screen. The sets were so over-detailed that it was ridiculous. They would even do things like, on the pirate's ship there would be a casket, you could open it up and there were individual gold dubloons inside... which were never going to be seen on film.

Every day they'd send a script, and every couple days I'd get another revised script, always with more nonsensical changes. I started to get these horrid visions of Hollywood producer types standing around an office saying, "If we did this, we could make a really cool toy!" So the plot would change and you'd have the whole thing drawn, and would need to redo it. I did do all the covers for the various formats, but most of them had to be redrawn by Romita's Raiders, because I'd draw a Lost Boy holding a spear and the movie's licensing people would say, "Well, they're going to be selling Happy Meals at McDonald's, so they have to be smiling," and those stern warriors would then be redrawn with huge smiles.

The movie was just... not lovely to look at. Since I've read almost every one of the scripts, I think there's a really good initial story idea buried deep down in its guts which was totally obscured by all the crap that was layered on it. That initial idea probably would have been a great film. It really should have been a ten million dollar independent film, and it would have been great. But, boy, they butchered it... and Robin Williams was/is not my idea of Peter Pan, grown up or otherwise.

Previous Page: For the *Hook* adaptation, Charles would provide rough layouts (2 pages on each 8 1/2" x 11" sheet) from which other artists—in this case Anne Marie B. Cool—would pencil. Charles would then ink the pages, sometimes altering details in order to make them consistent with his style.
Below: Layout and final inks for the cover of *Hook* #2. Charles penciled the covers himself.

MM: Shortly after that, in 1994, you wrote the *Prince Valiant* comic book for Marvel. I remember they were also doing *Flash Gordon* and *The Phantom*. Why was Marvel doing these old comic strip characters?

CHARLES: They wanted to compete with the licensed book that Dark Horse was producing.

MM: Really?

CHARLES: That was the whole idea. Fabian was acting as the overall editor of the line again,

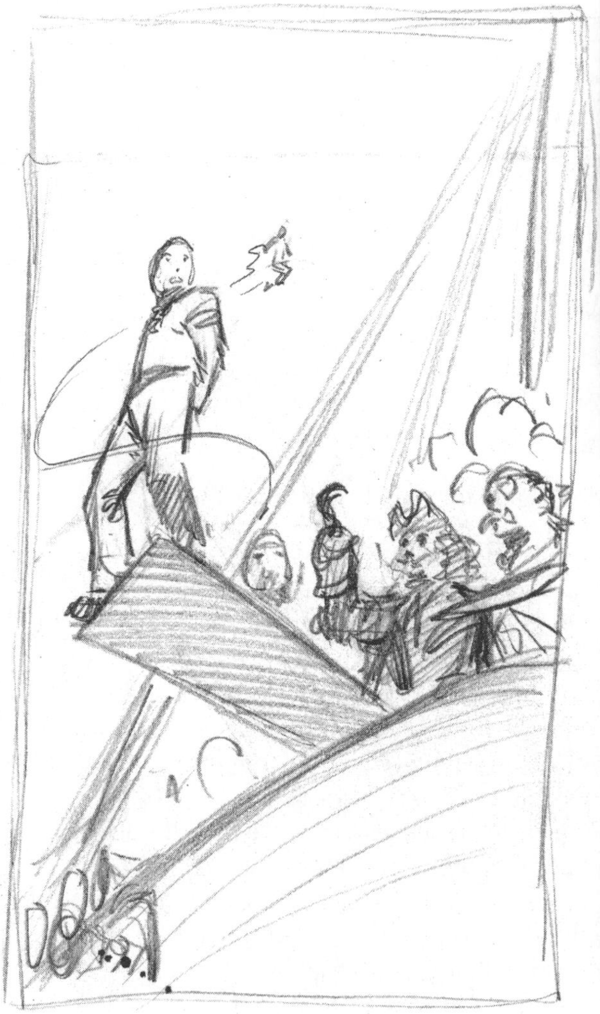

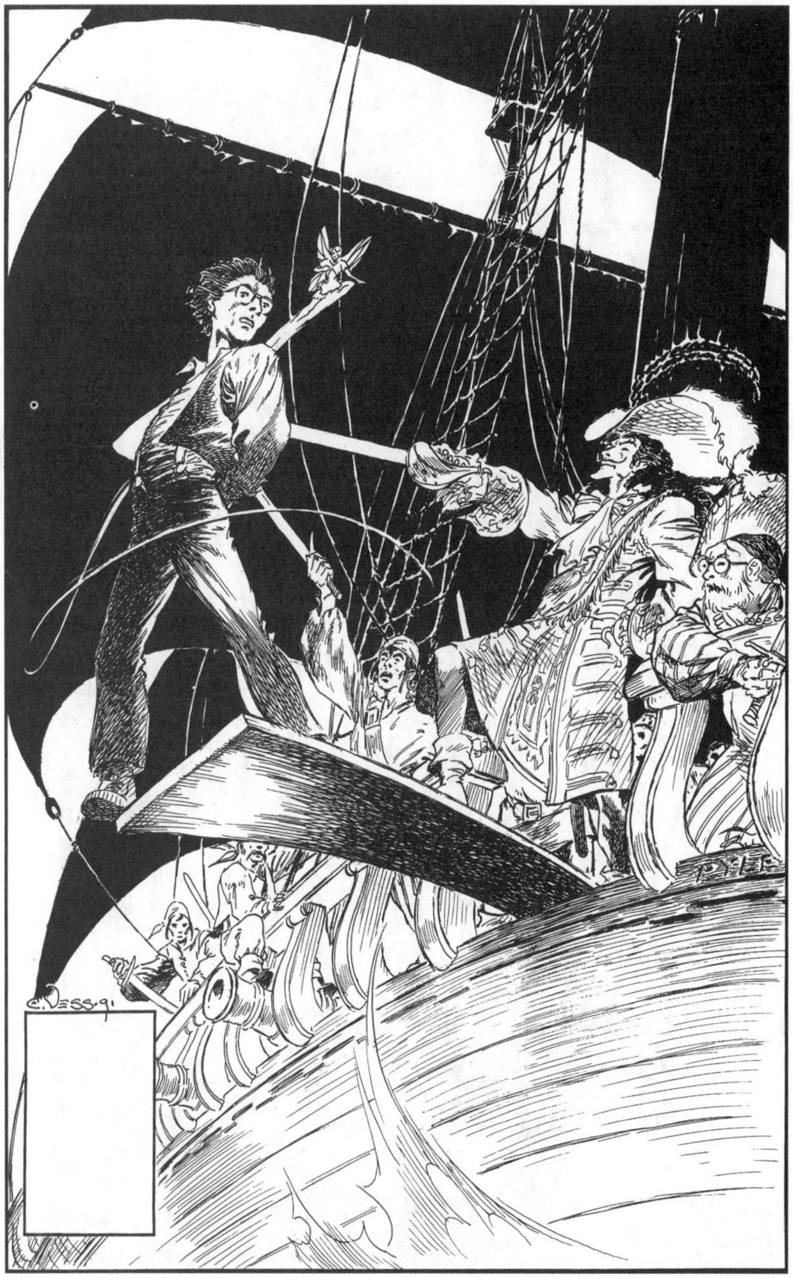

and they had gotten the licenses from King Features for Mandrake, Phantom, Flash Gordon, and Prince Valiant. Fabian asked for a 4-issue mini-series, with each issue being 48 pages long. That's 200 pages and I knew it would probably take me five years to draw and ink that many pages, so I asked if I could just write it. There were two reasons to say yes. First, I'm an absolute dyed in the wool Hal Foster fan, and second, there was at first no deadline attached to the series, so, being a novice writer, I could learn as I went along. At the time I had no computer and absolutely *no* typing skills so I hand-wrote the plots which were all about 40, 50 pages long, complete with lots of dialogue. I did quite a bit of research and really needed my story to not only to be informed by all the plot details from the old Hal Foster stuff—I went over to a friend's house and read his collections of *all* the Foster *Prince Valiant*—but to incorporate into it a lot of modern Arthurian mythology, as well as many characters and themes that have been written into the strip since Foster handed it off.

I thought, "Wouldn't it be cool to begin my story directly after the dream of Camelot has gone down in flames—Mordred dies killing his father King Arthur, all is doom and destruction—and then Prince Valiant has to pick up the pieces of that dream?" And then I thought "Well, y'know, it's going to be four issues, maybe we could name each section after the four books of T.H. White's *The Once and Future King*. I put in all sorts of references for people who knew about Arthurian mythos and would get them, and I thought that I developed an epic story line that, even if you didn't know anything about the myths, would be a rousing adventure.

I was working on this project all during the Marvel implosion, and Fabian was suddenly gone and his assistant, who was in his early 20s, was now my editor. He knew nothing whatsoever about the *Prince Valiant* strip or its legacy. One of my ideas was to get different guest artists to draw the back covers, because I thought, "Wouldn't it be cool to get Jeff Smith to do a drawing of Prince Valiant?" I sent Jeff's really nice portrait to Marvel and my new editor called me up and asked, "Do you really want to use this art? It doesn't have many lines in it." [*laughter*]

MM: "Where's the crosshatching?"

CHARLES: It was eventually used along with pieces by Paul Chadwick and Will Simpson. I also designed the entire look of the series, from the use of the Aubrey Beardsley drawings as the end sheets to getting Michael Kaluta to paint the covers.

Then, after all four plots were completed, which I consider to be the very best writing that I've ever done, suddenly my editor's telling me, "We have to put it on the schedule *now*, so we need the actual script in a month's time for the penciler to start drawing. I thought, "I'm just not comfortable enough with my writing abilities to finish this script in that amount of time." I called up my friend Elaine Lee

Below : Detail from the title page art for Marvel's *Prince Valiant* mini-series.
Next Page: Charles' try-out sample for the *Prince Valiant* newspaper strip.

Prince Valiant ™ and ©2007 King Features Syndicate, Inc.

OUR STORY: YUAN CHEN'S MESSAGE FROM THE EMPEROR OF THE MIDDLE KINGDOM IS A TONIC FOR THE WARRIORS OF CAMELOT: IT PROMISES ADVENTURE AND EXCITEMENT AND A CHANCE FOR GLORY. KING ARTHUR CONVENES THE ROUND TABLE. "THE LAST OF THE ANCIENT SPICE ROUTES HAS BEEN SEVERED BY THE HUNS AND THEIR ALLIES."

"THE EMPOROR PROPOSES A TREATY: A SHARE OF THE SPICE REVENUES IN RETURN FOR FINDING-- AND PROTECTING-- A NEW SPICE ROUTE."

AND WHO WILL LEAD THE QUEST? KING ARTHUR TURNS AS HE SO OFTEN HAS TO PRINCE VALIANT. "HAND PICK YOUR MEN AND COME BACK TO ME WITH A PLAN. WE MUST START AT ONCE." VAL SPENDS A DAY WITH YUAN CHEN AND HIS MAPS.

IT IS A DAZZLING PROSPECT. AT LAST THE KING WILL HAVE THE MONEY HE NEEDS TO FINISH THE REBUILDING OF HIS KINGDOM, RUINED BY MORDRED'S RULE. HIS OLD FRAME IS STRENGTHENED BY UNEXPECTED HOPE.

SOON A PLAN FORMS IN HIS HEAD. HE SAYS TO YUAN CHEN: "THE OLD SPICE ROUTES CROSSED THE DESERT WHERE CARAVANS WERE VULNERABLE TO BOTH THE HUNS AND THE WEATHER. LET US OPEN A NOTHERN ROUTE. RIVERS WILL CARRY US MOST OF THE WAY."

BY LAND AND SEA COURIERS CARRY A MESSAGE FROM KING ARTHUR TO THE EMPEROR OF THE MIDDLE KINGDOM: "WE ARE WITH YOU."
NEXT WEEK: BON VOYAGE

and asked, "What do you know about Prince Valiant?" She said, "Well, every Sunday morning my dad would place me on his lap and read me *Prince Valiant* to me." I replied, "Go for it!" She said it was the easiest script she'd ever written because I'd essentially already done all the work for her. If I'd known in the beginning that someone else was going to do the actual scripting, then I probably would have made my outline a lot looser. Then John Ridgway came along behind Elaine and drew some beautiful pages for the series.

MM: Did you ever want to do the Sunday strip?

CHARLES: I was actually offered *Prince Valiant* by Jay Kennedy, who's the editor at King Features. He'd liked my writing, and was aware of my drawing, and was interested in my trying out for the strip. John Cullen Murphy, who had been drawing it since after Foster left, was in his 80s and considering retirement, so they were starting to look around for a replacement. I was very flattered to be asked and did a full-page sample, which I really enjoyed drawing. But there were a number of constraints that made me choose not to pursue the opportunity. John's son, Cullen Murphy, was still writing it at the time, and I found his stories to not be very exciting and couldn't imagine drawing them. What Mark Schultz and Gary Gianni are doing now is very exciting, and I absolutely love their work. A great return to the hallowed days of yesteryear.

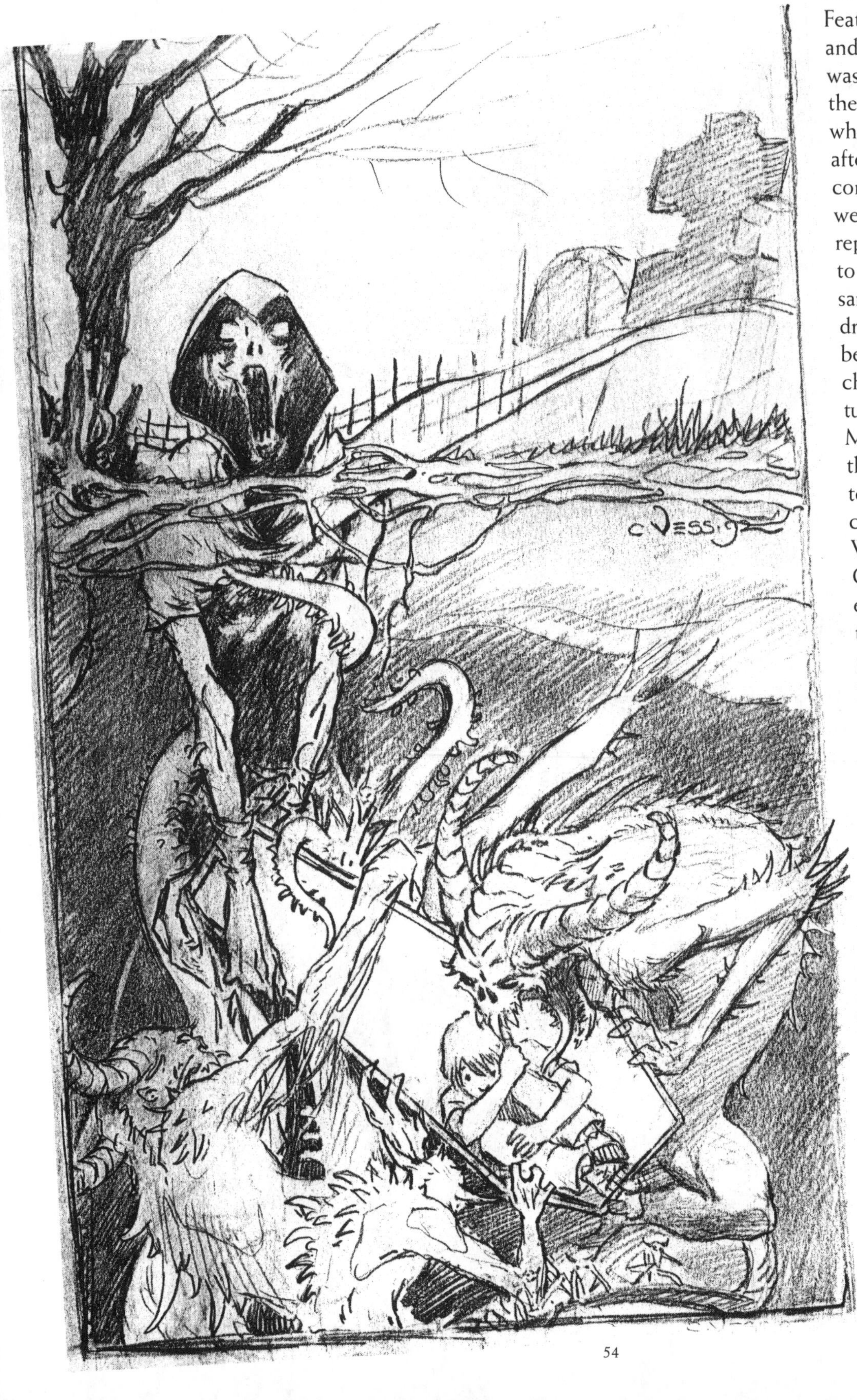

MM: I always thought of *Prince Valiant* as a textbook when I was a kid.

CHARLES: Probably by then it didn't have the gung-ho adventure of the early years.

MM: Mark makes me want to pick it up each Sunday.

CHARLES: They've been picked up by a few newspapers, which is nice, and they've started to talk about a collected edition.

MM: Good for them. They deserve it, and the strip deserves it. On to *Sandman* #75, the "Tempest" issue. Instead of your usual thin

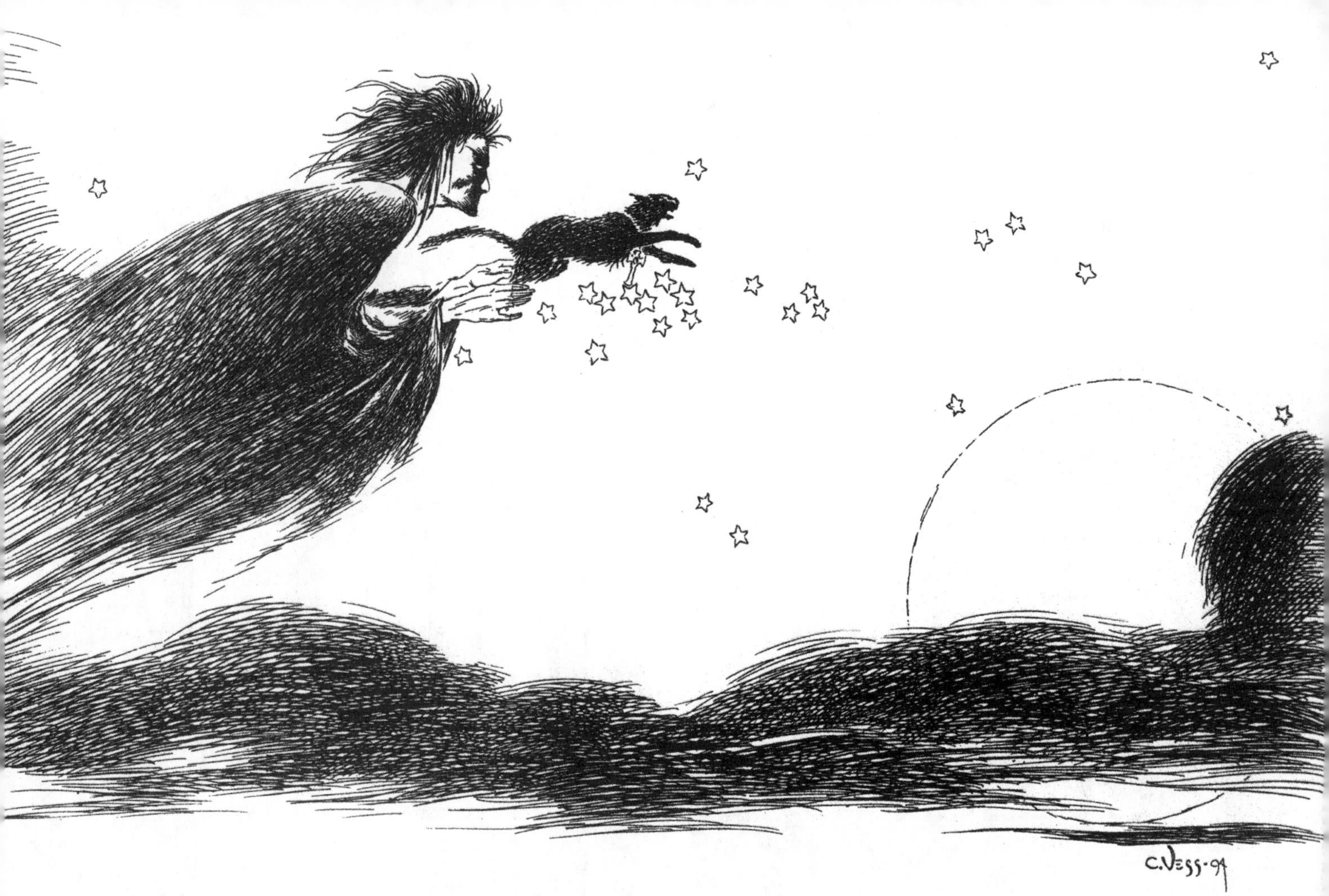

linework, this issue seems to be your first extensive use of crosshatching.

CHARLES: I had just come from drawing my self-published *Ballads and Sagas* series where I'd crosshatched the hell out of everything and loved it. I was channeling as much of Bernie Wrightson's work for Warren—especially the story, "The Black Cat"—as possible. Anyway, for some reason, when I got down to doing "The Tempest," I thought about the cross-hatching style and how it could look really cool; I could think of ways to color it where it would look good. Then Neil came up with the idea of doing pages that were directly out of the play that I would paint in full color. So I thought the contrast between the feathery cross-hatching and the pure line color pages would be interesting.

It should be noted that there is a feisty old woman in the story that runs an inn. I was starting to hang out with Jeff Smith about then, and asked him if I could make use of his Grandma Ben character. He said, "As long as she's

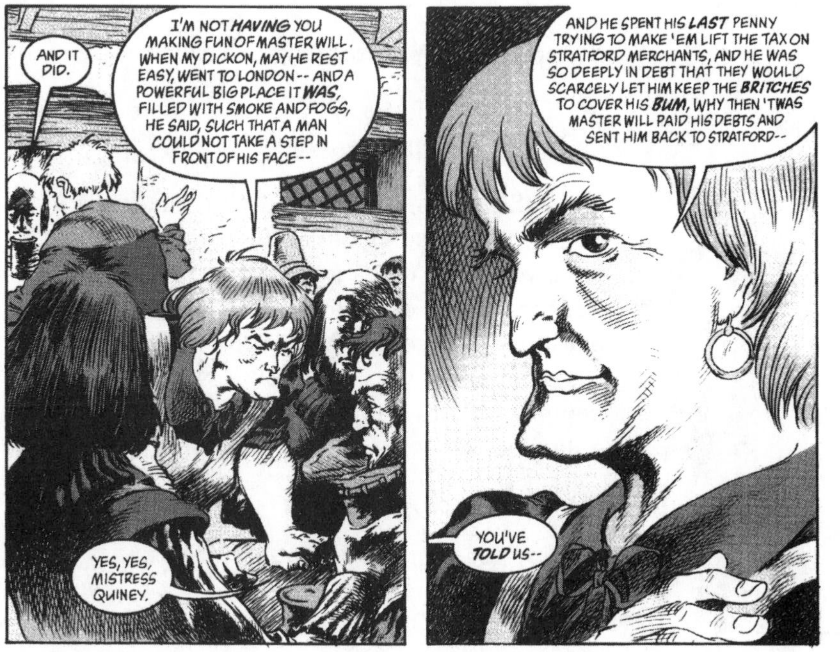
I'M NOT HAVING YOU MAKING FUN OF MASTER WILL. WHEN MY DICKON, MAY HE REST EASY, WENT TO LONDON-- AND A POWERFUL BIG PLACE IT WAS, FILLED WITH SMOKE AND FOGS, HE SAID, SUCH THAT A MAN COULD NOT TAKE A STEP IN FRONT OF HIS FACE--
AND IT DID.
YES, YES, MISTRESS QUINEY.
AND HE SPENT HIS LAST PENNY TRYING TO MAKE 'EM LIFT THE TAX ON STRATFORD MERCHANTS, AND HE WAS SO DEEPLY IN DEBT THAT THEY WOULD SCARCELY LET HIM KEEP THE BRITCHES TO COVER HIS BUM, WHY THEN 'TWAS MASTER WILL PAID HIS DEBTS AND SENT HIM BACK TO STRATFORD--
YOU'VE TOLD US--

Right: Not long before the final hurrah of *Sandman*, Charles painted the cover for *Spectre* vol. 2, #5. Shown here are his rough pencils.
Above: A Sandman commission sketch.
Left: *Bone*'s Granma Ben—or at least her likeness—makes her cameo in *Sandman* #75 in the form of Mistress Quiney.

This page: *Sandman* proved to be so popular that it was spun off into several other titles, including *The Dreaming*, which featured many of the *Sandman* supporting characters. Layout and final inks for a promotional piece intended for DC's 1994 sales catalog. **Next Page:** Speaking of X-Men, here's one of Charles' two pages of pencils for 1985's charity jam comic, *Heroes for Hope starring the X-Men*.

The Dreaming and all related characters™ and ©2007 DC Comics. Nightcrawler ™ and ©2007 Marvel Characters, Inc.

not wearing the same dress," so it's Grandma Ben with the jaw, and everything.

MM: Okay, I've got to look at it.... So now, when you worked with Neil, would he give you just a full script, or would he...?

CHARLES: Yeah, it was a full script with lots of funny asides, with Neil's notes to the artist saying that if you want to do anything different, then do it. It was a long, 48-page book, and Neil was funneling one or two pages of script out to me at a time. Both Neil and my schedules were loaded with various projects, so progress was

very slow on the book. To meet the publishing deadline more art needed to be finished sooner rather than later. So, again I thought, "Okay, if it worked on *Books of Magic*, it'll work on this book." So we asked Brian Talbot, John Ridgway, and Michael Zulli [*a.k.a., the Mysterious Mister Zed*] to help pencil the issue. They worked from my layouts and did pencils on approximately half the issue.

MM: Really quickly, did you have any trepidation on having the final word on *Sandman*?

CHARLES: No, it was just kind of fun. It was also one of those exciting but at the same time depressing revelations: When it came out, *Sandman* #75 was the number one selling comic of that month, but it had only sold 100,000 copies. This was in the brunt of the sales crash. Both Neil and I were going, "Well, it's really cool we're the number one selling book...."

MM: "...But 100,000 copies."

CHARLES: "...But it's 100,000 copies, y'know?" We had outsold *X-Men*.

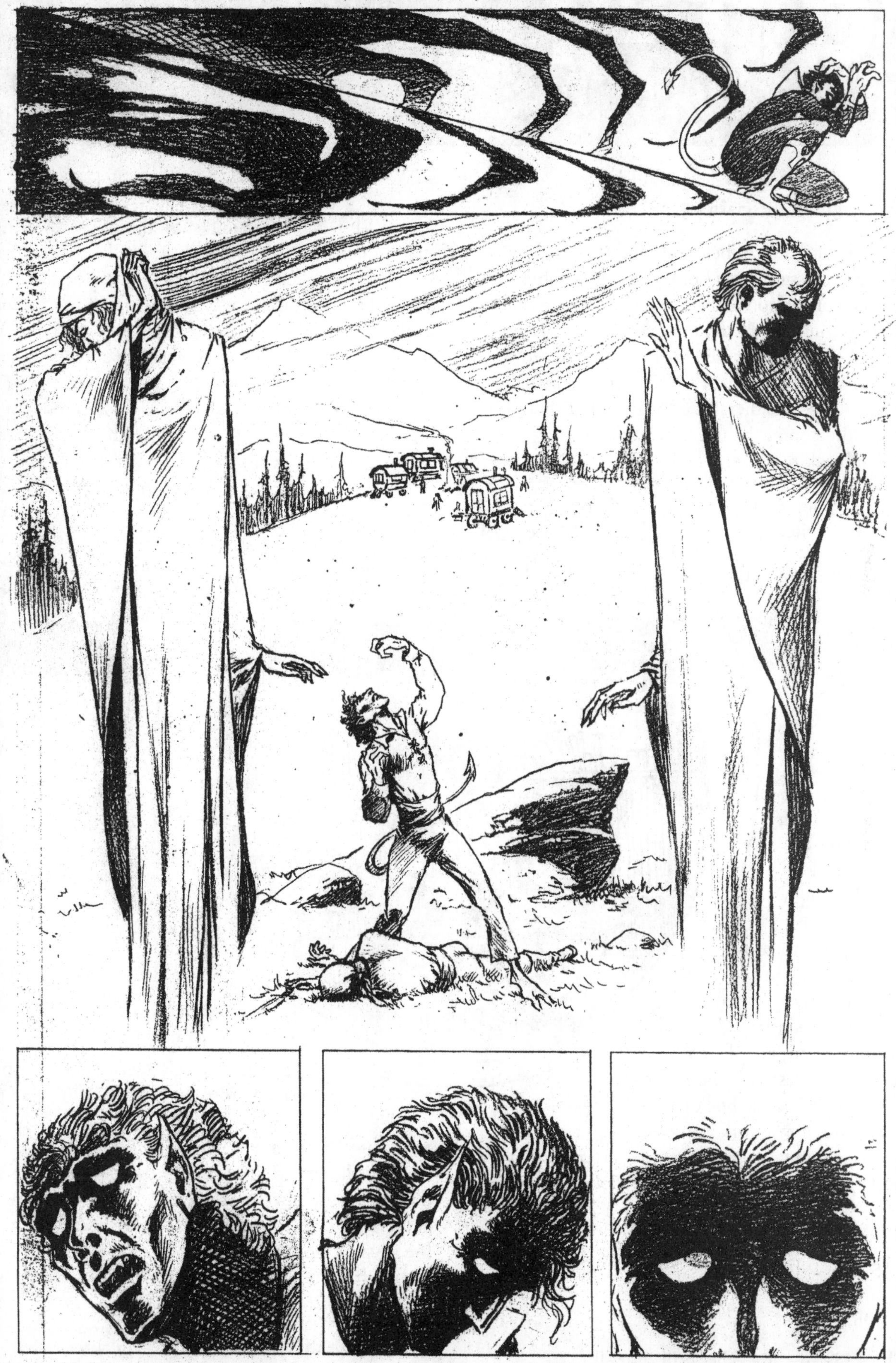

Part 4: The Saga of Self-Publishing

MM: So you were basically self-publishing *Ballads* around the height of the crash.

CHARLES: I started right before it, and I was selling 25,000 copies per issue of my book. I still remember being at some convention and I was talking to Shooter, who was publishing his third line of comics [*Broadway Comics*]. I could see in his mind that he was trying to figure out how I was doing what I was doing, and I still remembered him as the dictator of Marvel. But there I was selling more copies than he was, and my comic was in black-&-white.

MM: Well, Defiant wasn't really anything to be excited over.

CHARLES: No, it wasn't.

MM: So you just decided to self-publish?

CHARLES: Well, I was hanging out with Jeff Smith, Steve Bissette, and Rick Veitch. I came up with the idea of doing a comic based on Scottish and English ballads, and I thought, "It's got a really weird, broad based appeal to consumers, as I use well known authors from the mystery, science fiction, and fantasy fields to write most of my scripts; folk music aficionados are interested in the ballads themselves; and the comic book fans will hopefully buy it because of my work." And I was right. I even got a lot of folk music enthusiasts who subscribed that had never bought or looked at a comic book in their life.

MM: So were you packing and shipping these yourself?

CHARLES: Yes, I was! [*laughs*]

MM: Oh, my gosh.

CHARLES: Oh, the joy. The thrill of it all.

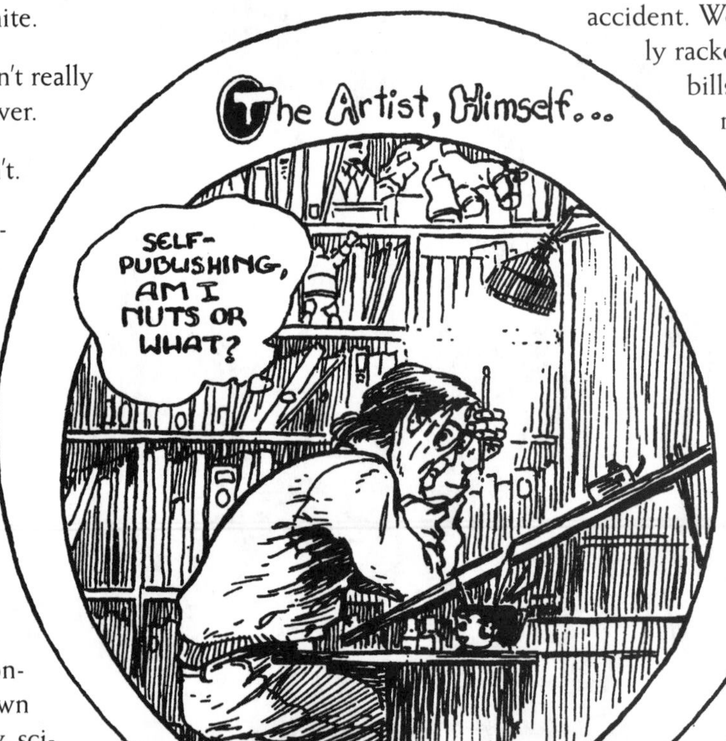
The Artist, Himself...
SELF-PUBLISHING, AM I NUTS OR WHAT?

MM: Yeah, even the wonders of bulk mailing?

CHARLES: Bulk mailing, subscriptions, answering e-mails, guerrilla marketing, all those things, which I really enjoyed for a long time, but there was a certain point where I realized that I was spending an entire week doing all those things and feeling like I'd accomplished quite a lot but I hadn't gone near my drawing board. I'm an artist, it's what I'm supposed to be doing. I had an assistant and I still only got the four issues out. At that time, too, my wife was in very bad shape from her accident. We had no insurance and quickly racked up some very high hospital bills. Although I'd always made money on each issue, it was never steady and nowhere near what we needed to start paying some of those medical bills. The comics industry came through in a very big and amazing way which helped put a serious dent in some of those bills, but I still needed a more substantial freelance income than what my self-publishing efforts brought me.

MM: What were your basic guidelines for the writers?

CHARLES: I asked that all the scripts be no longer than eight to ten pages using the actual narrative from a particular ballad as its basic plot. The writers could then do anything they wanted with subplots. They could set the tale in a different time period if they wanted. None of the contributors were paid until each book was printed and distributed. Later they also received a percentage of the royalties. Some of them managed to make more money from the process than if they'd been paid a flat fee for an 8- to 10-page pure text story.

MM: Were they mostly well known authors?

THE THREE LOVERS
·A PLAY·
ISN'T LOVE SUPPOSED TO BE A PLEASURE?
SCRIPT BY LEE SMITH
ART BY CHARLES VESS
YET HERE I AM TORMENTED.
TORN IN TWO!
I CANNOT DECIDE BETWEEN THEM!

Previous Page: Charles wonders what he's getting into with *The Book of Ballads and Sagas.* **Left:** By playing with the setting, Charles was able to make "The Three Lovers" work and not appear to be overly silly. **Below:** Charles used an almost bigfoot style of drawing when he teamed up with Jeff Smith for "The Galtee Farmer."

CHARLES: Most of them were familiar. Some of them were not. The funniest and most involved script was from Lee Smith, a wonderful writer. She's also been on the *New York Times* bestseller list, but she's sort of local, and a really nice person. I really liked her writing. After much begging on my part, she turned in the script. After reading it I was stunned, because I felt it featured some of the worst Victorian-style dialogue I'd ever read in my life. And I thought, "Oh, my God, I can't draw this!" I put it in a drawer, and it sat there for about six or seven years. It finally occurred to me that every time I mentioned the script to a friend, I was describing it as a melodrama, as if you were watching it being performed on a stage with a villainous man in black twirling his waxed mustache while spouting wildly melodramatic dialogue. And one day it struck me that the dialogue was perfect once it was actually coming from an old fashioned stage. So that's the way I eventually drew it, as a play.

"SAID THE SON (ALL TO THE FATHER),"
A GOOD PRICE CAN BE FOUND!
THE PRICE ON HER IS TWENTY GUINEAS...
BUT LOOK, I'LL TAKE 1 POUND.
20 GUINEAS
"UP COMES A DUBLIN BUYER, AND HE TAKES A LOOK AROUND."
THE PRICE ON HER IS TWENTY GUINEAS...
BUT LOOK, I'LL GIVE 1 POUND.
"SO QUICKLY THEN HE PAID FOR HER AND LED THE MARE AWAY..."
"AND HE SHOVED HER IN A STABLE AMIDST THE OATS AND HAY."

MM: Oh, yes, "The Three Lovers."

CHARLES: It's a doom-&-destruction story. Everybody dies in it. I added the clown character that introduces the story, but every other thing is just like it was in the script. I did do one long shot from the interior of the cottage looking out at the audience, and after I'd inked it and was ready to send the story to the printer, I thought, "Oh, my gosh! I did that wrong!" I was understandably a little nervous about showing my extreme interpretation of her story to Lee, since I had changed the entire context of the story. I sent it to her and got a note back saying, "To be honest"—it had been seven years, remember—"I don't remember writing this."

At the time she was still grieving over a personal family tragedy, and she appreciated the laugh. So, it came out and it got the best reviews. The new collected edition, *The Book of Ballads*, was published by Tor Books, who have done an amazing job of getting the book out into the real world of bookstores and

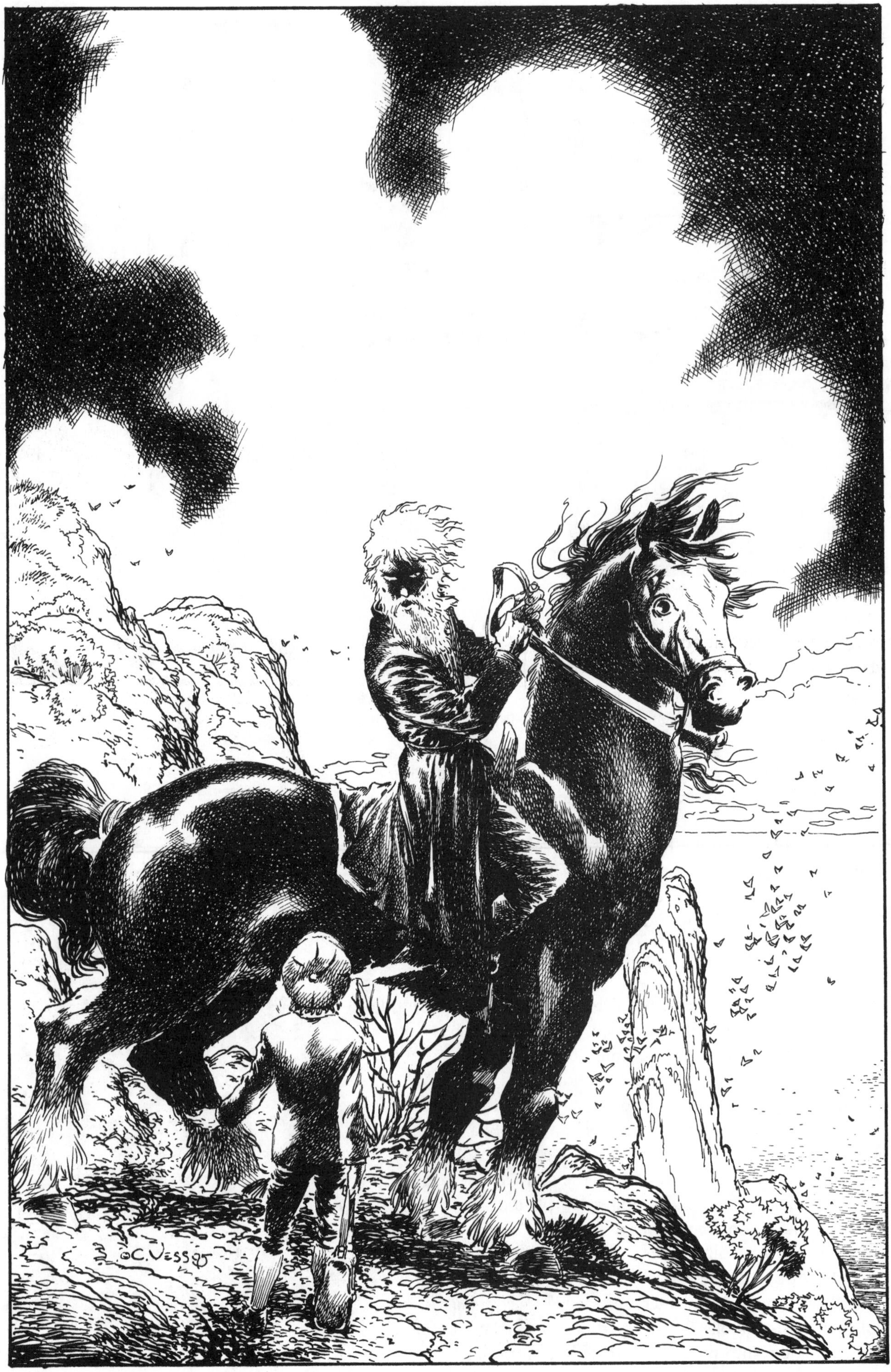
©C.Vess'95

libraries. It's garnered some lovely reviews from the *Washington Post*, *The New York Times*, on and on and on. Splendid!

MM: I like how you've adapted your style for each story. "The Three Lovers" reminds me of Winsor McKay.

CHARLES: From the very first story I always realized that I'd want to publish all of the stories in a single collection. I felt that there needed to be some variation in art style to retain a reader's visual interest. If it was all the same intensely crosshatched stuff....

MM: It would get old. You have a real Al Capp feel on "The Galtee Farmer," which you did with Jeff Smith.

CHARLES: When Jeff writes, he writes scripts with scribbles in it, so he basically hands you his layout along with the script. It was exhilarating diving into the comical simplicity of "The Galtee Farmer" after so very many gothic stories.

MM: How did you land getting foreign editions of *Ballads and Sagas* out?

CHARLES: They just contacted me. The thing that's interesting about the foreign edition is that they have a problem with translating the poetry of the ballad itself into whichever language is needed. The French translators came to me and asked, "Excuse me, please, but what is a 'woman's maidenhead'? Perhaps a woman's head cut off?" I started trying to explain that particular term, and every time I would type something, I would be using some sort of slang, which, of course, wouldn't translate either. I had to try to offer a scientific translation. And of course it's a woman's private womb that usually denotes when she's been raped. It was an interesting language problem.

MM: Looking back at *Ballads and Sagas*, do you plan on going back to it sometime soon?

CHARLES: It's very alluring subject matter for me, but I have a lot of projects that I might at some point want to do. There are still some particular ballads that I'd like to adapt, but they'll just have to keep their place in line and be patient.

MM: So what type of reactions did you get when you told people you'd be adapting ballads?

CHARLES: Within the comics field there was a general shaking of heads in disbelief at my chosen subject matter. Also, I can remember when I had my first issue in hand, I went to one of the local colleges that has an actual ballad studies department and attempted to show what I'd done to its department head. All he had to say was, "You can't draw music!" Of course not, but you can draw the story that

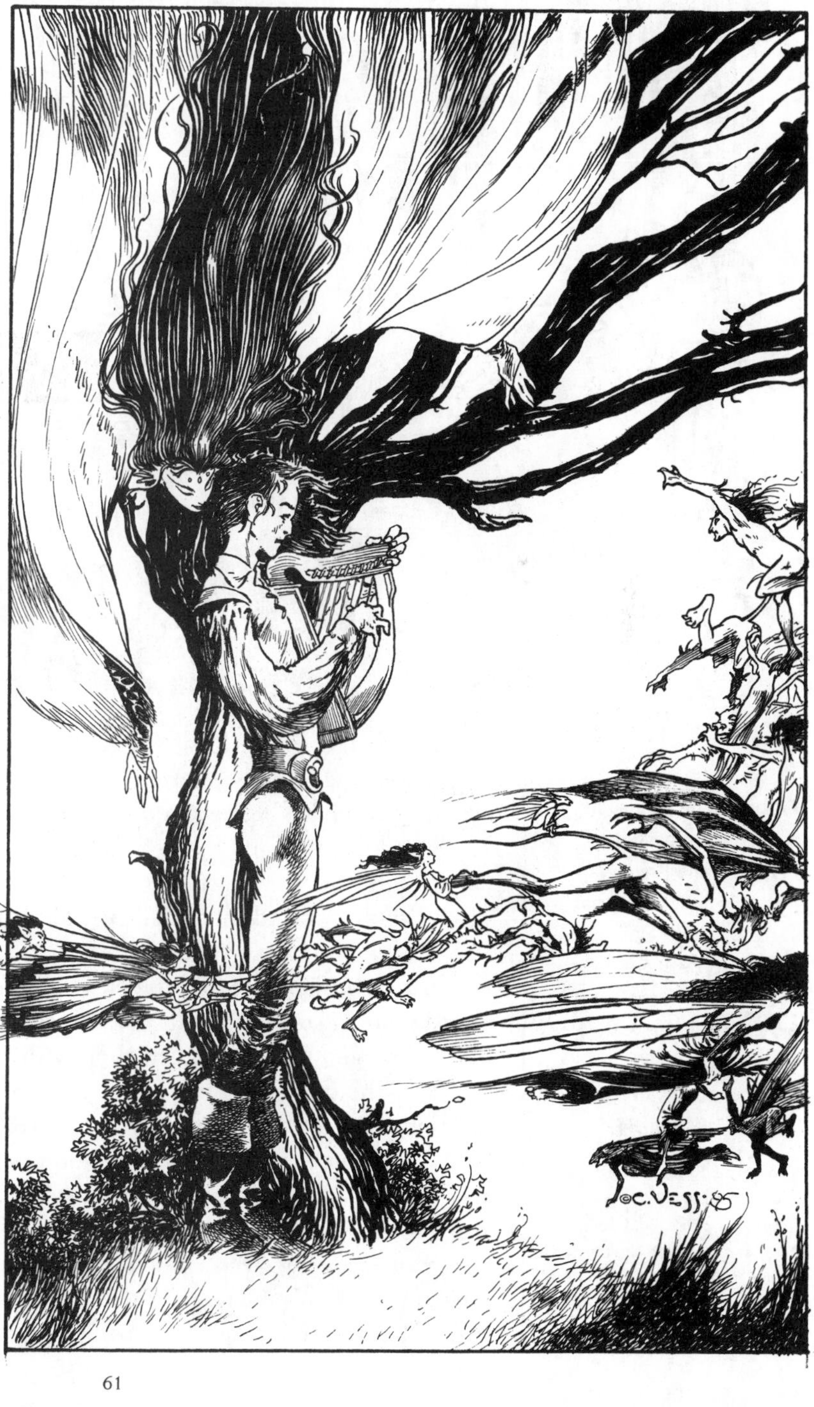

Previous Page: Line art intended for the cover of *The Book of Ballads and Sagas #1*, which was only used as the cover for a limited San Diego Comic-Con preview book of the series. **Below:** This line art of Thomas the Rhymer was used as the ad for *Ballads and Sagas #1*—the actual cover was a painted version of the image.

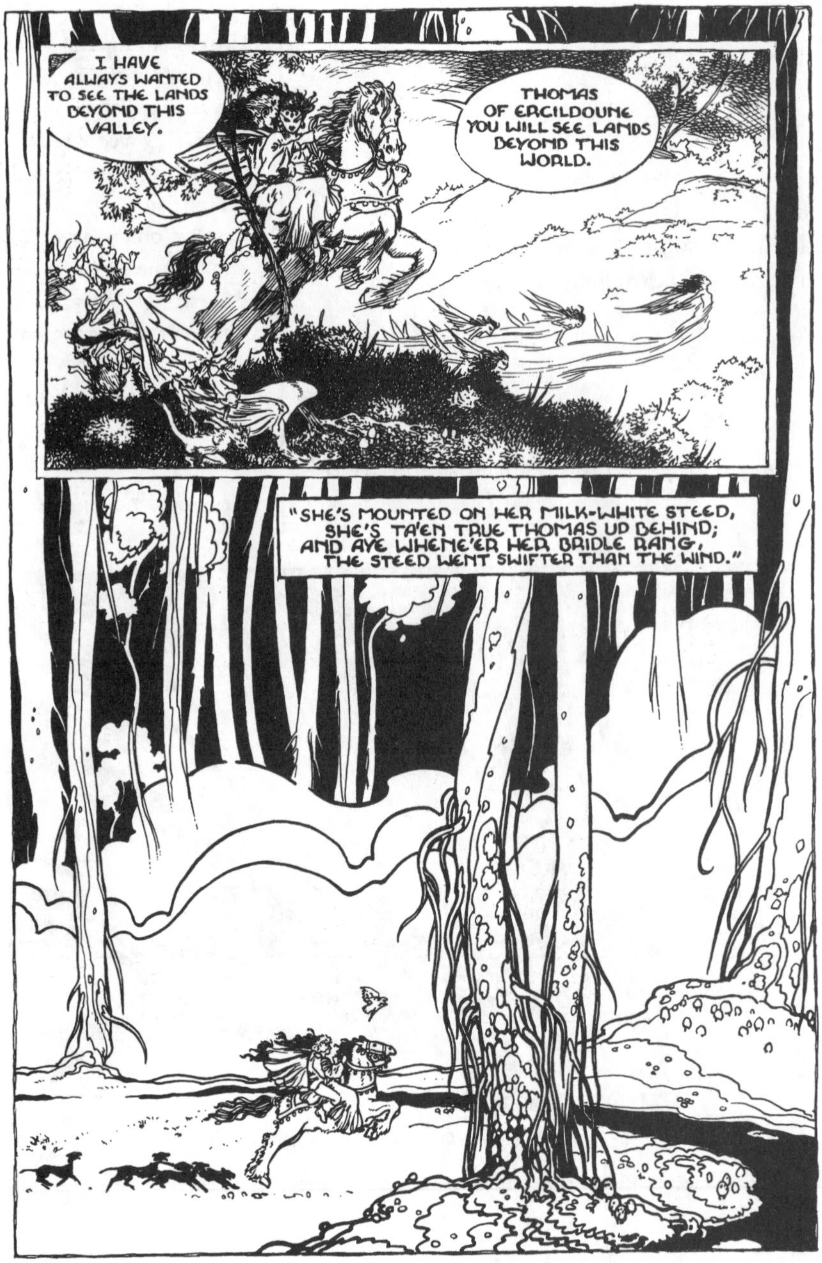
I HAVE ALWAYS WANTED TO SEE THE LANDS BEYOND THIS VALLEY.
THOMAS OF ERCILDOUNE YOU WILL SEE LANDS BEYOND THIS WORLD.
"SHE'S MOUNTED ON HER MILK-WHITE STEED, SHE'S TA'EN TRUE THOMAS UP BEHIND; AND AYE WHENE'ER HER BRIDLE RANG, THE STEED WENT SWIFTER THAN THE WIND."

inspires the music. The ballads themselves are seminal stories for writers of fantasy literature and have been used as the basis of many a contemporary fiction. Every element of a great story is there, and they lend themselves very well to all sorts of interpretations. There's something very appealing to me about that music that carries those stories, too.

MM: How long have you been listening to ballads?

CHARLES: Since about 1970. I won an art contest in Richmond, Virginia. I think I got a $15 gift certificate at the local record shop, and back then you could buy three records for that. I got two Moody Blues albums—a favorite band at the time—and I decided I'd blow the rest of the money on something I didn't know anything at all about. I looked through the whole store, and there was one album that had this beautiful cover by Albrecht Dürer. Is he Swiss or German? [*Note: Dürer (1471-1528) was German*] Whatever. That guy. I looked on the back and saw the titles of the songs, which all looked interesting, so I bought it. It was a group called Pentangle, a British folk/rock/jazz group, and they were using ballads as their jumping off place. I fell in love with their music, and ballads in general, from that moment on.

MM: So you did *Ballads and Sagas*, tried different styles for different stories... and then *Stardust* came out. Somewhere in all of that is The Trilogy Tour.

CHARLES: The Trilogy Tour.... At the end of San Diego one year I was standing there talking to Linda Medley [*who was self-publishing* Castle Waiting], and we both had our little booths, and I said "Maybe we need to get together and have bigger booth so we'll make more of an impression." And just about then, Jeff Smith went by and I said, "Jeff! Come over here." And he was like, "Yeah, yeah, what?"

So right there we started coming up with this grandiose scheme that was way more than just a simple booth display. We eventually developed a physical 3-D environment to exhibit in. We didn't want our space to be rectangular like most booths, but to reflect all of our preoccupation with nature and the environment. In the end we were sitting amidst giant styrofoam standing stones and all sorts of other decoration, all gathered around a large tree made with aluminum framing and covered with textured material and silk ivy. You could actually climb up the tree to the top and see the con from an entirely new perspective. You could also hide in it and listen to people's conversations about your work; that was fun.

We did three stops, three conventions, and three in-store appearances over the first summer—Dragon Con, Chicago Con, San Diego Comic-Con—and at each one of the stops we had a retailer party, because one of our theories was that most creative people never talk to the retailers and vice versa. But with self-publishing, you learn how important it is to develop a relationship with the retailers that sell your books. So we invited people like Frank Miller, Mike Mignola, Art Adams, etc., to the party, and it was just like a high school prom where all

Above: The change in art styles on page 3 of "Thomas the Rhymer" not only provides visual variation, but helps the reader to distinguish the "real world" from the fairy realm.
Next Page: Charles' cover sketches for *Books of Magic* #2 and #4.

the boys are on one side, all the girls the other, except that here, it was all the creators would be over on the left and all the retailers over on the right. It became our job to be the mixers and hosts. We gave out a jam drawing done by all the artists present that was 30" x 40" as a prize drawing to one of the retailers, and how they got it home would be their problem. [*laughter*]

It was successful enough to where we were going to do it again the next year, but we thought having a few more people to split the costs would be smart. So the next year we added Stan Sakai, Mark Crilley, and Jill Thompson with a bit more stuff, and had a slightly bigger booth. It was very splashy. Right in the middle of that was when my wife had her accident. The accident happened while I was attending the Chicago Comic Con.

MM: What year was that?

CHARLES: '98. Then about two weeks later it was San Diego, which for me was an incredibly emotional experience. The powers that be at Comic-Con gave all the proceeds from their art auction to me, and it seemed like every artist at the con donated art. When they presented me with the proceeds it was a huge pile of bills and checks. If someone'd stopped me on the plane going back, they would have thought I was a

BOOKS OF MAGIC #2 CVR. SKETCH REVISION
P.S. WHAT ABOUT THAT RAISE?
ATTN: STUART MOORE - THE MANTICORE (VERY DARK, VERY OMINOUS) STANDING IN HIS GARDEN. THE GROUND IS AWASH WITH BONES, BONES, & MORE BONES. THE ROSE BUSHES ARE WITHERING AROUND HIM.
☆ TIM—WOULD HAVE TO BE SMALLER

GO UP.
STUART / JULIE
DEATH SEATED & HOLDING HER TEDDY BEAR AND THE FEATHER THAT IS TIM. THE FEATHER IS BLOOD SOAKED & SEEPING ONTO HER HAND. THE DOOR BRONZES FROM THE SCRIPT FLANK HER WITH THE AMADAN PERCHED ON ONE SERPENT HEAD. TAM-LIN & TITANIA HOVER IN THE BACKGROUND. MOODY & SUGGESTIVE.
C. VESS 99

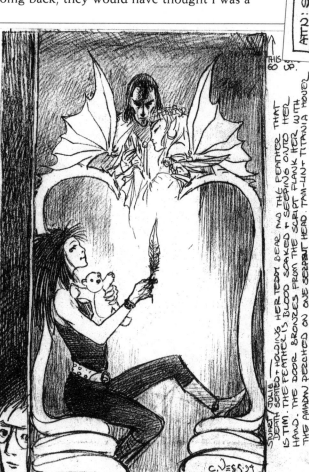

drug dealer, because I had so much cash, but I must say it really helped pay a lot of the bills.

MM: She was in a car accident.

CHARLES: A car accident... spinal cord injury, and we didn't have health insurance. The bills to just the neurosurgeons were phenomenal. If artists were paid half that much for an hour and a half's work....

MM: I can't even begin to imagine what it was like.

CHARLES: Yeah, it was tough having to deal with everything myself, learning about insurance, learning about Medicare, etc.

MM: Yeah, yeah, I bet. So how did that work, did you just stop work altogether to take care of her?

CHARLES: DC was especially great. They called me up and gave me a whole bunch of covers to do. They certainly weren't the best covers I've ever done in my life, some *Books of Magic*, but they were loading my work pallet so I could keep paying those bills.

And also, Neil and I came up with of doing the *Fall of Stardust* as a benefit portfolio, which was originally going to be a bound book. It had a story by Neil, one additional story by another writer, and 30 artists doing their interpretations of various scenes from our book, *Stardust*. Everything was falling into place when I got this very apologetic call from Karen Berger who said, "We would love to see you do this book, but there'd be a copyright issue if it's printed as you originally intended. Paul [Levitz] and I had an idea, though. If you resolicit it as a looseleaf portfolio—a non-bound book—then we'd have no legal problem with that." So that's what we did.

MM: I think it actually makes it more unique this way.

CHARLES: Yeah. So it was an interesting design. It did pretty well, especially for Susanna Clark. At that time, she was pretty unknown, but eventually she had a successful book called *Jonathan Strange & Mr. Norrell*. This book came out and it was an international bestseller. So the story that she had written in the *Fall of Stardust* all of a sudden was becoming a hot item, and it's now selling like crazy on eBay. People that have the portfolio can sell it for two to three hundred dollars.

MM: Wow.

CHARLES: Especially if she's signed it. It's sort of a collectible. When it's on eBay now, it doesn't even mention that Neil wrote a story in it. [*laughter*] It's sort of humorous.

MM: [*jokingly*] "Neil, you're old news, hate to break it to ya, buddy!"

When did *Stardust* first start to gel for you?

CHARLES: Well, it began life during the 1991 World Fantasy Convention, which was out in Arizona. We had just won the World Fantasy Award for *Sandman* #19. I was at a party and Neil came to get me. We walked out into the desert and gazed up at the stars, both of us had glasses of champagne in hand, and Neil began to tell me the story of *Stardust*. I said, "Yeah, I'll draw that." It took two or three years for us to get our act together, and then his literary agent took the book to auction. Eventually DC offered the best deal. So I guess it was close to '96, '97.

It was done in four separate issues, and because of Neil's schedule, it was written as we did it. It was never given to me in complete manuscript form, so I didn't really know how it was going to end until I actually got the end of the story.

MM: I heard Neil changed his method of writing for this one?

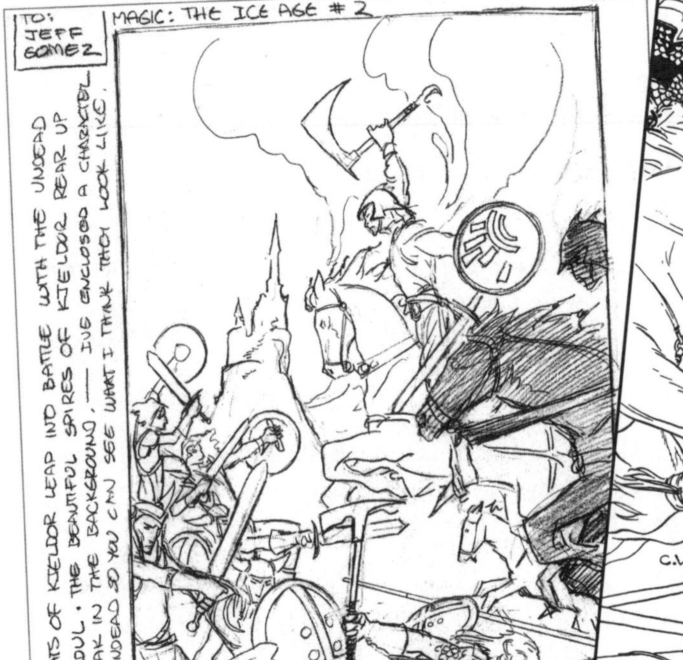
TO: JEFF GOMEZ
MAGIC: THE ICE AGE #2
JEFF: THE KNIGHTS OF KJELDOR LEAP INTO BATTLE WITH THE UNDEAD WARRIORS OF LIMDUL. THE BEAUTIFUL SPIRES OF KJELDOR REAR UP ATOP A MOUNTAIN PEAK IN THE BACKGROUND. — IVE ENCLOSED A CHARACTER SKETCH OF THE UNDEAD SO YOU CAN SEE WHAT I THINK THEY LOOK LIKE.
C.VESS 94

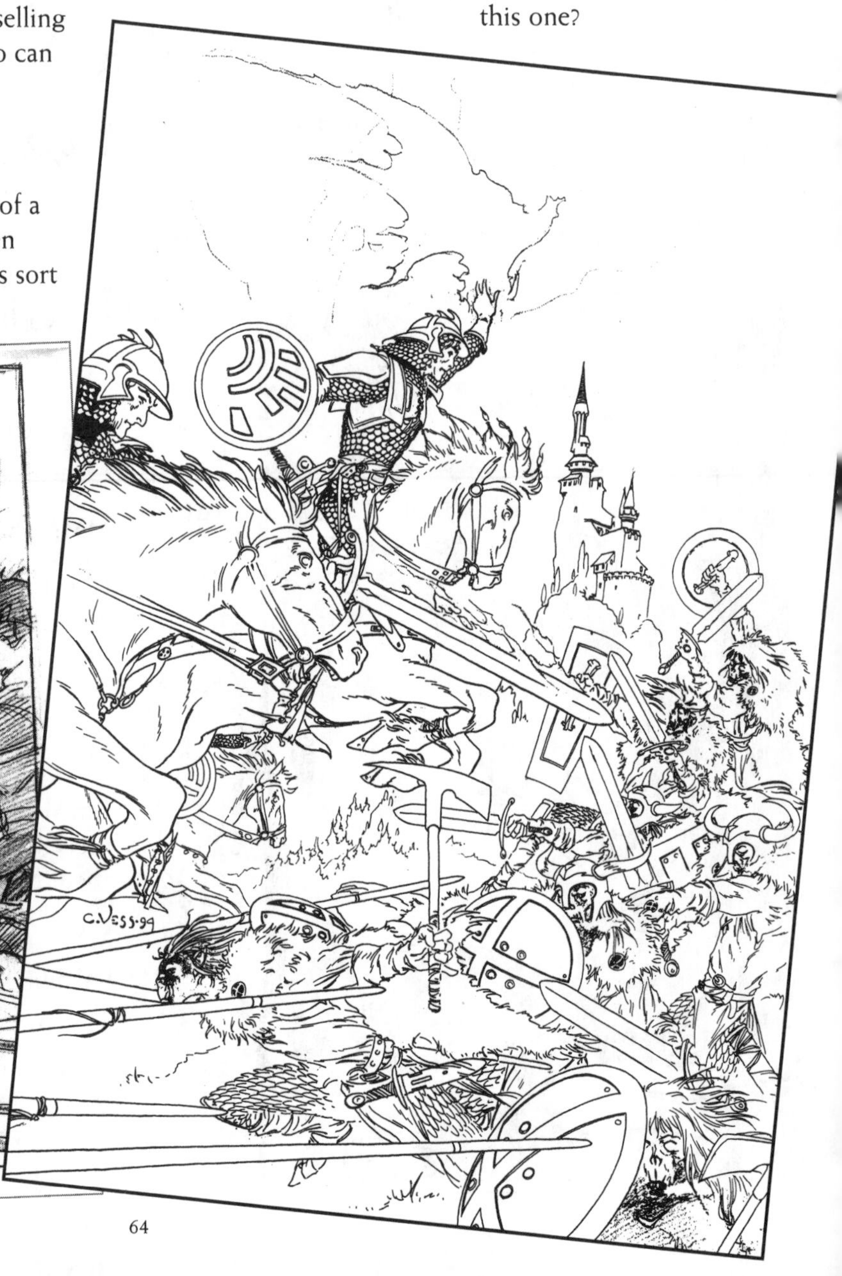
C.VESS.94

CHARLES: Well, he was charged by the idea of writing mountains of text in longhand because he'd never done this before. He had grown up on computers and word processors, but this was our grand Romantic novel, so he'd write it the grand Romantic way [*in longhand with a fountain pen*]. The next time we were going to see each other was at the next San Diego con, and he sent me a Xerox of the first couple of chapters he'd written. The plan was that I'd read his manuscript on the plane flight to the convention. So I got on the plane, and began to read. His handwriting is eccentric to say the least; about every third word I'd circle because I couldn't read it. I gave up after five or six pages thinking, "I don't even know what any of this means, because I can't decipher enough of the words."

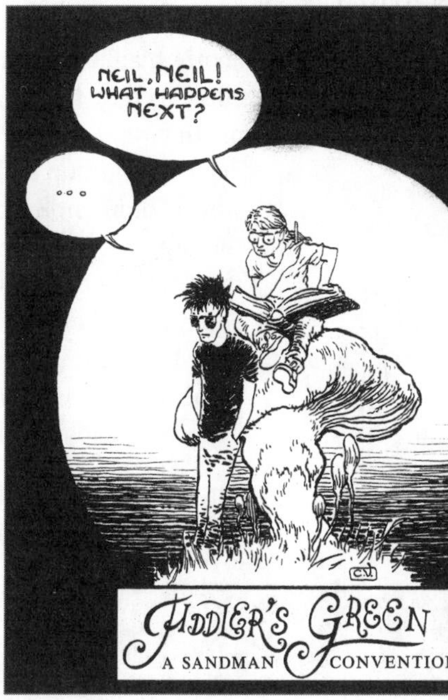
NEIL, NEIL! WHAT HAPPENS NEXT?
...
FIDDLER'S GREEN
A SANDMAN CONVENTION

MM: He could have been a doctor?

CHARLES: Yeah, he could have been a doctor. So plan B became Neil sending me a cassette tape of him reading the first two chapters, also stumbling across words and going, "I don't know what that is, let's just skip that." And that was what I began to work from. Eventually his wife, Mary, volunteered to transcribe his handwriting for him. But the greatest pleasure was Neil ringing me up and reading the latest chapter that he'd just finished, just to see if I would laugh at the right times.

This method caused an interesting design problem in that I couldn't thumbnail the entire book at once. We were told that each of the four serialized book would be 48 pages and thus the final collection would be close to 200 pages in length. It was very difficult to achieve a pleasing balance of text and images without knowing what Neil was going to be writing next. This was almost pre-computers, and you couldn't just flow out some text to fill in the spaces between images. There was a lot of semi-educated guesswork used so that sometimes after the artwork would be done, it would then have to be shrunk down a whole lot to accommodate the text. Or sometimes the text had to be edited to give the art a bit of breathing room. There was some give and take on both our parts, depending on how close to a text or an art deadline either of us were.

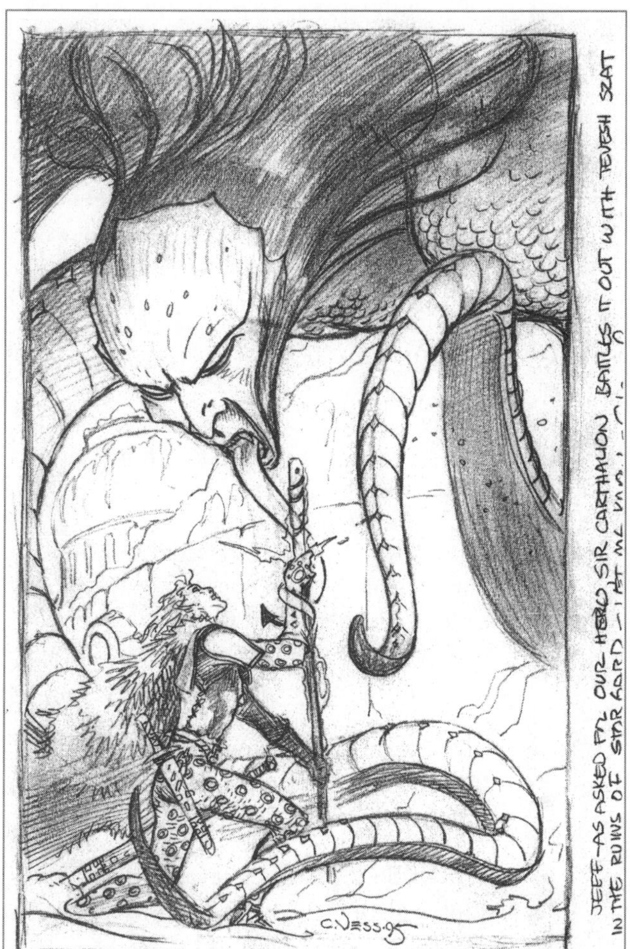
JEFF—AS ASKED FR. OUR HERO SIR CARTHALON BATTLES IT OUT WITH TEVESH SZAT
C.NESS-95

Every once in a while I might forget something pertinent and have to alter my finished painting, or not. The most significant of these edits was in the last part of the story, when Tristan wakes up, there's a badger there. In the text he's supposed to be wearing a heliotrope robe, and I just clean forgot about it and just drew a plain badger. Neil went "Oh, that's no problem," and edited his text. So, again, there were certain scenes that I couldn't draw and some scenes that I conceptualized differently, especially the village of Wall. Neil described it as an

Previous Page and Left: During his run of *Books of Magic* covers, Charles also painted the covers for the *Magic: The Ice Age* mini-series, based on the collectible trading card game. Shown here are the cover layout and final inks for *Magic: The Ice Age* #2, as well as the cover layout for issue #4.
Above: Advertising art for the annual Fiddler's Green *Sandman* convention.

Below: In this *Stardust* illustration, only the foreground is inked, giving the piece a greater sense of depth.
Next Page: *Stardust* illustration done in conté crayon on colored paper.

ancient village with one building after another, all leaning against each other in an effort to defy both age and gravity, but all of my drawings of Wall were going pretty much straight up and down. I don't know why, it didn't sink from my hand and through my fingers out on the page. So for the new edition I've been able to go back and draw certain images to more directly reflect Neil's text. These new images couldn't be inserted into the actual book, but will be in the supplemental material.

MM: That's why I just realized it was literally just a huge wall.

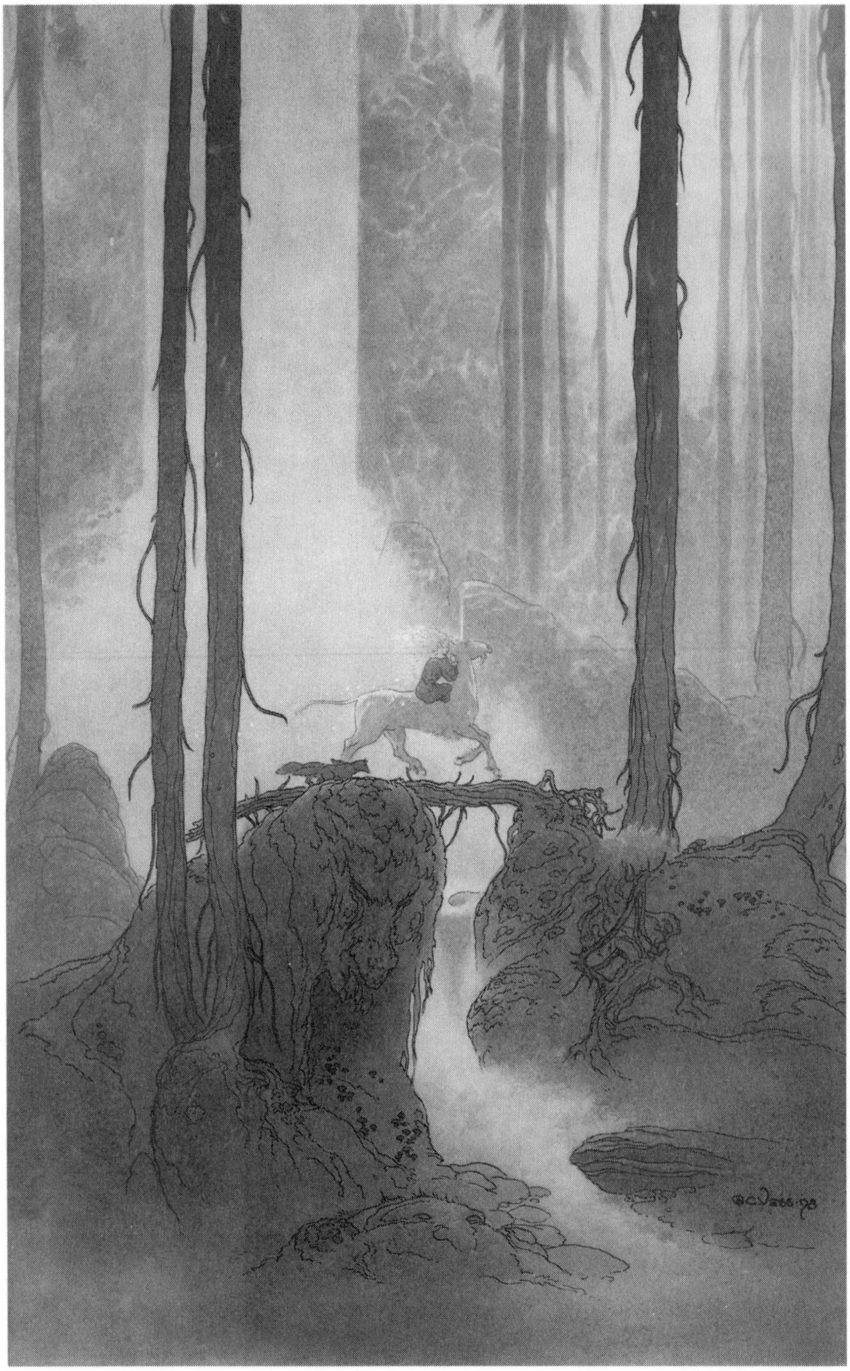

CHARLES: There's a photograph of the village that Neil clipped out of a magazine. He said, "This is what it should look like."

MM: I want to ask more about the process, but one thing I really picked up on that I see more of in *Stardust* is that you create a depth of field by your foreground objects. You go over the foreground object—is that in ink?

CHARLES: Ink.

MM: You give it an ink line, but then you're creating this atmospheric difference by just painting... or even just painting without a drawn outline.

CHARLES: Painting, or you outline the further away objects in a lighter color. It's sort of an animation effect.

MM: Yeah, very much so. When did you start doing that? Was it something you just did one day?

CHARLES: After you've done a billion paintings, you start to learn when to leave out which lines. A lot of the covers I've done—I did a year's worth of *Swamp Thing* covers and then a year's worth of *Books of Magic* covers before I started on *Stardust*, and it was pretty much learning where to leave out lines and where to just paint.

MM: In a lot of those, like you mentioned, you had a lot going on in your personal life, so I imagine you couldn't really worry about fine detail.

CHARLES: Yeah, and I experimented a lot at that time.

MM: There's a lot of "less is more," especially with this.

CHARLES: Yeah. And earlier on, three or four years earlier, this picture, the Golden Galleon picture [Stardust, *pg. 161*], probably would have had an outline around the clouds. And that would look really dumb.

MM: I also noticed some of the illustrations look like conté crayon on colored paper?

CHARLES: Yes. Some of it is done on colored paper.

MM: Is that—?

CHARLES: For variation. One of my biggest problems with graphic novels, say, for instance, *Kingdom Come*—I can't read it. There is no variation.... It's beautifully done, but there's the same intensity of detail on page one as at the end, y'know, and there's no visual rhythm to the story. I always want a bit of white space on the page so that my eye will relax. A lot of people like it the other way—full-bleed art from corner to corner—but I don't. It's the same thing with a movie. You can always have too much of the same thing.

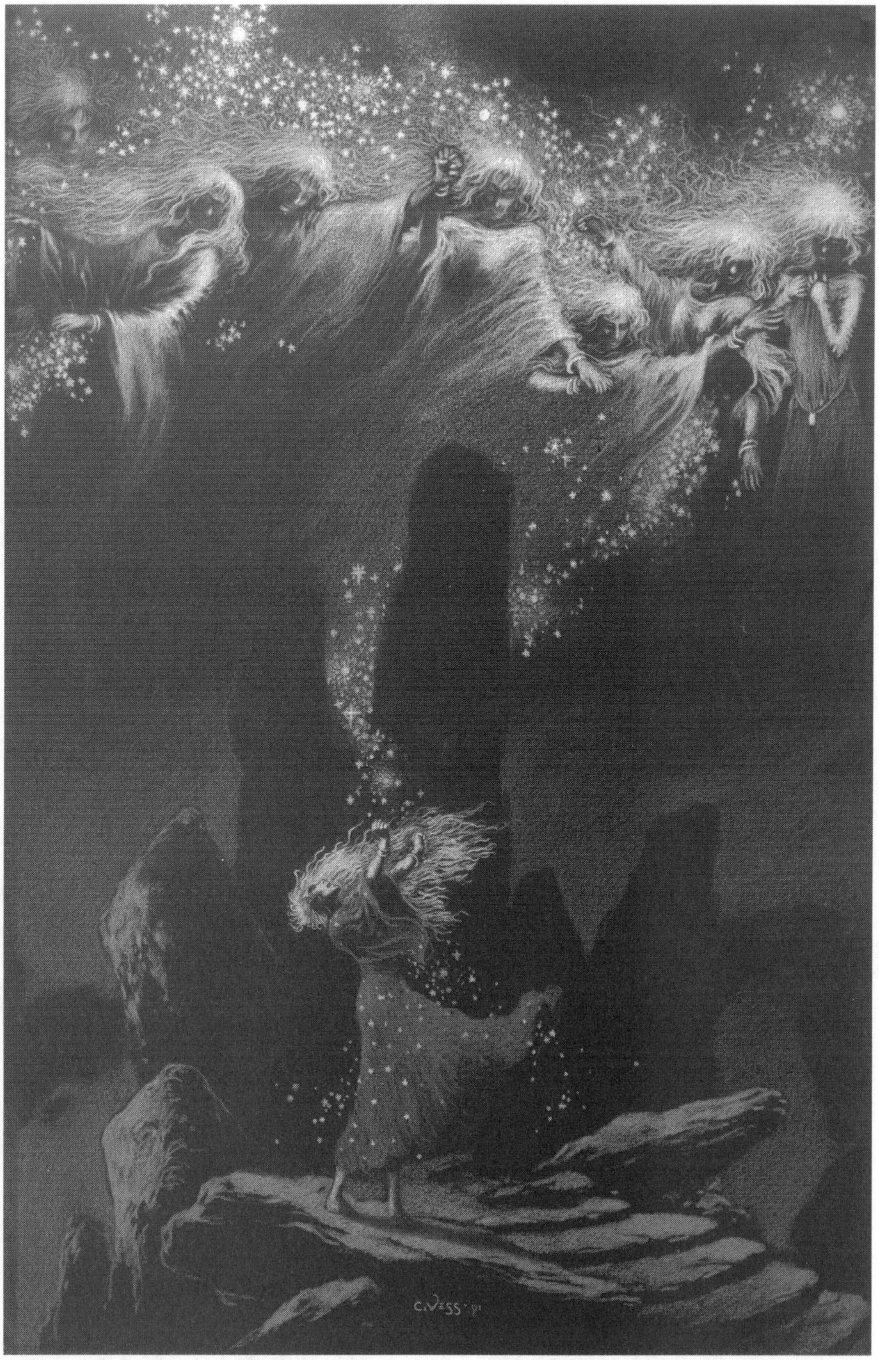
C.VESS

MM: Right. You can have too many of the same shots repeated. It's like when I saw some zombie movie based on a video game, I can't even remember the name....

CHARLES: Oh, yeah, one of those.

MM: Yeah, *Resident Evil*, I think, or....

CHARLES: How many times can you kill him?

MM: Well, that, yes, but, it's like, how many times can you go, "Boo!" Y'know? And literally every two minutes that happens; you become numb to it, so the effect is gone and rather pointless. All you have left is this annoying loudness.

CHARLES: Yup. It's the problem I had with early Frank Miller *Daredevil* is that every page was oomphed up to the eighth power, and after a while that's just as boring as six panels of white, because it's exactly the same thing page after page after page.

MM: When *Stardust* came out as four separate issues, was it just the *Sandman* bandwagon jumping on it, or was it something that you found lots of people who'd never read *Sandman* were picking it up?

CHARLES: There was a lot of that. DC did try to do some advertising outside of comics, and they did a bunch of music magazines. They were just at the tip of the iceberg of realizing what they had happening with Neil's audience, and they hadn't quite learned how to take as much advantage of it as they can now. So it's going to be really interesting to see how the film goes. Now the problem is we've got this book that's usually described as a graphic novel, and of course it's not a graphic novel, it's an illustrated book.

MM: It's a novel with graphics in it, but it's not a graphic novel.

CHARLES: Right, but there's also a prose version of it, and that's out there, too. There's a confusion with the identity of the property. With this movie, we've got a contractual guarantee of a full-screen credit of "Neil Gaiman and Charles Vess's *Stardust*." And the website's supposed to have a button that takes you to the book.

MM: Nice.

CHARLES: Yay! Woo! [*laughter*]

MM: I noticed that Tori Amos is the tree, right? The red tree with copper leaves?

CHARLES: Yes.

MM: How'd that happen? Did Neil just say to model the tree after her? I know that they have a friendship.

CHARLES: Yes, they have a longstanding friendship, but before the book happened, I had to produce about four or five paintings that were done before the text was written, to be used as promotional pieces to help sell the project. One of those pieces was based on a dream I'd had. I usually don't remember my dreams, but in this

one Neil and I were walking through a deep, deep woods, and he was telling me the story of *Stardust*. I kept feeling like someone else was watching us or listening in. When I looked up, above us in the trees was the Greek god, Pan, smiling back down in approval. I woke up and thought, "Good heavens, what a great image!" So I did a painting using that concept, but peopling it with *Stardust* characters. For some reason, and I don't remember why I did it now, in that painting there's a red tree— a sort of explosion of color.

MM: Did Neil base it on Tori, or did she see it first?

CHARLES: Apparently, when Tori saw that image she asked Neil if she could be a tree in the story.

MM: Any chance she'll be voicing the tree in the movie?

CHARLES: Well, in the best of all possible worlds, yes. I don't even know whether that scene will be in the finished movie or not.

MM: When did you first hear about the movie?

CHARLES: Well, it's been optioned before. But sometime in the spring, Neil was starting talking about the possibility, saying, "I think this might happen." Then I began to hear that Matthew Vaughn, a friend of Neil's who's a producer/director of a number of films, was attached, and it just started happening. Matthew raised half of the budget in England, and that's being matched by Paramount Studios who will be releasing the film. The script reads very smoothly. I think that it's the strength of that script that got all these A-list actors on board. It will be a very different fantasy world than the norm, and if it works right, will have a really nice balance between romance and fantasy and horror. Michelle Pfieffer makes a really terrifying witch. You feel that she could indeed rip your heart right out. What I've seen so far looks really promising.

I visited the sets, and they were all really impressive. Matthew Vaughn doesn't really like CGI very much, and once they did some research they realized it's actually cheaper to build the sets than to develop CGI models.

MM: Are these set designs based off your work?

CHARLES: Oh, they started with my art and then went off in their own direction. They're extensions of concepts that Neil and I came up with.

MM: I can't get over the casting on this movie.

CHARLES: Robert DeNiro, Peter O'Toole, Rupert Everett, Sienna Miller, Claire Danes... Charlie Cox, who is actually the star of the movie, is a talented young actor. Apparently he was the only one who auditioned who could do both the nerd part of Tristan and the hero part of Tristan.

Time-wise, it's going to come out the weekend of San Diego. That's both really cool, and a real headache in scheduling my life. There's nothing I can do about it, though; I just have to sit back, relax, and enjoy the ride.

They also just started doing test screenings, and they're getting really good feedback from those, and a lot of commentary on what might and might not work. Neil has seen the same rough cut, which still has unfinished special effects and music from other movies—which I'm told is a bit distracting—but he really liked what he saw.

MM: So, it's your first real movie experience, other than *Hook*. [*laughter*]

CHARLES: We won't go there!

MM: What tie-ins are coming out with this?

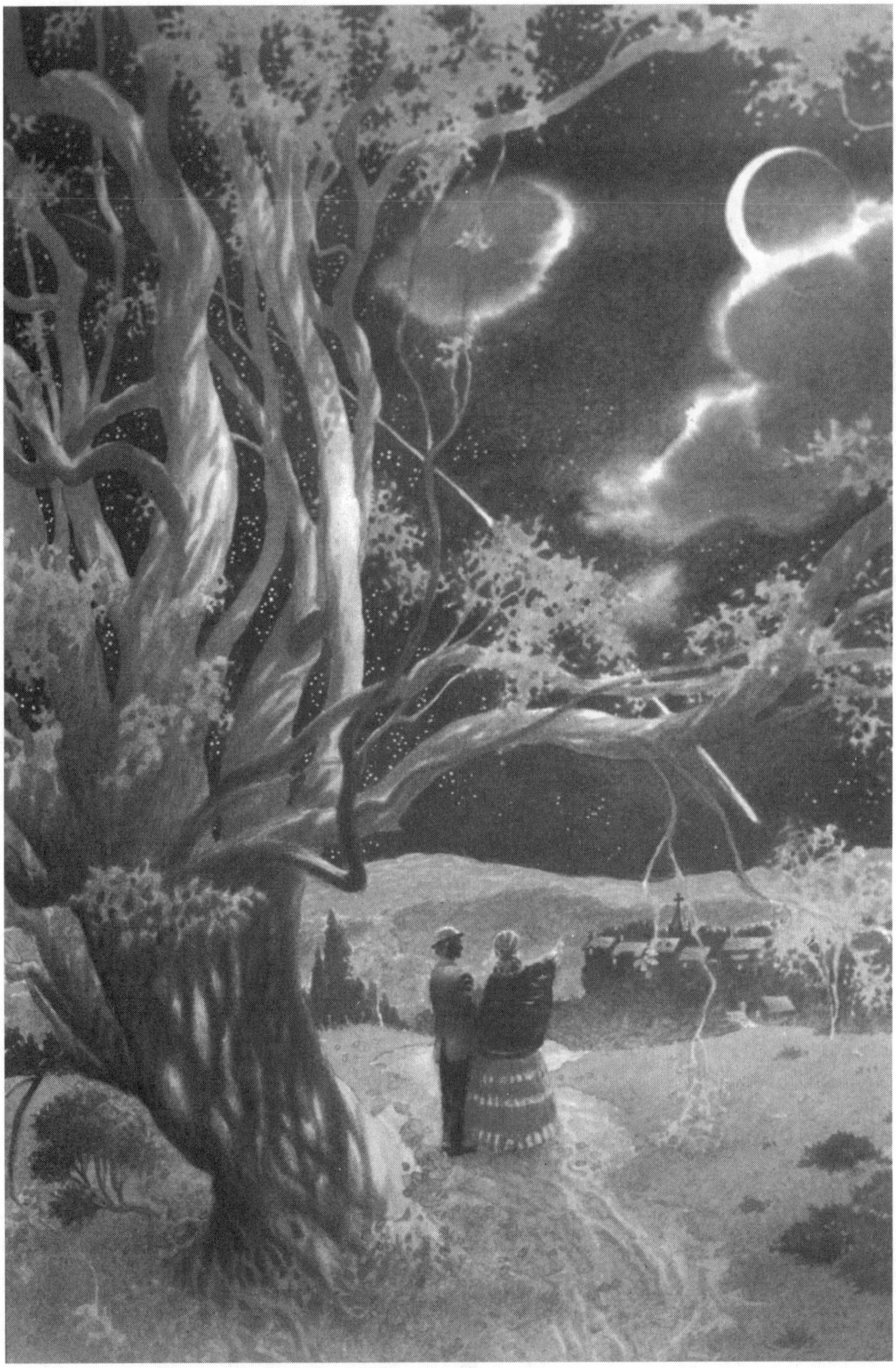

CHARLES: DC's doing an *Absolute Stardust* edition. I just did a full sculpture scene of Stardust and a fairy piper and several animals around a pool of water. DC is also producing four busts of Yvaine, Tristan, Primus—one of the major lords of Stormhold—and one of the Lillum; they all look really cool. They're doing a boxed set of notecards, two posters, and a new edition of the book, of course.

The Paramount website is going to do a whole section on the book. It took them months and months to realize the secret fan weapons they have with us; the value

Previous Page: Sandman meets Stardust. **Above:** Illustration from *Stardust*.

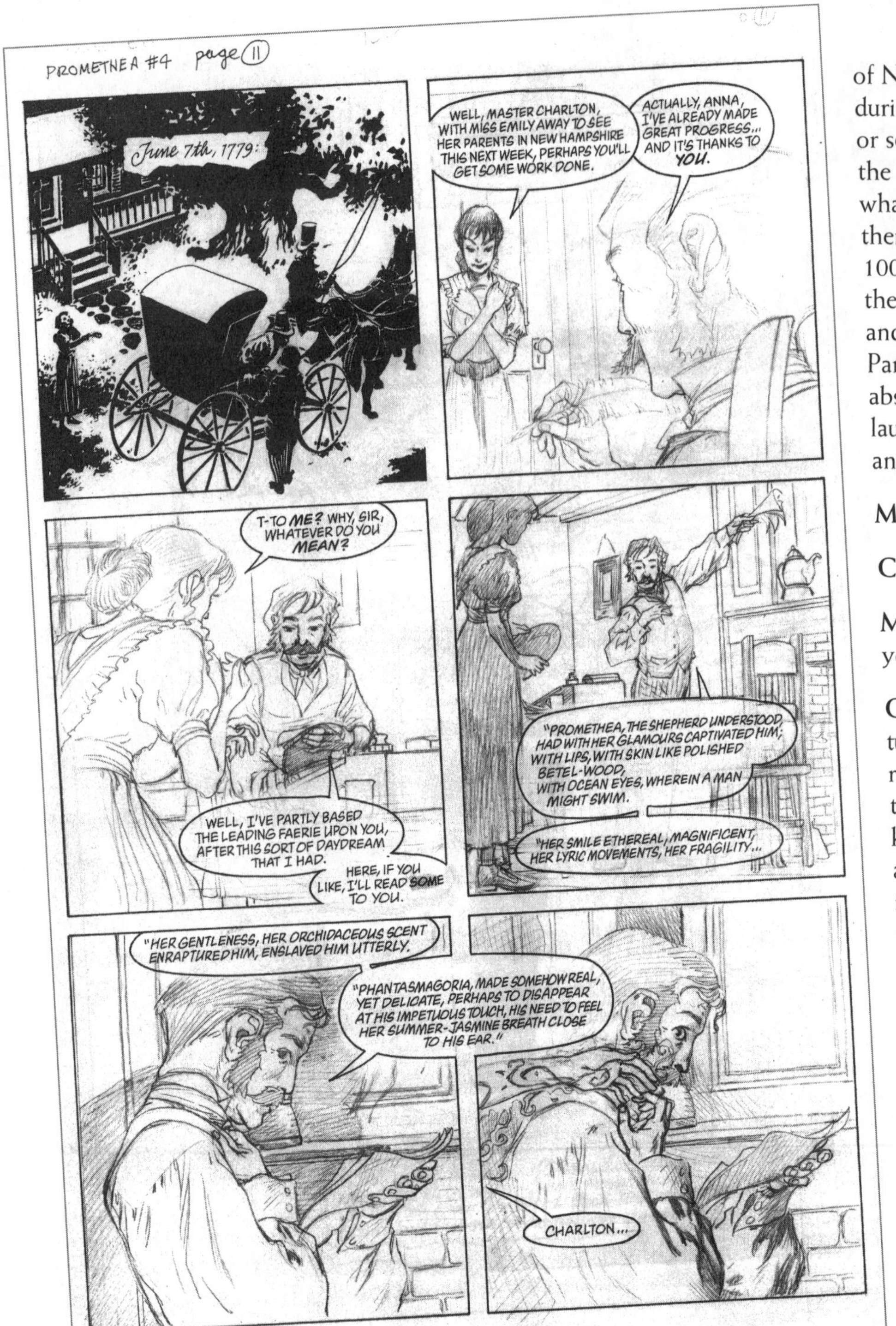
PROMETHEA #4 page 11
June 7th, 1779:
WELL, MASTER CHARLTON, WITH MISS EMILY AWAY TO SEE HER PARENTS IN NEW HAMPSHIRE THIS NEXT WEEK, PERHAPS YOU'LL GET SOME WORK DONE.
ACTUALLY, ANNA, I'VE ALREADY MADE GREAT PROGRESS... AND IT'S THANKS TO YOU.
T-TO ME? WHY, SIR, WHATEVER DO YOU MEAN?
WELL, I'VE PARTLY BASED THE LEADING FAERIE UPON YOU, AFTER THIS SORT OF DAYDREAM THAT I HAD.
HERE, IF YOU LIKE, I'LL READ SOME TO YOU.
"PROMETHEA, THE SHEPHERD UNDERSTOOD, HAD WITH HER GLAMOURS CAPTIVATED HIM; WITH LIPS, WITH SKIN LIKE POLISHED BETEL-WOOD, WITH OCEAN EYES, WHEREIN A MAN MIGHT SWIM.
"HER SMILE ETHEREAL, MAGNIFICENT, HER LYRIC MOVEMENTS, HER FRAGILITY...
"HER GENTLENESS, HER ORCHIDACEOUS SCENT ENRAPTURED HIM, ENSLAVED HIM UTTERLY.
"PHANTASMAGORIA, MADE SOMEHOW REAL, YET DELICATE, PERHAPS TO DISAPPEAR AT HIS IMPETUOUS TOUCH, HIS NEED TO FEEL HER SUMMER-JASMINE BREATH CLOSE TO HIS EAR."
CHARLTON...
11

of Neil's message board is enormous. It was during the San Diego Comic-Con that six or seven thousand people showed up for the *Stardust* panel that they started to get what we had to offer. Also, Neil linked to them through his website and they got 100,000 hits. They're really trying to make the connection between the original book and the movie. I don't know what else Paramount is doing. I'm sure it'll be absolutely bizarre and I know I'd just start laughing if I walked into a Burger King and there are the characters!

MM: A Tristan figure with kung-fu grip!

CHARLES: I'll have to buy a Whopper, Jr.!

MM: What are some of the challenges you saw in sculpting Yvaine?

CHARLES: I started dabbling with sculpture several years ago, and the thing that really surprised me is that for me it's easier to sculpt than it is to draw figures. I don't know why that is, but I'm very happy about it. The thing with this one is that it's so small and there are so many details to it. There's some very tedious things you have to deal with. I got a lot of advice from Georg Brewer at DC on how to deal with some technical aspects.

MM: Back in 2002, you'd done some children's book illustration with Charles de Lint. How does that work compare to what you did on *Stardust*?

CHARLES: Well, De Lint and I have known each other over 20 years. I actually met him while answering an ad in the back of *Comics Buyer's Guide*. He was looking for illustrators, so I would do drawings for some of his fanzines. I love his work, loved eventually meeting him, and we'd been trying to work together for a long time. A significant project finally clicked about five or six years ago, and we've now done a number of books together. On each one we've tried to make it a more collaborative effort on both our parts. I always really enjoy the act of collaborating. When it does work, it produces a third entity that can do things that neither one of the individual artists can do alone, and it's wonderful. It feels really good.

The very last book we really collaborated on was called *Medicine Road*, and it's based on a road trip Charles, his wife, and Karen and I made between Tucson, Arizona, and all the other places we stopped at. So the landscape was familiar, and we knew we were doing the book when we were doing the road trip. To start with Charles wrote up a very short plot synopsis with brief character descriptions. Then I would do drawings of these characters and certain significant landscapes, and hand those back to him. Sometimes he would ask for a few visual changes. We had photographs from our trip to work with.

Above: In 1998, Charles drew a sequence for Alan Moore's *Promethea*, in which an aspect of the character's past is revealed. Partially inked pencils for page 11 of *Promethea* #4.
Right: *Promethea* #4, page 12.

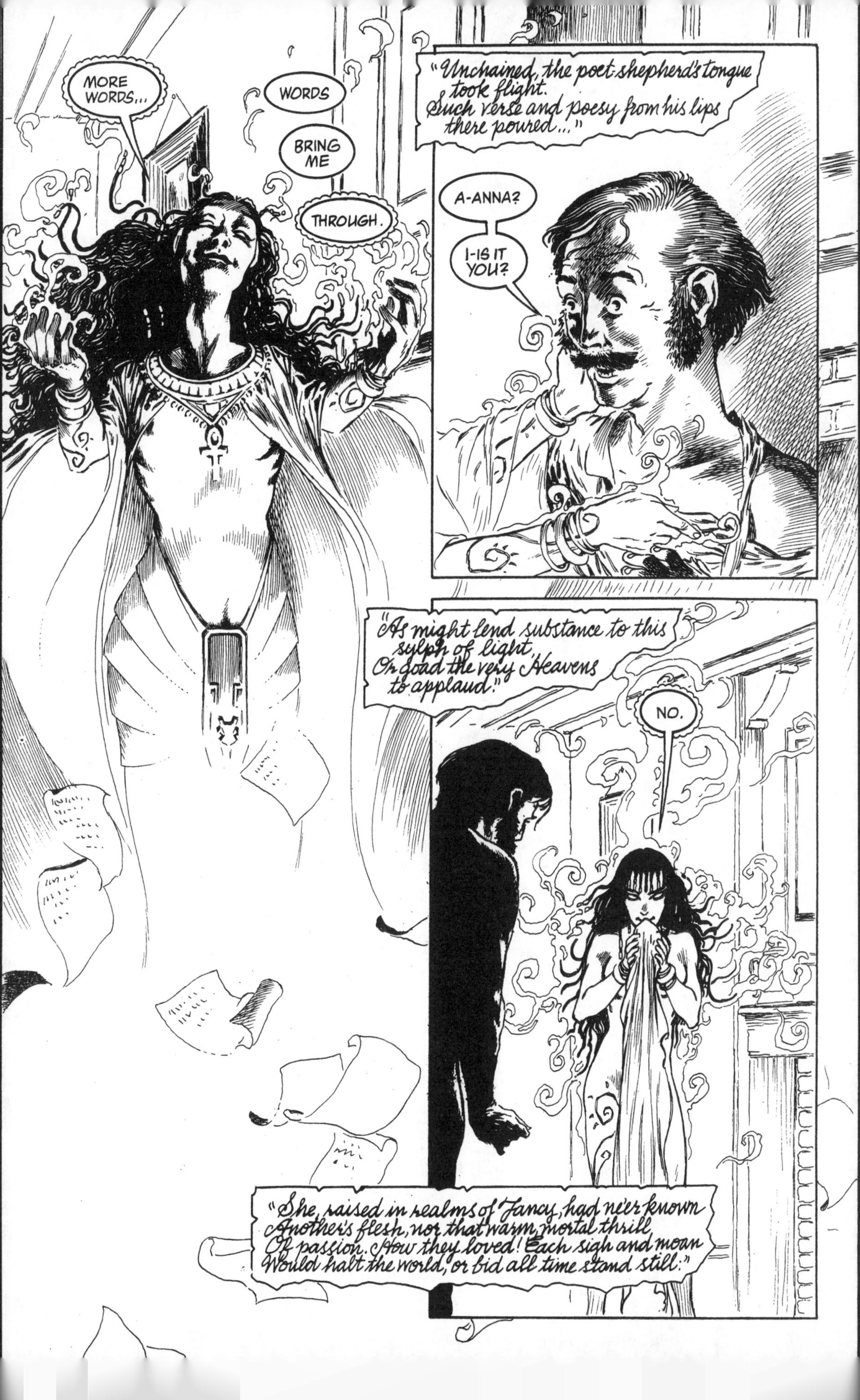
MORE WORDS...
WORDS
BRING ME
THROUGH.
"Unchained, the poet-shepherd's tongue took flight.
Such verse and poesy from his lips there poured..."
A-ANNA?
I-IS IT YOU?
"As might lend substance to this sylph of light,
Or goad the very Heavens to applaud."
NO.
"She, raised in realms of Fancy, had ne'er known
Another's flesh, nor that warm, mortal thrill
Of passion. How they loved! Each sigh and moan
Would halt the world, or bid all time stand still."

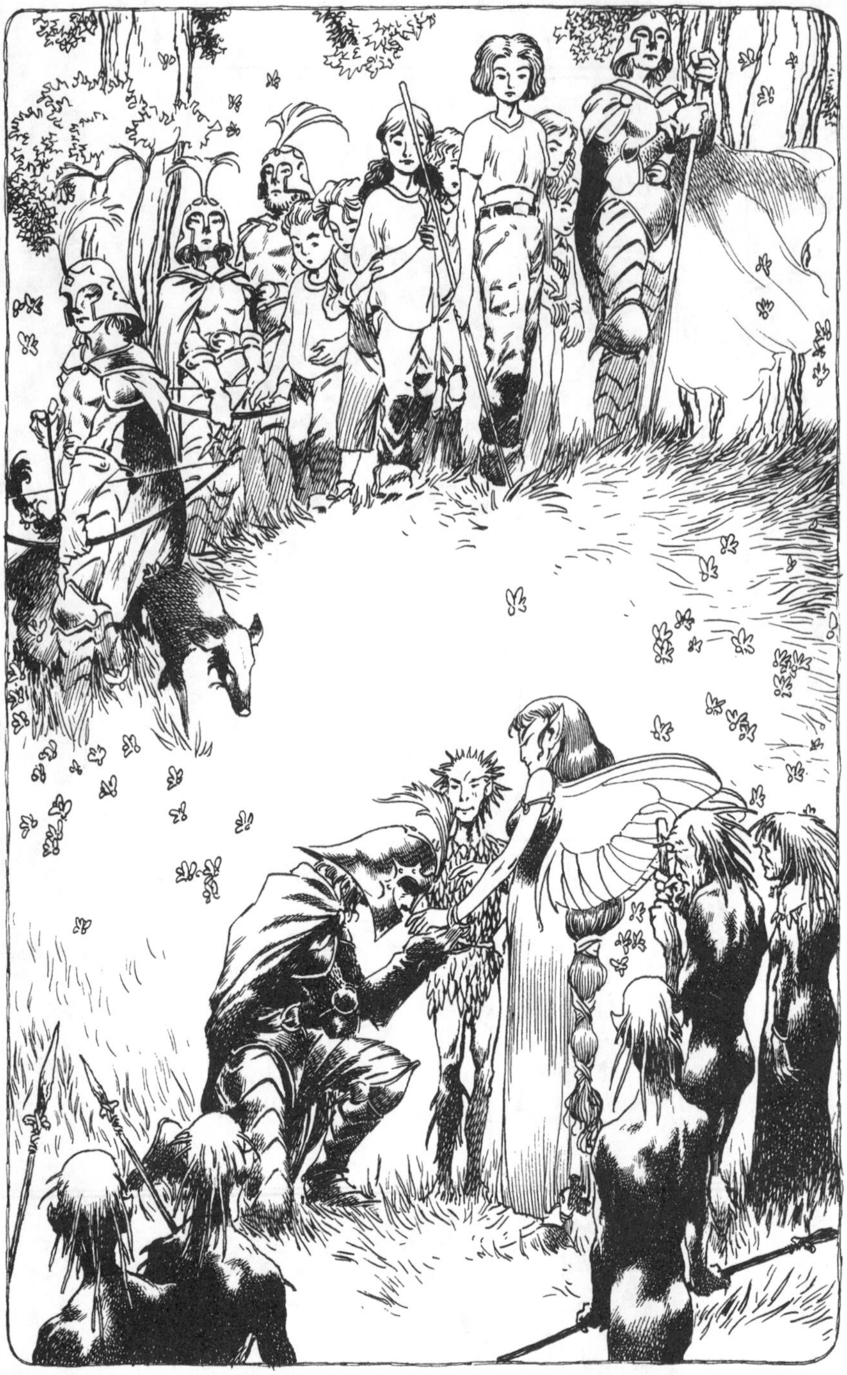

Above: A full-page illustration from Charles de Lint's *Seven Wild Sisters*.
Next page: "The Sushi Shot"—shown here at the panel's actual painted size—from *Rose* #3.

He's really good at developing characters. You want to be friends with them for the rest of your life. All that work produced a very good book. At least I think so.

MM: The first time I heard about *Rose*, actually, was when I interviewed Jeff Smith for *Comics Buyer's Guide* a few years back. One of the first things he said was "Yeah, he's doing this really cool thing with the word balloons, where you kind of see through them!" How did *Rose* come about?

CHARLES: Well, I'd known Jeff for a while and was a big fan of *Bone*. It's just one of my favorite comics, and I'm really happy it's getting as much worldwide recognition as it is. Over the years we've gotten to be pretty good friends. Several years ago I was up visiting Jeff and his wife and they took me downstate to visit Old Man's Cave in Ohio, the actual state park where his comic, *Bone*, is set. It's a small, natural valley where the Native Americans used to spend the winter. There are gorgeous waterfalls, caves, and trees all through it.

So we're walking through this park on a beautiful September day, and I just asked him, "What happened before the Bone cousins came to the valley?" He started rattling off this elaborate history which was a wonderful action/adventure, pure fantasy story. And he said, "Well, y'know, I've built this entire world from the ground up, because I've been making up *Bone* stories since I was eight years old, but I don't think I'll ever attempt to draw it." I just looked at him and said, "Then let me." He just sort of stopped and thought about it for a while, and then we agreed to work on it together. At first there was going to be a tagline on it, "Pure fantasy, no Bones about it!" Because, of course, the Bones aren't in it. [*laughter*]

We knew what the end of the story was going to be from the very beginning, as our story is based on a famous British folk legend called "The Lamptom Wyrm." In the actual tale, the dissolute heir of the local castle is out fishing on a Sunday when he should be dutifully in Church and he reels in a wyrm—which in medieval parlance is a dragon without wings. He pulls it up out of the water, becomes frightened, and runs away. The wyrm begins to devour all the people in the region and scours the landscape for years on end. Finally, the dissolute heir comes back and decides he has to do something about this, and he goes to the wise man for advice. He's told that he needs to build a suit of armor that is covered in small, sharp blades, then the wyrm will be cut to pieces when it tries to eat him. Each of those small slices wash away in the water unable to regenerate. But he's also told that he must kill the first thing he sees after he's vanquished the wyrm or his family will be cursed for generation after generation. He kills the wyrm, it floats away in various pieces, and the first thing he lays his eyes on is his father, who he hasn't seen in 30 years. Instead of killing his father, he kills his favorite dog instead. Doom and destruction reign for all the time that his family still lives in that land.

So we built our story around the bones of that folk tale, knowing that our ending was not going to be something that people would expect.

MM: You know, it's funny, because I wasn't quite sure what to expect of this. It's more adult than I expected, because *Bone* is generally all-ages, and this is... a lot of things getting lobbed off—

CHARLES: The sushi shot! [*laughter*] That's what we called that.

MM: That's aptly named. What was your collaboration like with Jeff on this, because the dragon, the red dragon, is very—did Jeff actually go back and do retouches on it?

CHARLES: Well, the first time we started on our story was an 8-page segment that appeared in the second Trilogy Tour book. Jeff did redraw the red dragon on those pages, but after that he just let me go my way. He was doing the layouts so I couldn't stray too far afield. Sometimes we did mildly butt heads on different approaches to a particular piece of storytelling. And you know who won? He did! He was the publisher! [*laughter*]

MM: The lettering font looks familiar.

CHARLES: It's the same font that I developed for *Ballads and Sagas*, but I didn't want to cover all the artwork with the balloons.

MM: Yeah, it's cool.

CHARLES: The color's about 75% there. It still loses a lot of color.

MM: Photoshop?

CHARLES: No, Jeff had never done color before, so it was like a new deal for him.

MM: Oh, yeah! I didn't think of that. Your ink line looks a little bit cleaner in this dragon shot.

CHARLES: I learned from *Sandman* #75. I did not want millions of little lines to just make them look furry. And I love Jeff's clean style; I wanted to draw that way. So I did a more broad, animation kind of thing.

MM: It's like the lovechild of your style and his. Do you have any more sequential art plans coming up soon?

CHARLES: Well, Jeff and I every once in a while talk about another *Rose* serial.

MM: She's still got some more gaps to fill in.

CHARLES: Oh, yeah, there's a lot to that story. But, in order to produce a graphic narrative the way I want to do a graphic narrative is an intense amount of work, and the older I get, the less continued concentration I have. So I don't know. And I'm having a great time, as long as I'm doing work that combines words and pictures; I don't care what form it takes. But I love that interaction. It's a sort of silent collaboration between a text and your images, and you can do that in a picture book, you can do it in an illustrated book, you can do it in a graphic novel. Who knows?

Stardust actually started off as a graphic novel. After imagining the 18 or so years it would have taken me to do it as a graphic novel I called up Neil and suggested the profusely illustrated form it finally took. Even with a sort of stripped-down style, such as I used in *Rose*, it still takes a very long time to finish a book, and I know at this point I'm not going to get any faster, so all I can do is work longer hours. I really don't want to spend every waking moment in my studio drawing. So there are some of the choices you have to make.

Part 5: Comics and Creativity

MM: You once mentioned Lorenzo Mattoti. When did you discover him?

CHARLES: Ten, twelve years ago.

MM: When I first looked up his work I went, "But he's an abstract painter," and I was like, "Wait a minute." I thought he would be one of those 1920s fantasy illustrators or something. But, y'know, I noticed that a lot of the hatching effects you do are very similar to his. What is it about his work, aside from his color, that you've picked up on?

CHARLES: There's this extreme sense of personality to his work. No one else draws like him and the color is brilliant. There's also a number of French, Belgian graphic novels that are gorgeous.

There's also Hermann, and Andres Juillard, who's a French cartoonist. I have a wall full of French and Belgian graphic novels. The only thing that's been printed in the US of his is contemporary mystery—*The Blue Notebook*... his storytelling is always superb. And his sense of history in his other work, I mean, you are there. But Juillard's done 10 to 15 albums concerning the Louis XII time period in France. All of them are quite beautiful. He is very popular in France. I have a portfolio that a small press produced of his work—a dozen plates, all loose with tissue paper dividers, and they're all in color. Absolutely beautiful production values. It's really amazing to look at, but nobody can make any money off of something like this. It's just some little comics group that wanted to do it. I've even struck up a general correspondence with him, but since neither of us speak or read the other's language we just send art back and forth.

MM: You don't even know each other's language, but art is the universal. I really wish we had the sophistication that they seem to have; maybe we're on our way. I like to think we are.

CHARLES: With all the, especially, small press stuff coming out right now, that's hand-done—they're gorgeous. I have a whole bunch of them somewhere.

MM: You know, I think on the small press level there's that personal touch that you just don't have with a lot of the major publishers.

CHARLES: It's a big world with room enough for all types of genres and art styles. One of the things that I enjoy most about going to San Diego Comic-Con is that you realize just how big our world really is. There are plenty of niche markets within it with a plethora of thrones for individual kings and queens to sit atop their own particular fiefdoms.

BACK 'N KANSAS WHEN I WAS JUST A KID THEY USED TA SPIN TALES 'BOUT OL' FARMER HARKLIN 'N HIS...

SCARECROW

· STORY AND ART · C. VESS ©86

IF YA LEFT TOWN BY TH' WEST ROAD 'N TURNED RIGHT ONTA HOBB'S LANE YOU'D HAVE TA PASS RIGHT BY TH' HARKLIN FARM.

'N THERE IT WOULD STAND, RIGHT SMACK 'N TH' MIDDLE OF HIS FIELDS. A TALL THIN PECULIAR TYPE A SCARECROW. ITS STICK FINGERS JUST A SCRATCHIN' AT TH' SKY.

EVEN ON TH' CLOUDIEST A DAYS TH' SHADOW FROM IT WOULD COME SPILLIN' CROSS TH' ROAD. CHILL YA TA TH' BONE THAT SHADOW WOULD, IF YA WALKED THRU' IT. MOSTLY FOLKS WALKED ROUND.

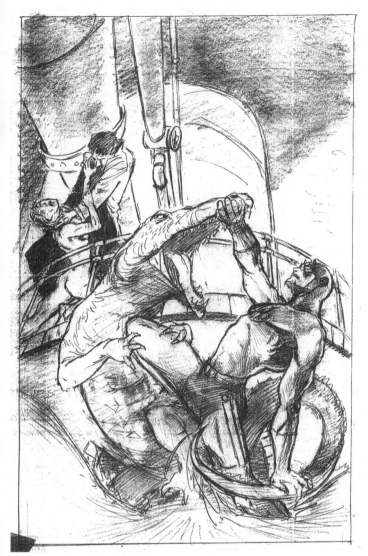

I remember at the height of the Image madness, when Rob Liefeld in particular was a godling. Every comics-orientated magazine was full of his exploits, his deals, his art, as if his was the only "voice" worth hearing. That summer I was there at Comic-Con, busy at my table and I never once heard a word about his antics, wasn't even particularly aware of his presence at the con. I left thinking, "Right! There's more than enough wiggle room for us all." It seems crazy to me to put blinders on and to think, "I'm only gonna read one certain type of book." I was always amazed at people saying that they would only read comics that were in color, or only read comics that were black-&-white, or only ones that are self-published, or only alternative comics, or only if they're about super-heroes.... they'll only read fantasy, they'll only read science fiction... and I'm like, "There's plenty to like all over the board. Just pick and choose and look at what's interesting."

MM: It's like watching only one channel or one kind of movie.

CHARLES: Yeah! I remember when Dave Sim made the pronouncement of "If it's not self-published, it's not any good." And I thought, "Are you nuts?" That's like saying, "If Warner Books didn't publish it, then it's not a good novel." There's always a chance that good material will rise to the top in any genre that you pay attention to. There's always a way to sneak under a radar and do something interesting.

MM: When you get started on a project, do you work with really tight thumbnails?

CHARLES: Sometimes. Sometimes there's nothing. Of course, with *Rose*, it was just over Jeff's layouts. I looked at his quick sketches and drew from them. Most of the time, at this point, in book illustration, the editors ask for a certain number of illustrations and I just turn them in when I'm finished. Except with a

Previous Page: Opening page of "Scarecrow," which was originally published in the black-&-white anthology, *Taboo* #1.
Above: Charles' pencils and inks for 1987's *Daredevil* #247. Upon reflection, Charles points out, "The bottom jaw on that alligator doesn't work that way!"

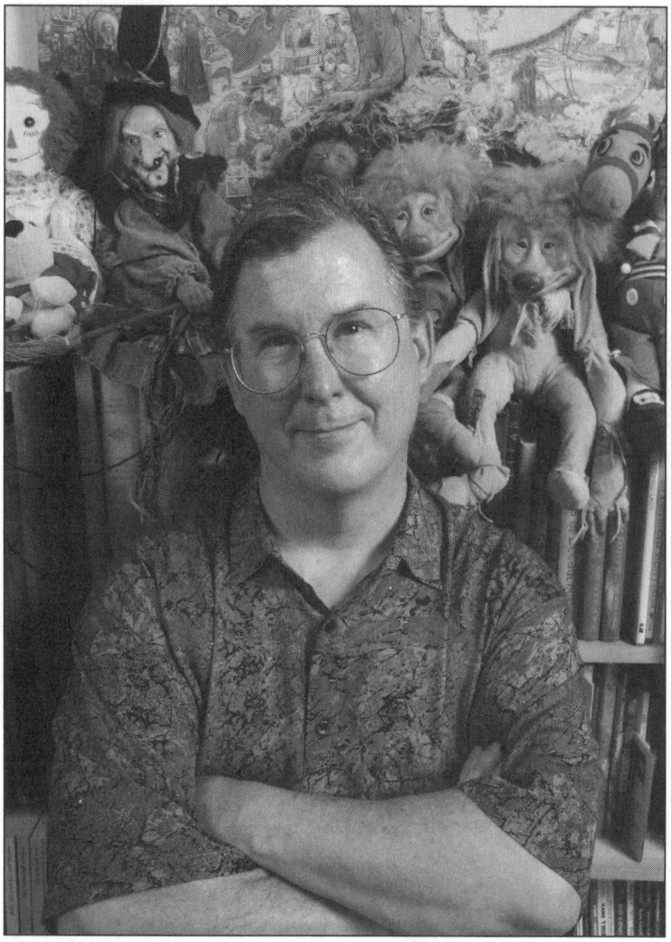

cover. With the cover, more so than in comics, the book cover, jacket art, you're not so much dealing with the author or the editor... you're dealing with the marketing division. They know how they want to market a particular book and base their cover decisions on that plan. That's why you can't just send a sketch in and expect to go right into paint, because you may think it's the greatest thing in the world, but it still has to go through all these marketing channels.

MM: You'd mentioned the *Art of Stardust* show in Abingdon this summer, as well as the arts scene here. How did you first get involved?

CHARLES: Well, there are a lot of artists in the area, unfortunately none of them work as illustrators. Most of them paint beautiful landscapes or flowers. Having a mindset than can apply my artistic problem solving to a variety of circumstances makes me very unique in amongst these other artists. Pretty soon architects and interior designers become aware of what I can do and started asking me to be involved in certain projects.

A community college about 45 minutes from here approached me about designing a 30' x 50' wall sculpture of bas-relief brick, which I did. It's based on the Appalachian Jack tales. Every time I take someone they go "Gosh, that's big." It took about two years for Johnny Hagerman to sculpt the bricks based on my designs. I've also just designed and will be doing a lot of hands on sculpting of a 16' bronze fountain

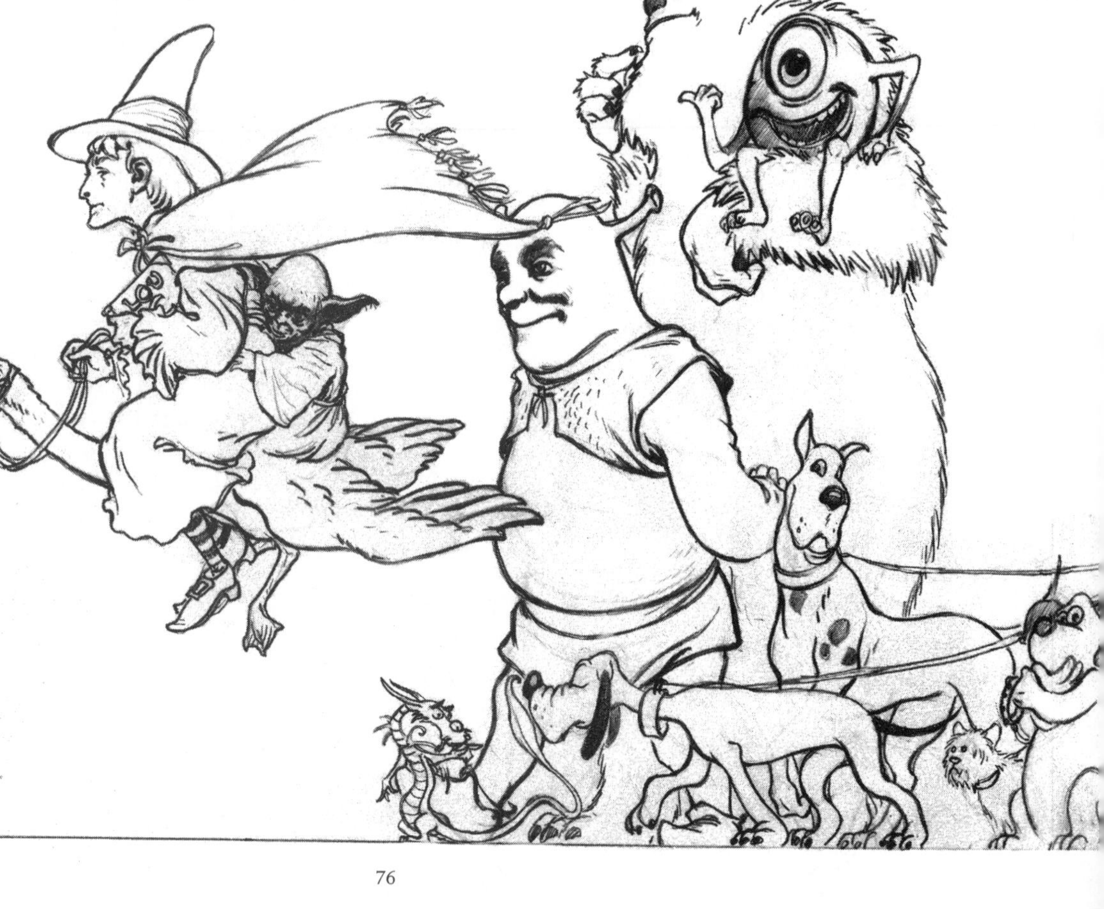

Above: A recent photo of Charles and a few of his friends.
This Page and Next: Charles' layout drawing for the mural which will be on the wall of the CineMall—the local movie theatre in Charles' hometown.

which is based on *A Midsummer Night's Dream* for the State Theater of Virginia here in Abingdon.

Also, there's a locally owned movie theater called the CineMall, where we will be having a regional premiere of *Stardust*. I don't believe that anyone but me—that's connected to the movie—is going to be there. [*laughs*] It's only local, but it'll be really fun and the proceeds will benefit several local charities. I had the idea to repaint the exterior of the walls to the CineMall with a mural of mostly animated movie characters and turn it into a community-wide art project. We decided to put characters that would be funny or cool next to one another together. I've already spent way too much time on the original drawing, which is 20" x 4' for each side of the wall. The actual wall will be 14' x 200'. I do the drawing, then Pat takes it off, and they project it large on to the building and redraw it. All sorts of community artists come in to work on it, from high school, college and up. Seeing it go up is fun.

We've been giggling when we see Cruella De Vil up next to Shere Khan, and then beside those two we put Gollum, thinking to ourselves that Gollum could be the lovechild of Khan and Cruella.

MM: All through this interview, I've noticed these two giant charcoal illustrations on the wall.

CHARLES: Well, when I lived in New York for twelve years, I had an 8' x15' room. When I moved to upstate New York for three years, my studio room was 10' x 10'. When I moved down here and got my studio space in the arts center, the room was 20' x 30' with 15' ceilings. I thought, "Hot damn, I'm going to draw me some big pictures!" Originally they were going to be sketches for oil paintings, but once I got them done, I just thought that they were just fine the way they are. The one on the left is based on a Scottish ballad, and

the one of the right is based on Deirdre of the Sorrows, which is known as the third great sorrow of Irish storytelling. It's sort of an Irish Helen of Troy story. When Deirdre is born she is quickly declared to be the most beautiful woman in the world; that is why you do not see her face. Everyone's got a different version of the most beautiful woman in the world. Over the years I've had several long arguments with art directors, who always win, of course, over who the most beautiful woman in the world is. [*laughter*] At a certain time I was told that that would be Cheryl Tieggs. But as I said, everybody's got a different ideal. So I simply wasn't going to clarify the features on this woman. I hid them in the shadows of her cloak so that, hopefully, each viewer can produce their own distinct features.

MM: So how often do you do things like this just for yourself?

CHARLES: Not nearly often enough. Sometimes you just need to not have a deadline, and just do something for yourself that feels really good.

C. Jess

Charles Vess

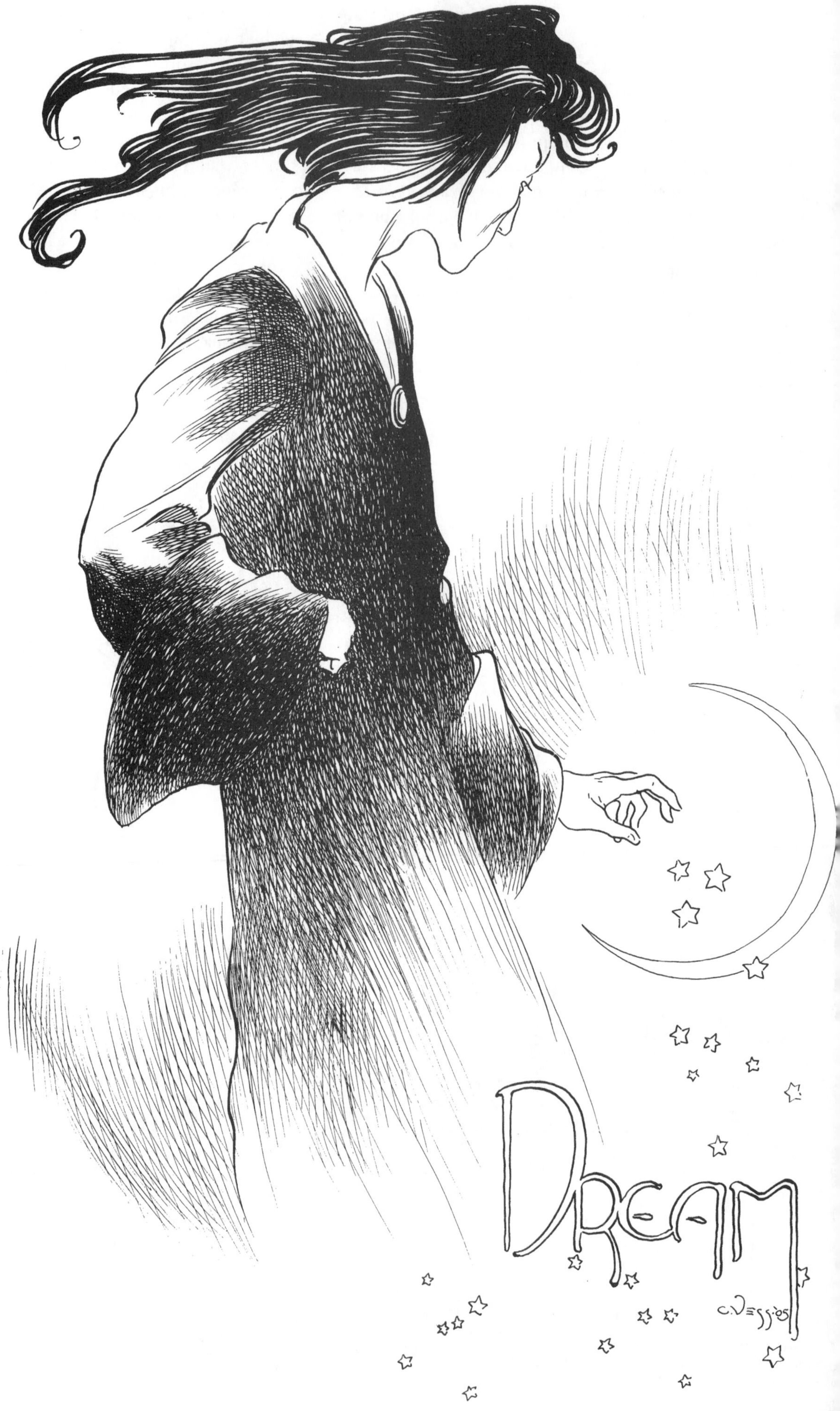
DREAM
C. Vess '05

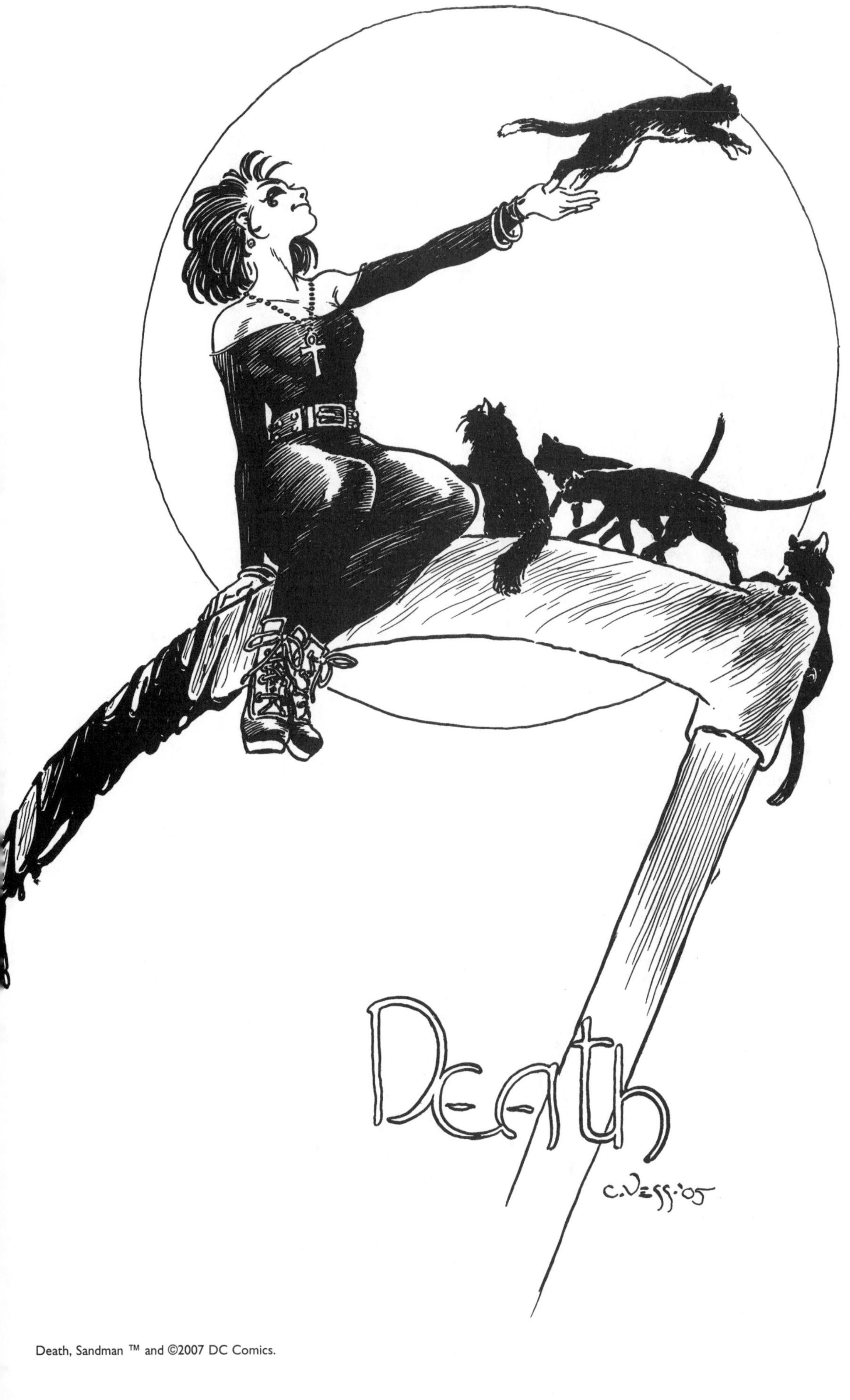
Death
C. Vess '05

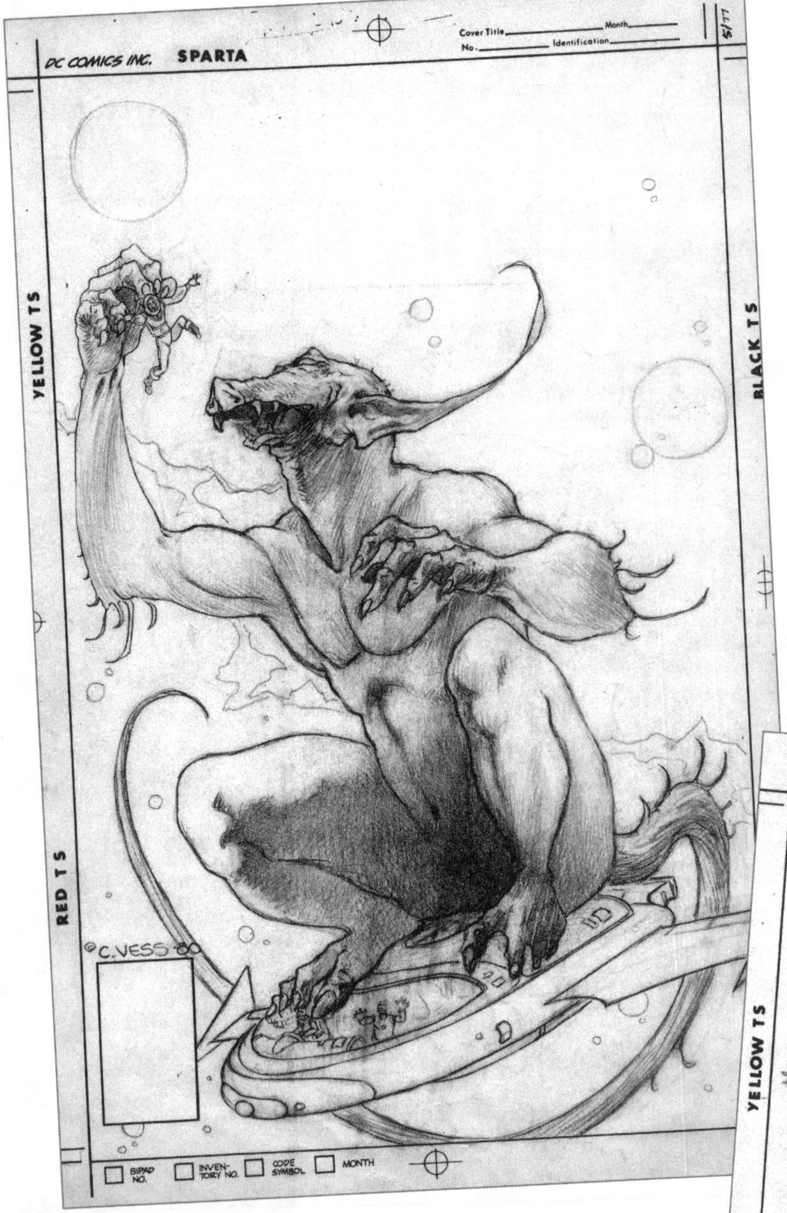
DC COMICS INC.
SPARTA
Cover Title
Month
No.
Identification
YELLOW TS
BLACK TS
RED TS
©C.VESS'80
BIPAD NO.
INVEN-TORY NO.
CODE SYMBOL
MONTH

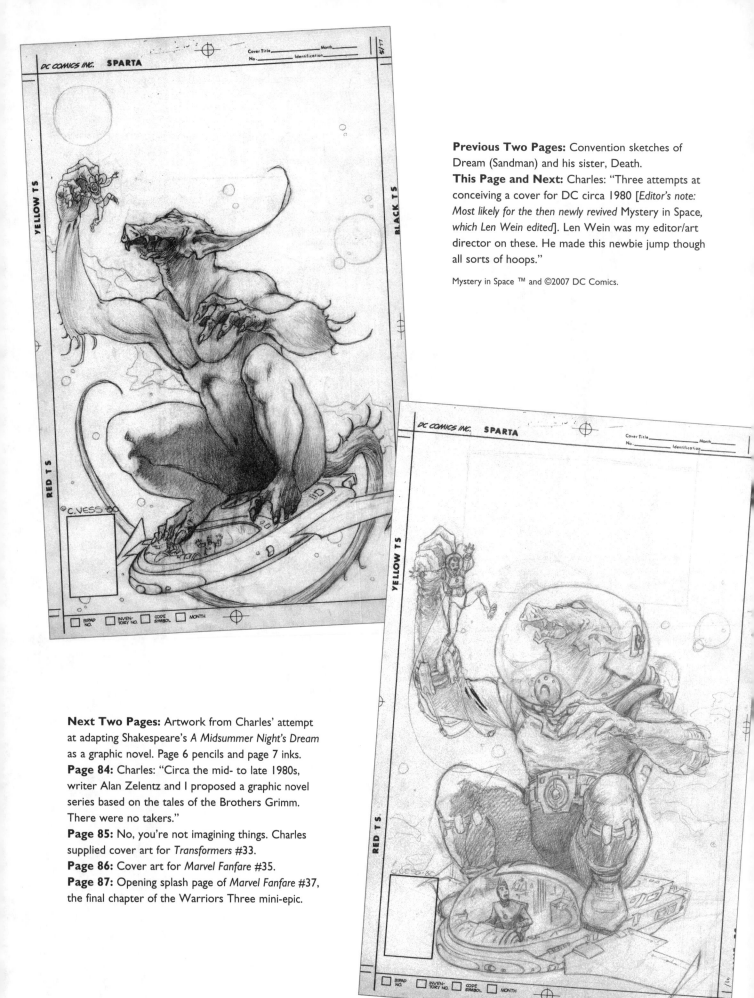

Previous Two Pages: Convention sketches of Dream (Sandman) and his sister, Death.
This Page and Next: Charles: "Three attempts at conceiving a cover for DC circa 1980 [*Editor's note: Most likely for the then newly revived* Mystery in Space, *which Len Wein edited*]. Len Wein was my editor/art director on these. He made this newbie jump though all sorts of hoops."

Next Two Pages: Artwork from Charles' attempt at adapting Shakespeare's *A Midsummer Night's Dream* as a graphic novel. Page 6 pencils and page 7 inks.
Page 84: Charles: "Circa the mid- to late 1980s, writer Alan Zelentz and I proposed a graphic novel series based on the tales of the Brothers Grimm. There were no takers."
Page 85: No, you're not imagining things. Charles supplied cover art for *Transformers* #33.
Page 86: Cover art for *Marvel Fanfare* #35.
Page 87: Opening splash page of *Marvel Fanfare* #37, the final chapter of the Warriors Three mini-epic.

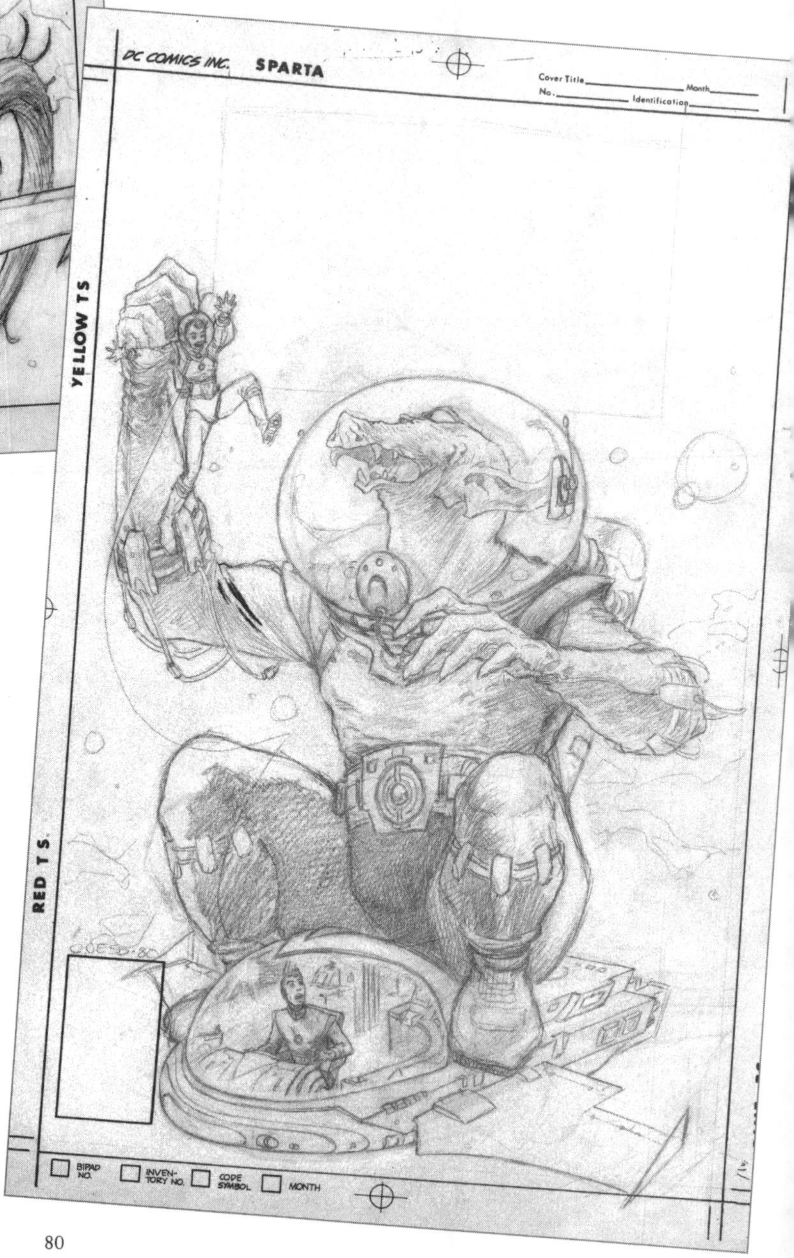
DC COMICS INC.
SPARTA
Cover Title
Month
No.
Identification
YELLOW TS
RED TS
BIPAD NO.
INVEN-TORY NO.
CODE SYMBOL
MONTH

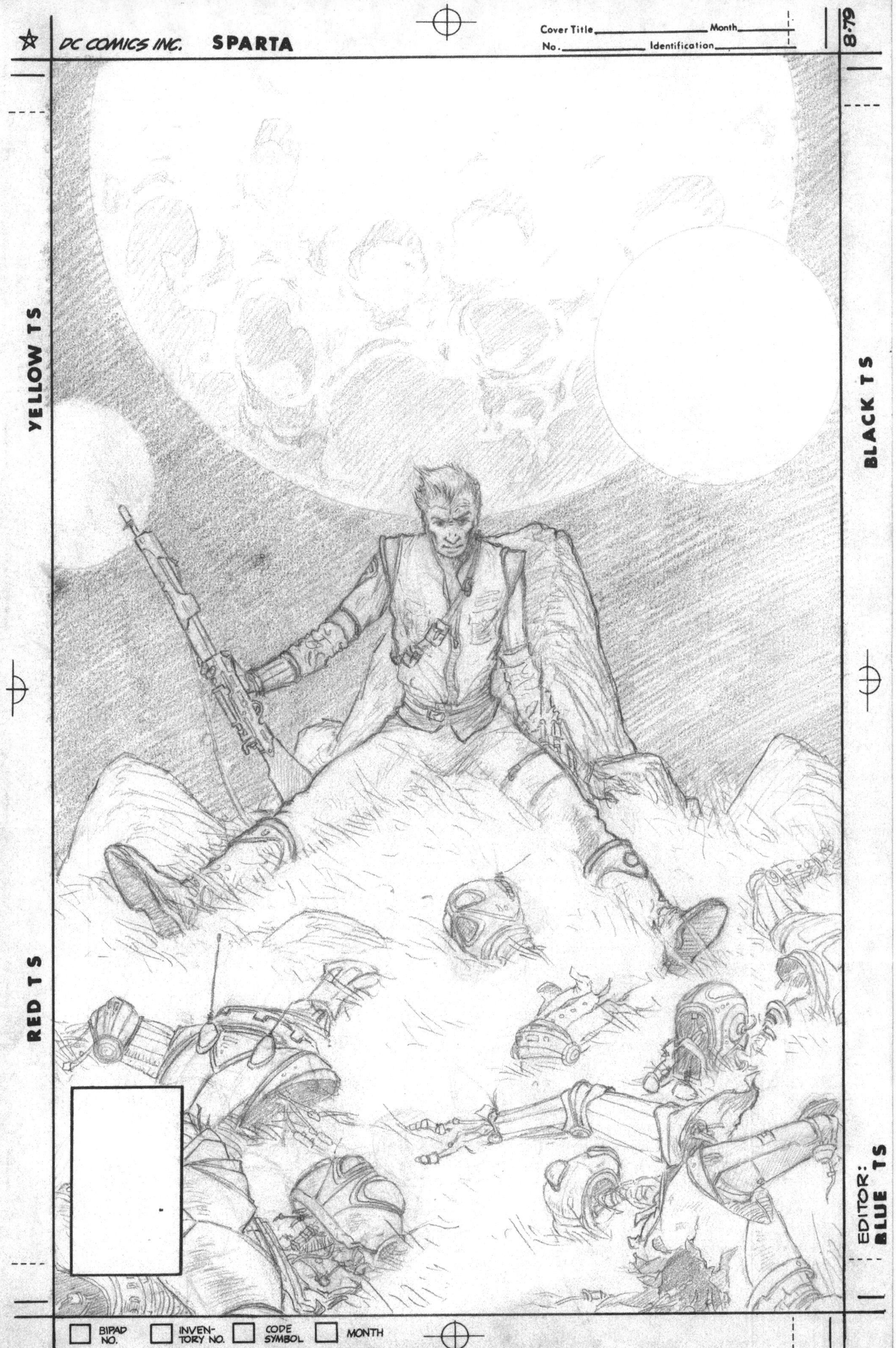
DC COMICS INC.
SPARTA
Cover Title
Month
No.
Identification
8.79
YELLOW TS
BLACK TS
RED TS
EDITOR:
BLUE TS
BIPAD NO.
INVENTORY NO.
CODE SYMBOL
MONTH

FAIRIES, SKIP HENCE:
I HAVE FORSWORN HIS BED AND COMPANY.

— TARRY, RASH WANTON: AM NOT I THY LORD?
— THEN I MUST BE THY LADY.

WHY ART
THOU HERE?

NEVER
SINCE THE
MIDDLE
SUMMER'S
SPRING
MET WE
ON HILL,
IN DALE,
FOREST
OR MEAD,
BY PAVED
FOUNTAIN

OR
IN THE BEACHED
MARGENT OF
THE SEA TO
DANCE OUR
RINGLETS
TO THE
WHISTLING
WIND, BUT
WITH THY
BRAWLS THOU
HAST DISTURBED
OUR SPORT.

⑤

— DO YOU AMEND IT, THEN: ITS LIES IN YOU:
WHY SHOULD TITANIA CROSS HER OBERON.
DO BUT BEG A LITTLE CHANGELING BOY.

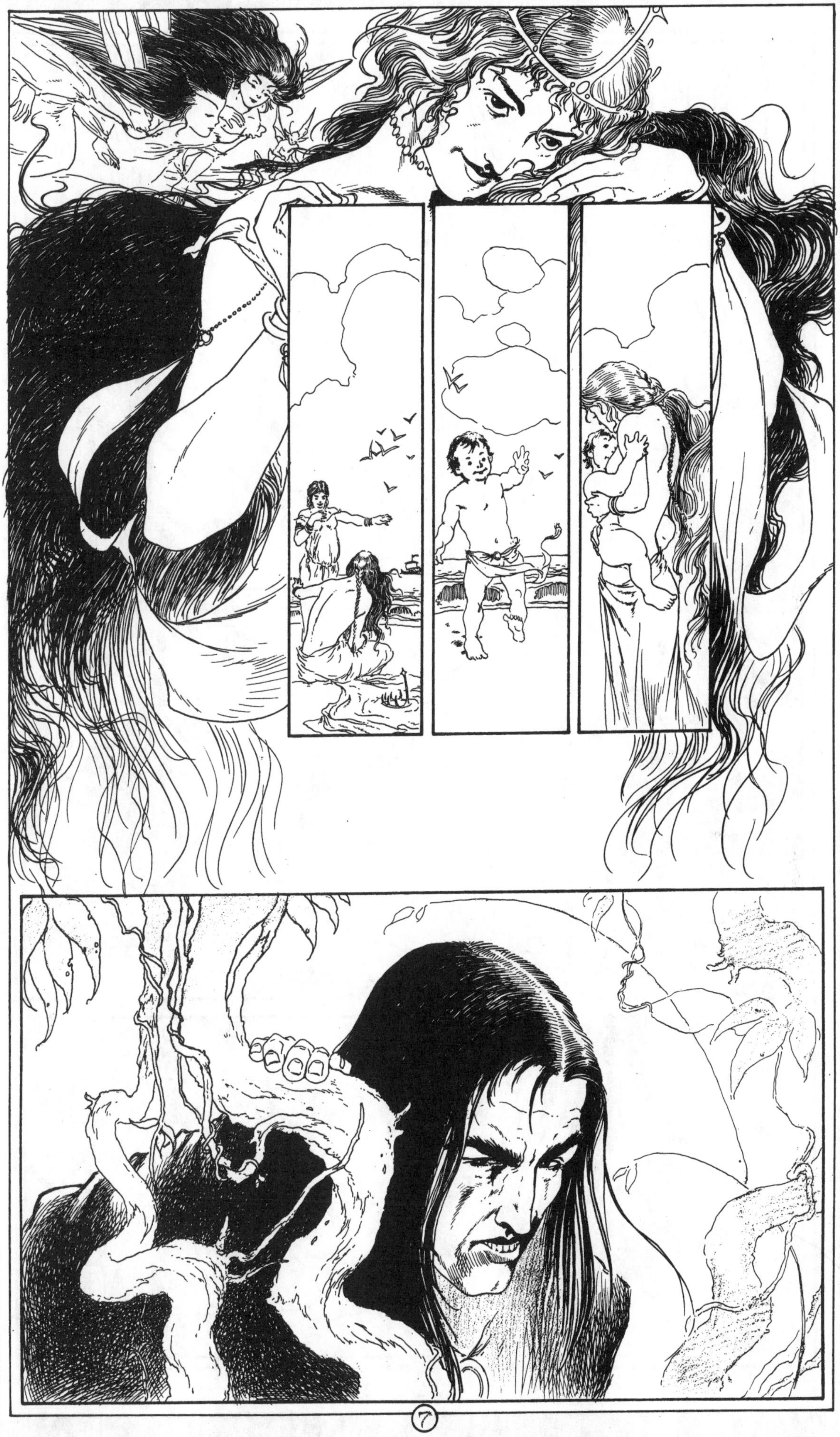

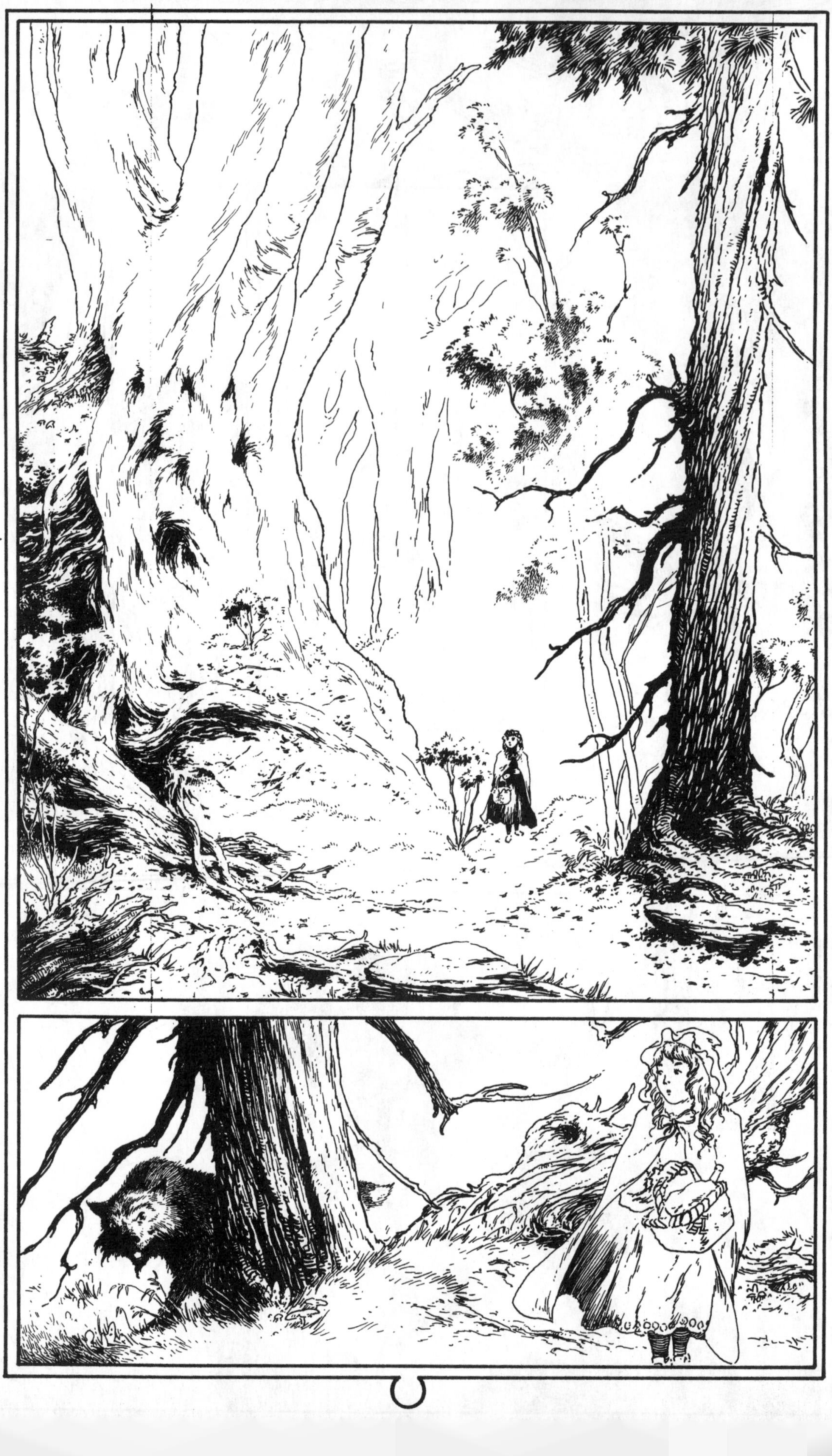

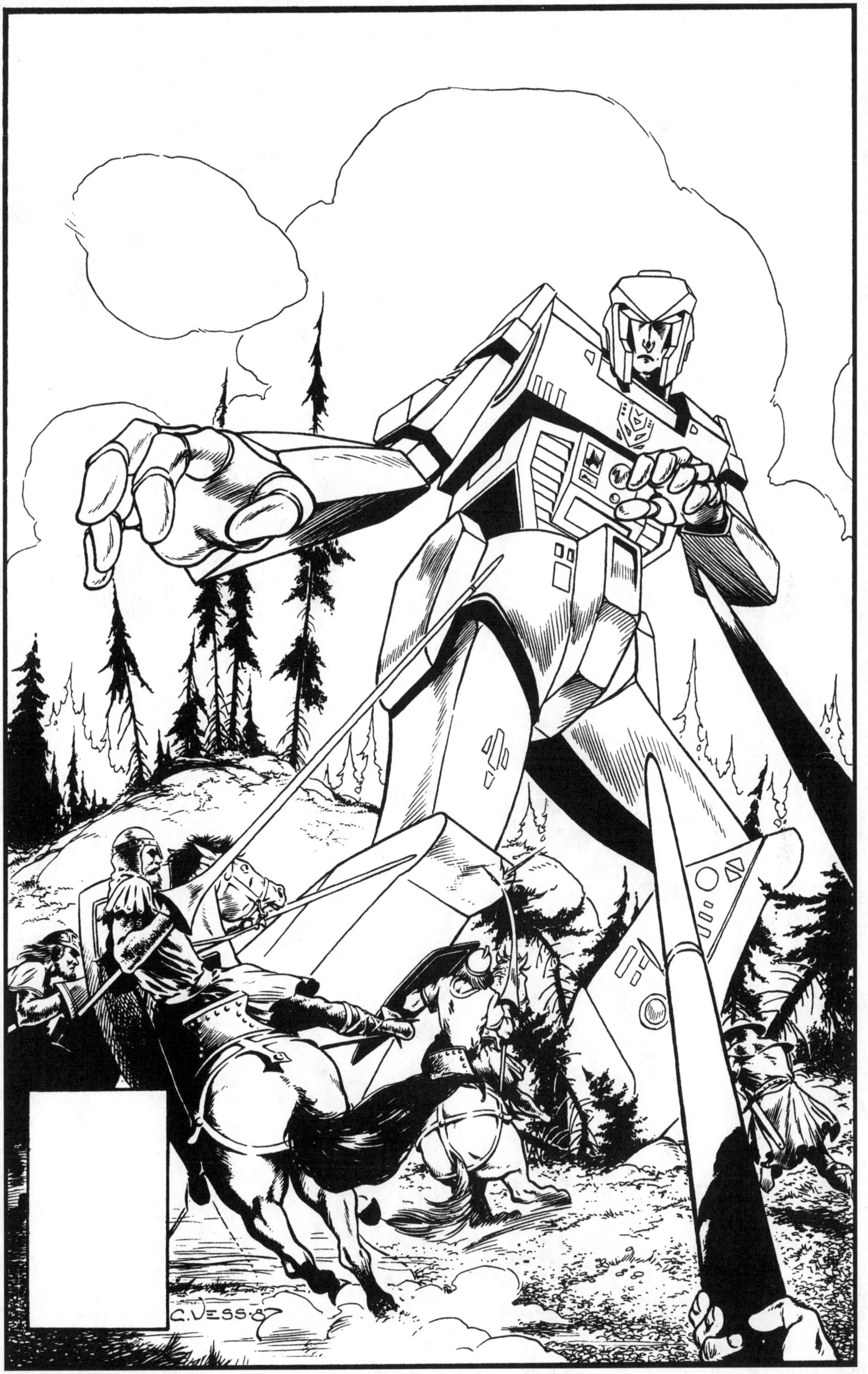
C. VESS '87

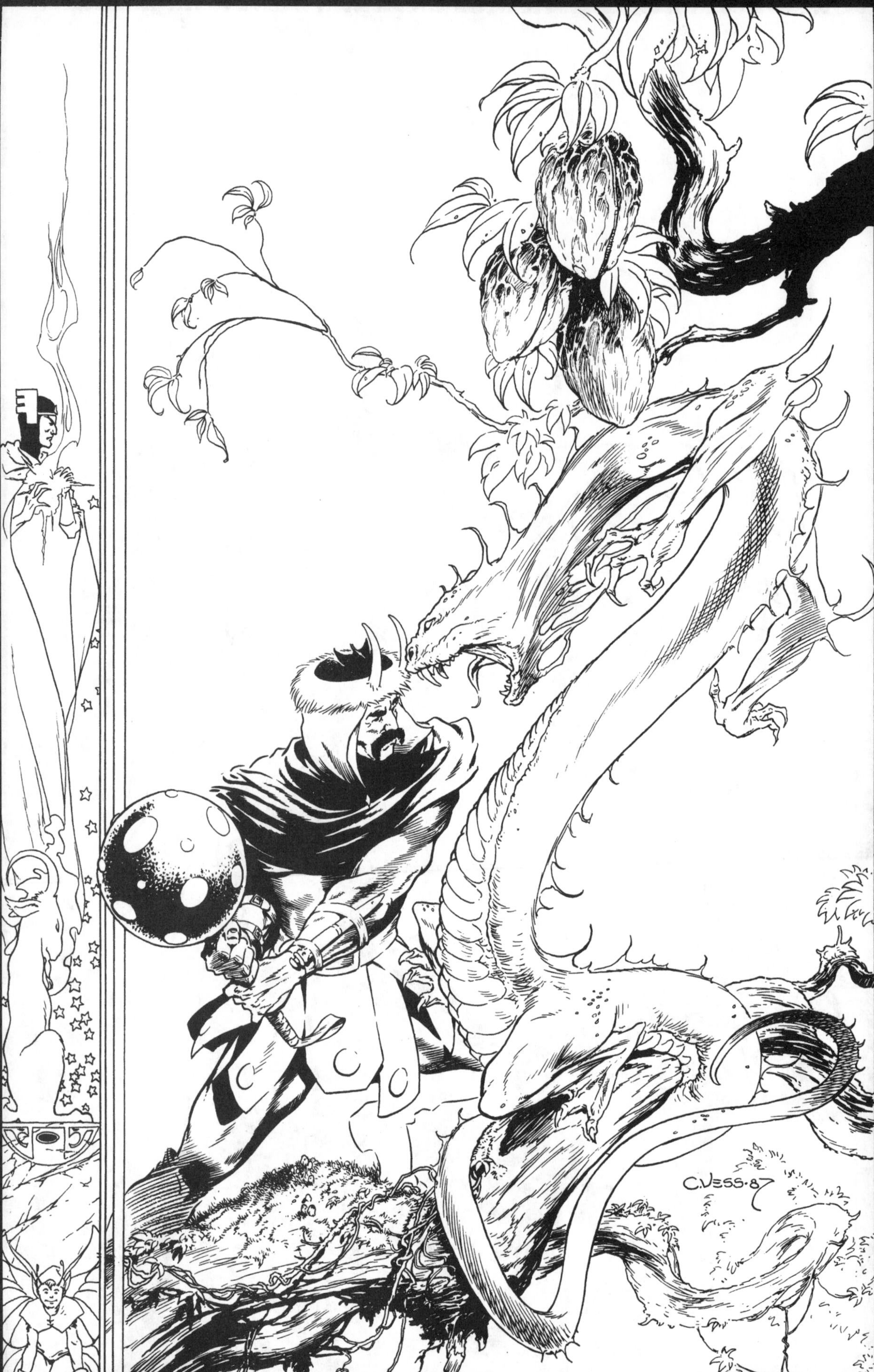
C.VESS·87

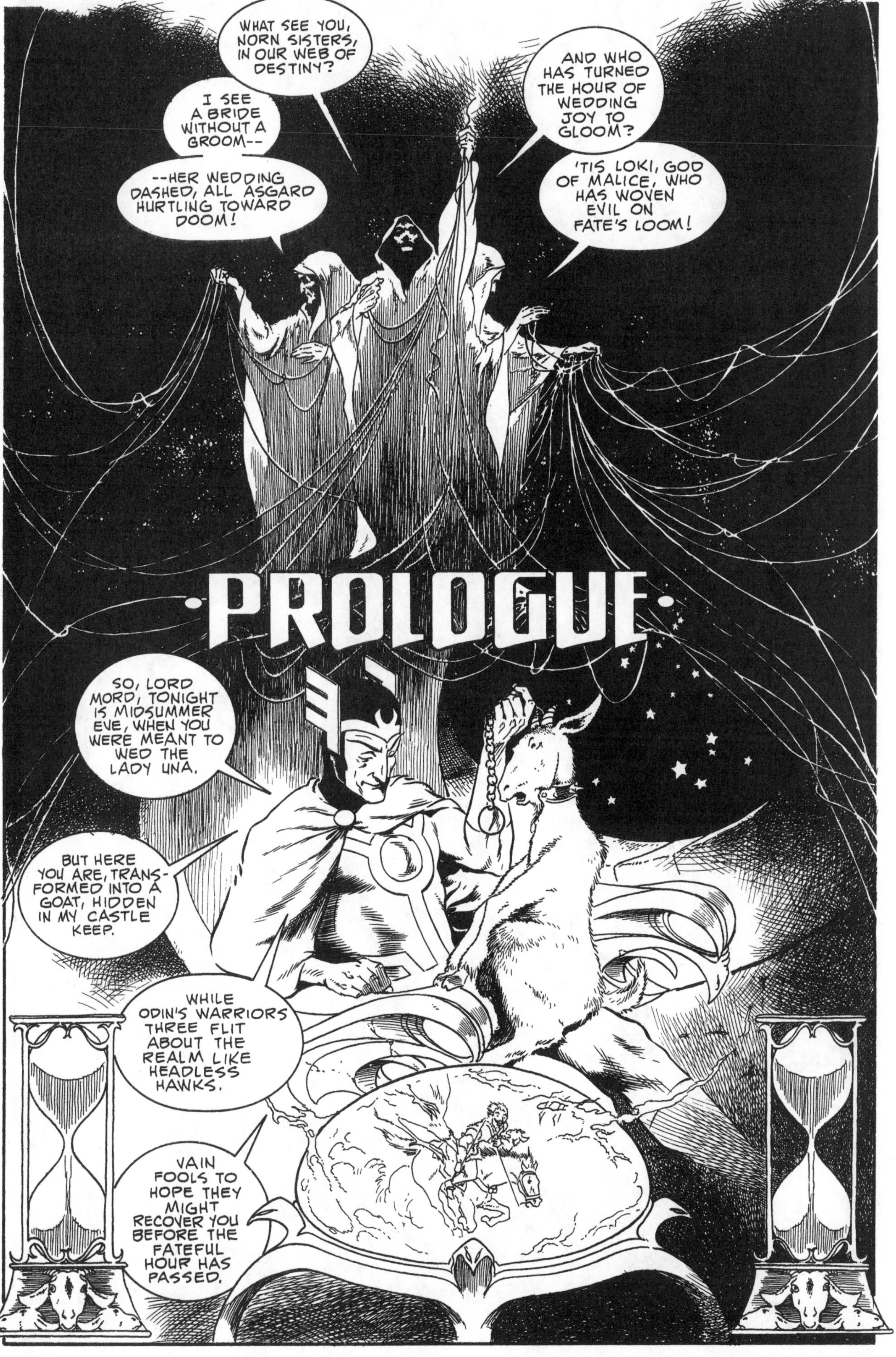
WHAT SEE YOU, NORN SISTERS, IN OUR WEB OF DESTINY?
I SEE A BRIDE WITHOUT A GROOM--
--HER WEDDING DASHED, ALL ASGARD HURTLING TOWARD DOOM!
AND WHO HAS TURNED THE HOUR OF WEDDING JOY TO GLOOM?
'TIS LOKI, GOD OF MALICE, WHO HAS WOVEN EVIL ON FATE'S LOOM!
PROLOGUE
SO, LORD MORD, TONIGHT IS MIDSUMMER EVE, WHEN YOU WERE MEANT TO WED THE LADY UNA.
BUT HERE YOU ARE, TRANS-FORMED INTO A GOAT, HIDDEN IN MY CASTLE KEEP.
WHILE ODIN'S WARRIORS THREE FLIT ABOUT THE REALM LIKE HEADLESS HAWKS.
VAIN FOOLS TO HOPE THEY MIGHT RECOVER YOU BEFORE THE FATEFUL HOUR HAS PASSED.

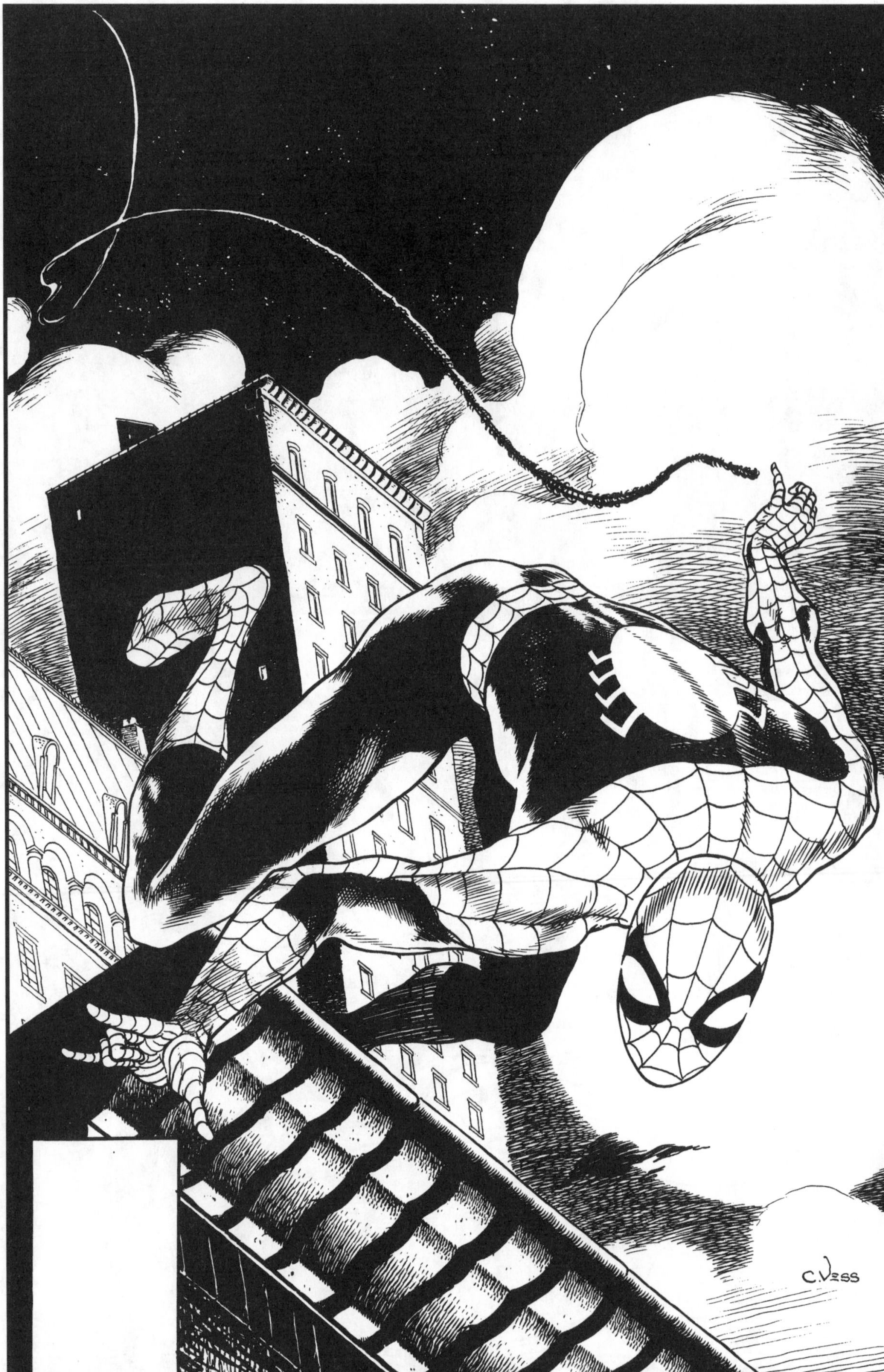
C.Vess

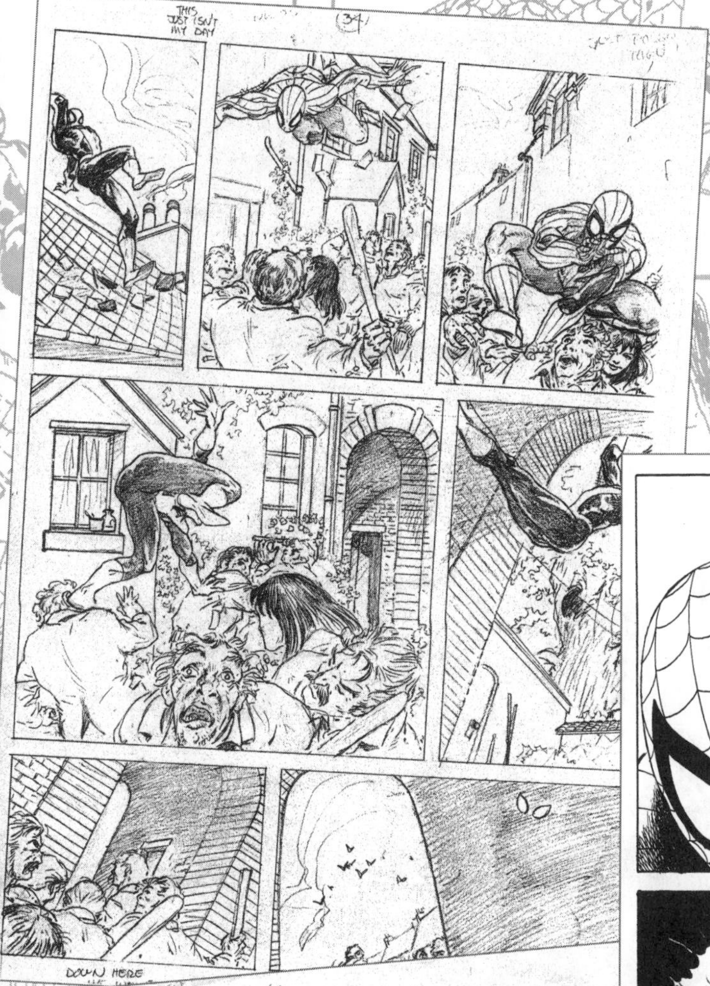
THIS JUST ISN'T MY DAY
DOWN HERE

Previous Page: Cover art for *Web of Spider-Man #49.*
This Page: Pencils for pages 34 and 41, along with the inks to page 41, from *Spider-Man: Spirits of the Earth.* The background image is inked version of page 41.

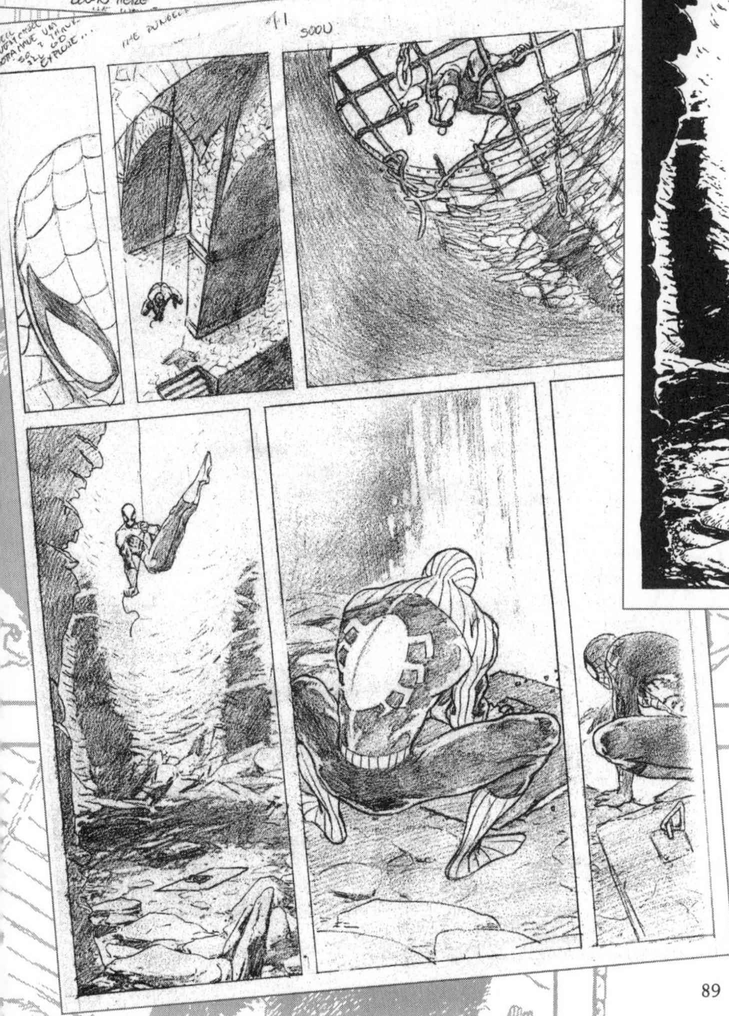

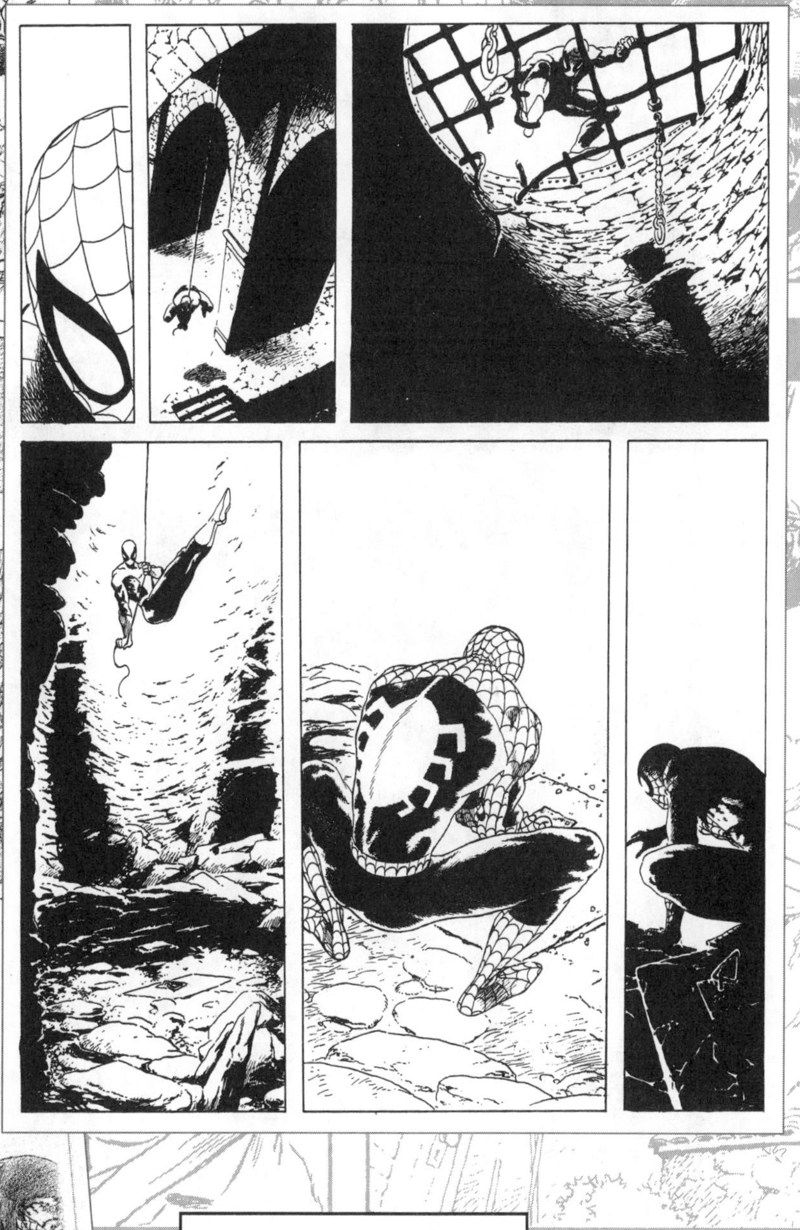

Next Two Pages: Cover art for *Spectre* vol. 1, #13 and 14.

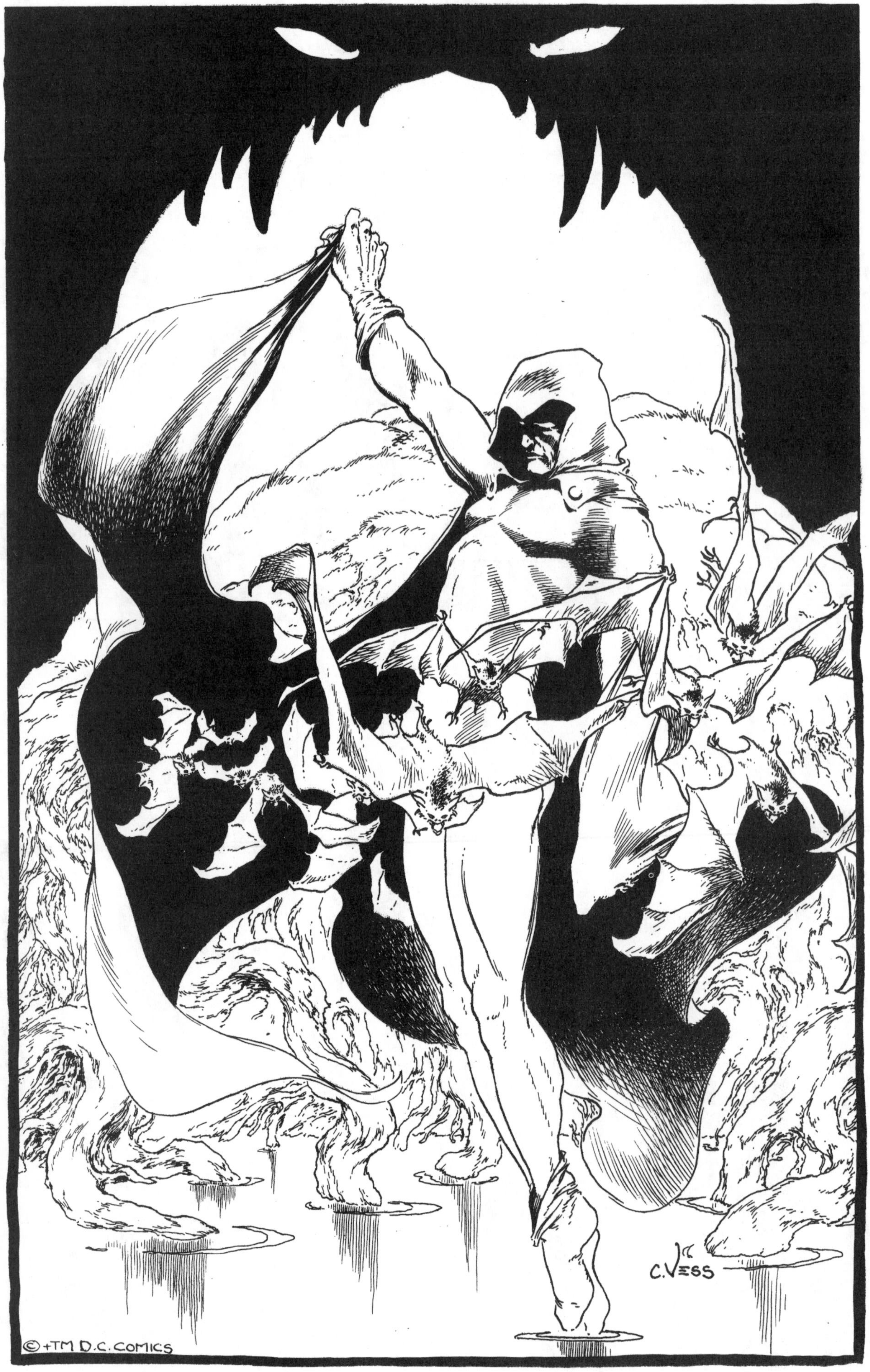
C. Vess
© +TM D.C. COMICS

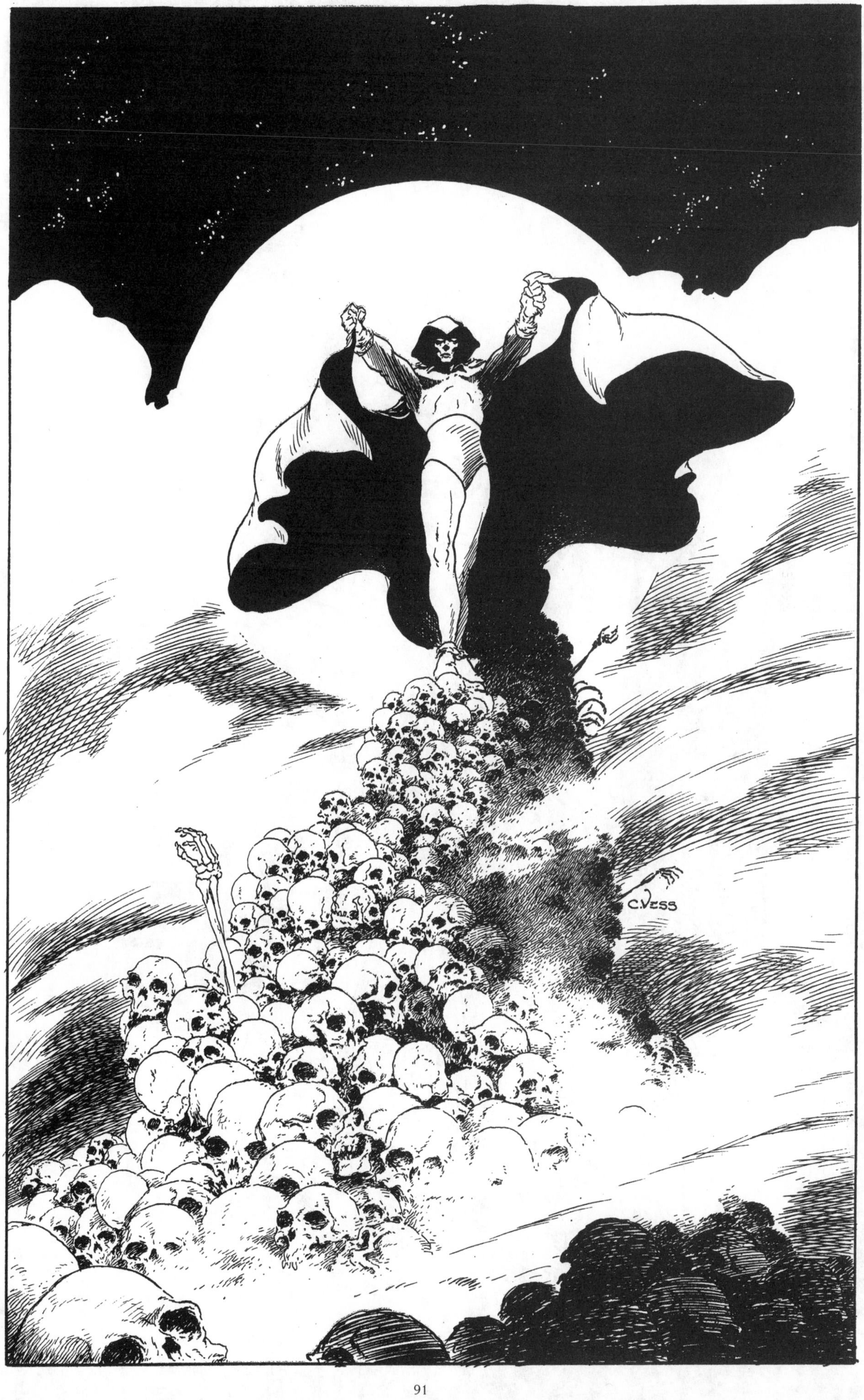
C.VESS

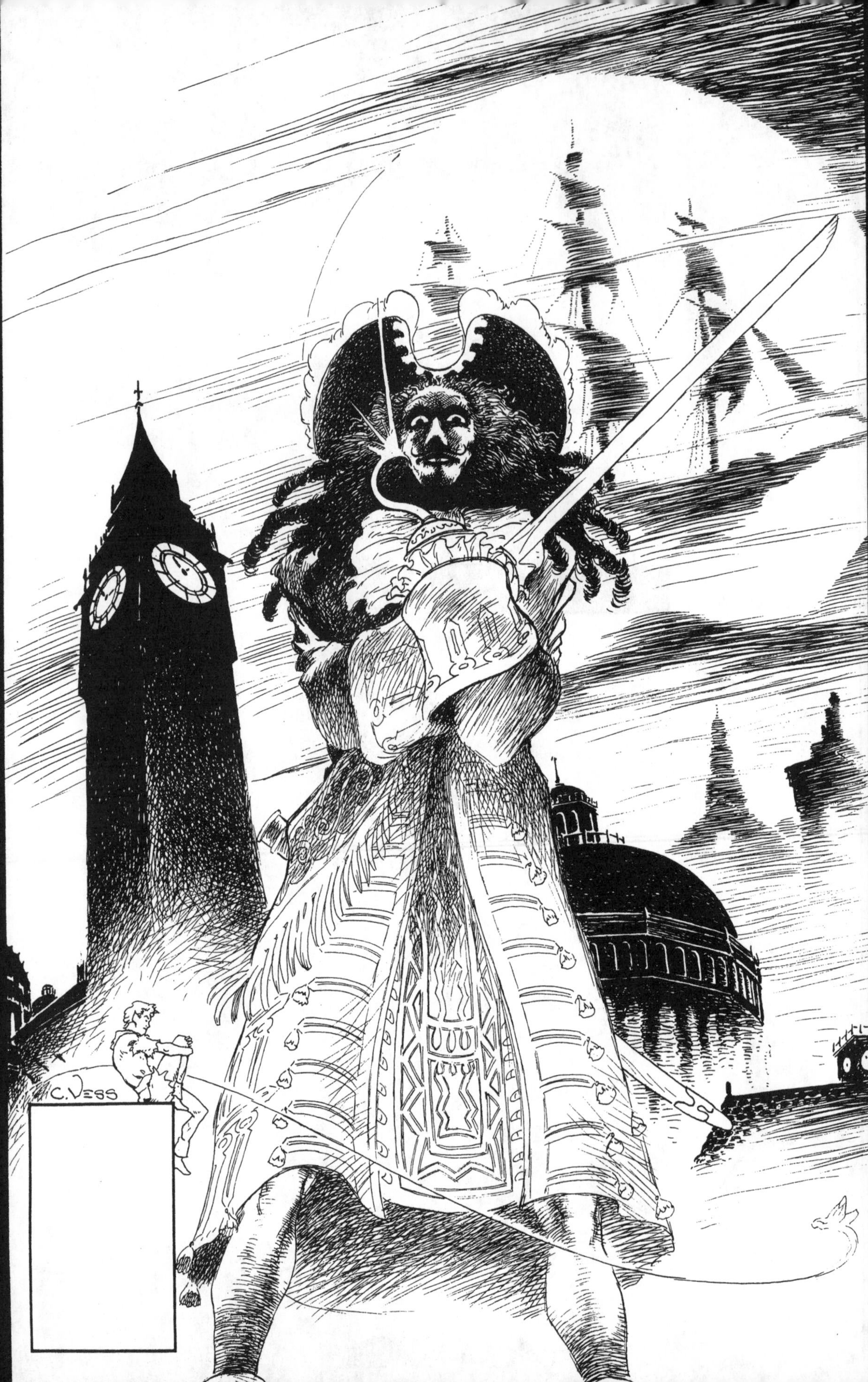
C. VESS

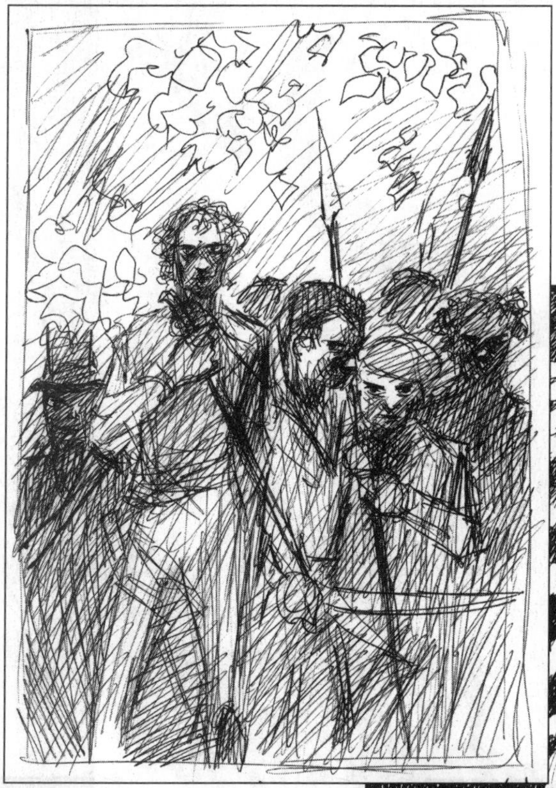

Previous Page: Line art for the cover of *Hook* #1, adapting the movie of the same name.
This Page: Charles' initial sketch and final inks for the cover of *Hook* #3.

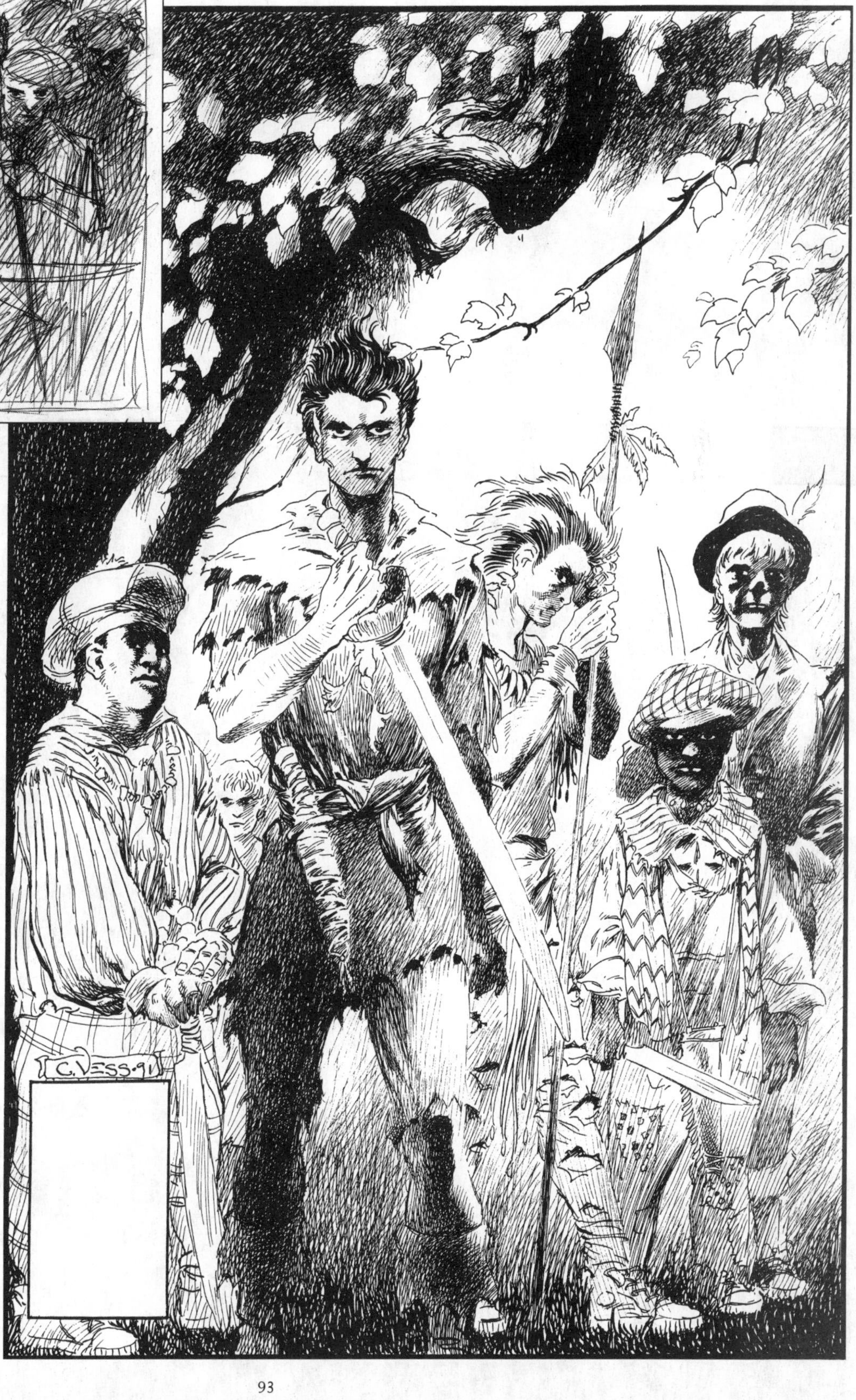
C. VESS·91

Next Two Pages: Dr. Occult gives the young Tim Hunter the 50¢ tour of the hidden worlds—including Skartaris and the Dreaming. Page 36 inks and page 40 pencils from Book 3 of the *Books of Magic* mini-series.
Pages 96 and 97: Charles: "They ended up using this piece as a pin-up in some issue of *Swamp Thing*, but used the black-&-white and colored it in comic book color. I draw women better than that now—that Abby has a big butt!"
Page 98: Painting for the Arzach portfolios published by Tundra. Charles: "I vividly remember seeing Moebius' first 'Arzach' strip in *Metal Hurlant* way back in 1974. I could sense the possibilities of what could and couldn't be done in the world of comics altering even as I turned those pages."
Page 99: "Caesar's Last Breath," a one-pager done for Klutz Press.
Pages 100 and 101: This piece ran as a fold-out poster in *Spectacular Spider-Man* #189. Charles: "The comic ran the piece with the roof tops cropped off thus eliminating the horde of kitty cats racing in pursuit."

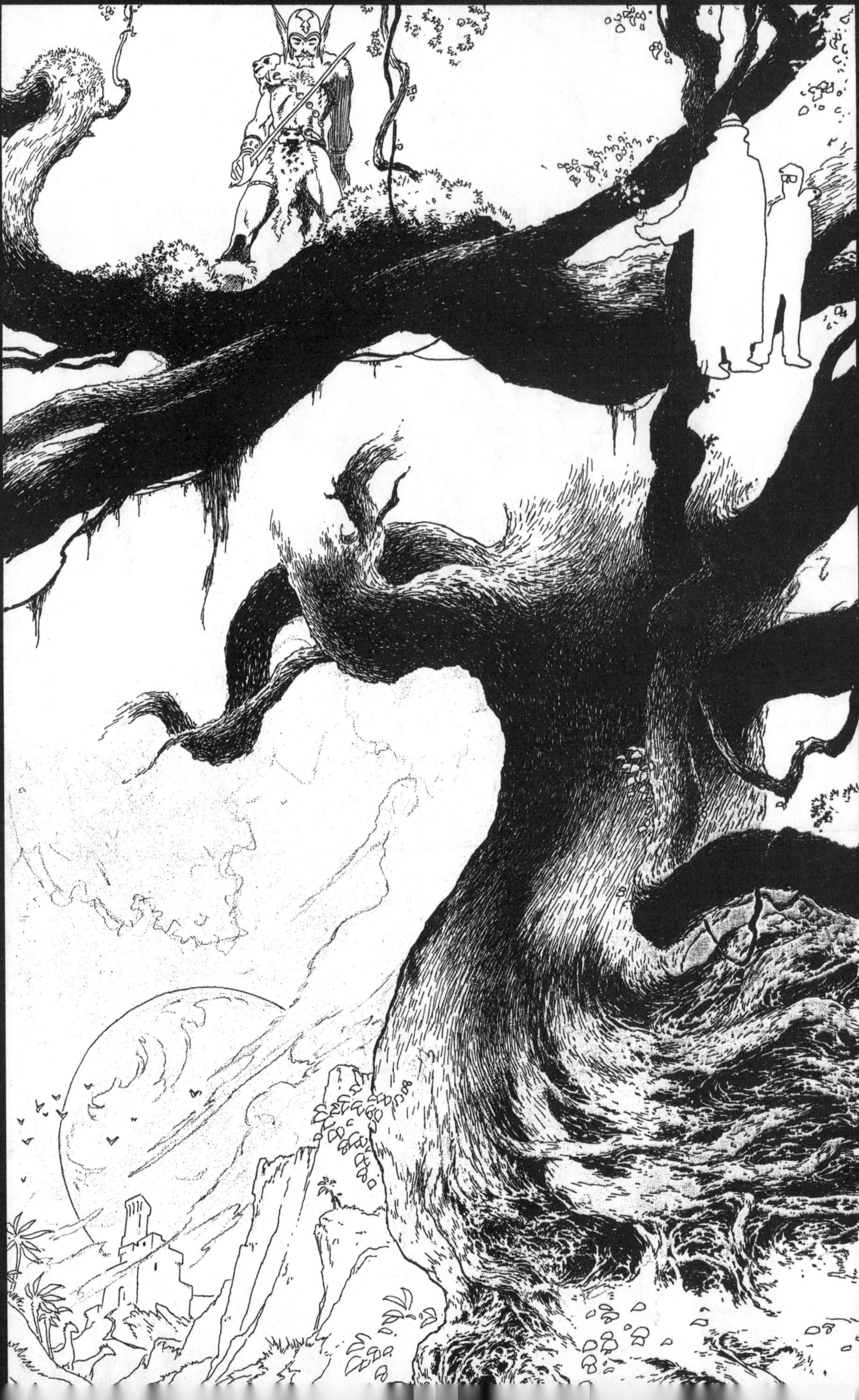

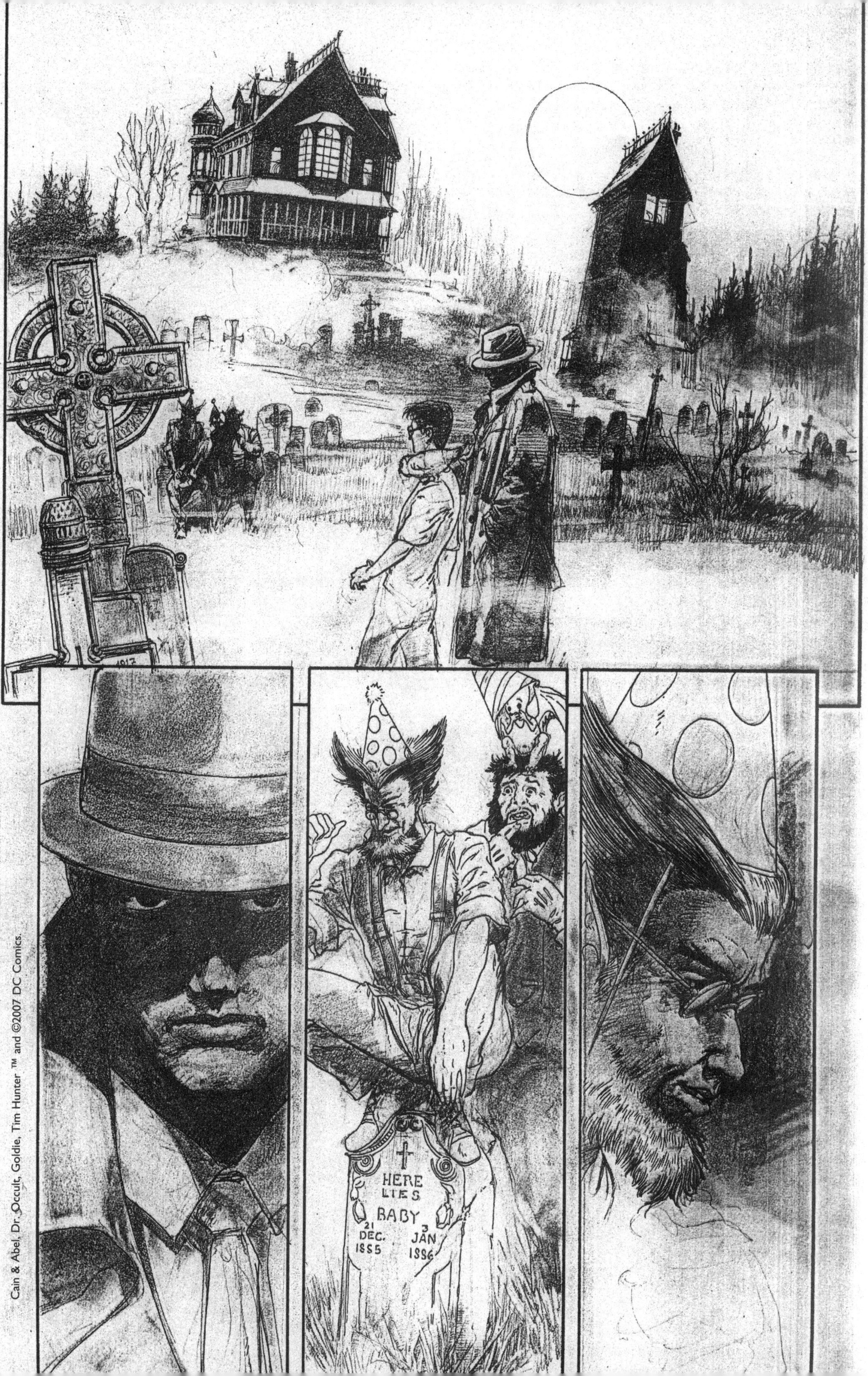
HERE
LIES
BABY
21 DEC. 1855
3 JAN 1856

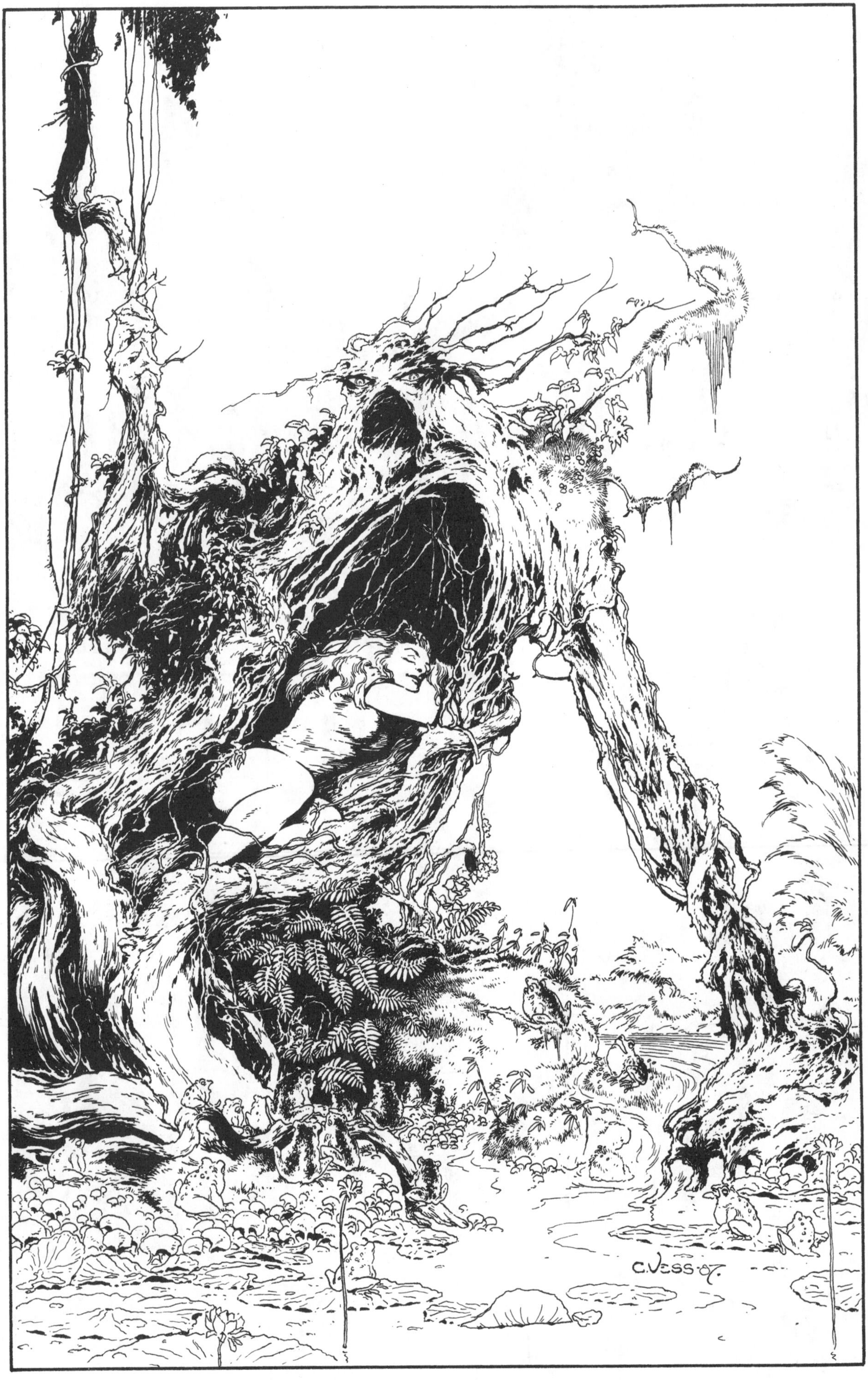
C.VESS 07.